TABLE OF CONTENTS

Part I: Ancient History

Part II: Religion

Part III: Secret Societies

PART I

ANCIENT HISTORY

1

THE ANCIENT ASTRONAUTS

AS FAR BACK as we can peer into mankind's past through the meticulous examination of ancient texts and archaeological remains of civilizations lost, striving to unveil the secrets of our origins, a common legend pervades every culture. The legend of people that descended to Earth from the sky and created mankind.

As of today, the oldest known writings that mankind has been able to decipher come from the ancient Sumerian civilization and stem back to around 4000 B.C. The Sumerians described in detail how there was a time, *before mankind existed*, when people descended to Earth from the Sky. The Sumerians called these people the DIN.GIR, which means Righteous Ones of the Rocketships (Rf1). In Sumerian pictographic writing, DIN.GIR was drawn in the shape of a multi-stage rocketship (Fig. 1.1).

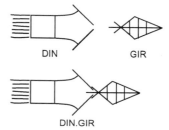

Figure 1.1

Interestingly, this image is very similar to a drawing that was found in the Egyptian tomb of Huy (Fig. 1.2). Huy was the governor of Nubia and the Sinai during the reign of Pharaoh Tut-Ankh-Amon. The drawing is believed to depict a multi-stage rocketship in an underground silo. You can even see two people standing in the rocketship awaiting takeoff! (Rf2).

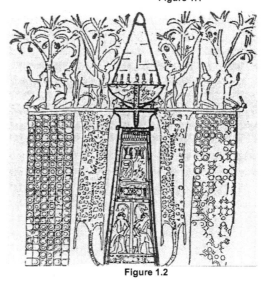

Figure 1.2

According to the Sumerians the Ruler of the DIN.GIR was called AN. Over time AN became known as ANU in the Babylonian and Assyrian texts. In the Akkadian texts ANU was known as ILU, and in later Canaanite and Hebrew texts, ANU became known as EL. (As you will see later, EL is the singular noun of the plural ELOHIM which we find used in the original Hebrew texts of the Torah. It is this word ELOHIM which later became mis-translated into the singular noun "God" which we see in English language Bibles). Anu was the Lofty One, the Supreme One, the Ruler of the planet from which these people had come (Rf3).

Figure 1.3

While the DIN.GIR were collectively known by the pictograph shown above, the "star" symbol (Fig. 1.3) became used as a simplification to identify Anu. In the ancient cuneiform writings the "star" symbol preceded certain names to indicate that the written name was not of a human, but was the name of one of the DIN.GIR. The "star" sign eventually evolved further into a crosslike wedgemark (Fig. 1.4)(Rf4).

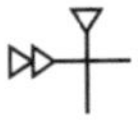

Figure 1.4

Anu had a wife named ANTU (who was also his half-sister), and had six concubines. While the texts say that Anu had some 80 children, for the purposes of this section it is only necessary to discuss three of them: ENKI, ENLIL, and NINHURSAG (Rf5).

Anu's first born son was EN.KI (meaning Lord of Earth). In Sumerian "EN" meant Lord and "KI" meant Earth (Rf6). Enki was a master architect, engineer, scientist, geneticist, and astronomer. Enki eventually became known by many epithets. He was Lord of Wisdom, Lord of Mining, Lord of the Sea, and others we will discuss later. A text labeled by scholars, *Enki and the World Order*, explained how

Figure 1.5

he brought the arts of brickmaking, construction of dwellings and cities, metallurgy, and all other arts and sciences to Earth (Rf7). Enki was sometimes depicted with streams of water flowing from him (Figs. 1.5 and 1.6) and sometimes as Lord of Mining (Fig. 1.7).

Anu's second born son was EN.LIL (meaning Lord of the Airspace, Lord of the Storm, and Lord of the Command) (Fig. 1.8). Enlil was the commander of the mission to Earth and was known as a strict

Figure 1.6

"by-the-book" disciplinarian (Rf8). He would eventually become the most powerful ruler on Earth. Enlil was the archetype and father of the later

2

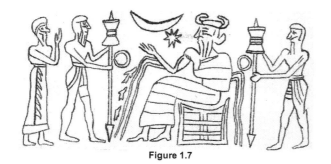

Figure 1.7

Figure 1.8

(so-called) "Storm Gods" (Rf9). Enlil was also known as ILU-KUR-GAL (Lord of the Mountain) (Rf10).

Even though he was the younger brother, Enlil was the Crown Prince (heir) because his mother was Antu. Antu was Anu's half-sister; therefore Enlil was born with a greater percentage of the family's genetic strain than Enki, whose mother was a non-related concubine. Under the succession rules of the DIN.GIR this entitled Enlil to the right of succession to the throne even though he was the second born (Rf11).

The practice of procreating with an immediate family member in order to ensure the strongest possible genetic strain in the child was passed down from the DIN.GIR to the royal courts of all ancient cultures. In Egypt it was a common practice for a Pharaoh to marry his sister and a child born of such union always entitled that child to succession even if he was not the first born. As you will see in Part II, this was also practiced by the biblical patriarchs: Abraham (who married his sister Sarah) Isaac (who married Rebekah, a close blood relative), and Jacob (who married Leah and Rachel, two close blood relatives).

Anu's third child was a girl, NIN.HUR.SAG (meaning Lady of the Mountain). Ninhursag was the Chief Medical Officer and was generally depicted by the Womb symbol (Figs. 1.9 & 1.10)

Figure 1.9

which is also known as the Omega symbol (Rf12). Ninhursag is the archetype of all the mother goddesses.

The gateway to Anu's palace was depicted in an Assyrian drawing showing Two Pillars flanked by

Figure 1.10

3

"Eaglemen" (Fig. 1.11). Between the pillars is the Winged Disc emblem representing the planet from which they came. From the palace's view point, by the right pillar are seven stars representing the Earth. By the left pillar is a crescent representing the Moon. Also in the image is a representation of the original twelve member solar system (Rf13).

Figure 1.11

> Anu sat on his throne, flanked by his son Enlil seated on the right and his son [Enki] seated on his left. (Rf14)

Only Anu could anoint people to rule as King and even the traditional insignia of kingship (crown, tiara, scepter or staff, and coiled measuring cord) stem from his Anutu (Anu-ship)(Fig. 1.12) (Rf15).

Anu's family and staff (his chief chamberlain, commanders in charge of the rocketships, justices, assistants, etc.) were given the term ANUNNA (Those of Anu) (Rf16). The term ANUNNA with KI (meaning Earth) formed the term ANUNNAKI, meaning: Those of Anu who came to Earth. It was this term, ANUNNAKI that eventually replaced the original word DIN.GIR.

Figure 1.12

The Anunnaki were described as being very tall (9 to 10 feet), with big eyes, white skin (which earned them the name "Shining Ones"), and the men were generally bearded. As you can see from the above pictures they were usually drawn wearing a conical shaped horned headdress. These were originally antennas for the headsets in which they used to communicate with each other. Because our early ancestors did not understand their significance, they assumed that they were decorative and in future generations horned helmets became a symbol of superior status among various cultures. We see

4

this at work in Egypt where Pharaohs wore a horned headdress with the Uraeus, and again among the Vikings who wore horned helmets.

While eventually there were hundreds of Anunnaki on Earth, only (12) made up the Circle of Great Anunnaki, the Supreme Pantheon of Twelve:

Rank / Name	Rank / Name
60 - Anu	55 - Antu
50 - Enlil	45 - Ninlil
40 - Ea/Enki	35 - Ninki
30 - Nannar/Sin	25 - Ningal
20 - Utu/Shamash	15 - Inanna/Ishtar
10 - Ishkur/Adad	5 - Ninhursag

The numerical rank next to their name was sometimes used in texts to identify them. As you can see, multiples of ten were assigned to men and multiples of five were assigned to women. The rank was accompanied by an equal number of epithet names (Rf17). The Pantheon was made up of 6 males and 6 females. Only when an opening became available could a successor be initiated into the Pantheon of Twelve. This was the archetype of all future Pantheons: 12 Titans, 12 Olympians, 12 Tribes of Israel, 12 Stones in the Magical Breastplate of the Hebrew High Priest, 12 Princes of Ishmael, 12 Apostles of Jesus, 12 Gates of Heaven, 12 Gates of the Great Temple Esagila, 12 Stars in the woman's Crown in the Book of Revelation "12", 12 Houses of the Zodiac (which also contains six males and six females), etc.

In addition to being identified by numerical rank, each of the Anunnaki adopted one or more animals or symbols by which he or she was identified. Some of which paralleled the Zodiac. From this, in much later times we see the Pantheon of Anunnaki being depicted using animals and symbols during the Kassite Dynasty (2nd millennium B.C.) (Fig. 1.13) and during the reign of King Nebuchadnezzar I (1125-1104 B.C.) (Fig. 1.14) (Rf18).

Because of these associations eventually all the Anunnaki collectively became known as the Serpent People, demonstrated in Fig. 1.14 by the snake/serpent symbol that overshadows the entire Pantheon. This also resulted in future generations describing the Anunnaki as half-human and half-serpent.

While the oldest texts that we have come from Mesopotamia, they were not the only people to record the history of the Anunnaki (Those of Anu who descended to Earth from the sky).

Figure 1.13

Figure 1.14

The ancient Egyptians also recorded the history of how the Anunnaki descended to Earth in their "Celestial Boats" (aka rocketships), created and then ruled over mankind. The Egyptians called the Anunnaki NETERU. The term described people who were mighty, strong, powerful, and eventually became translated as Guardians/Watchers because they were the rulers over mankind. While the term Neter does not mean "god," most contemporary Egyptologists have incorrectly translated it as such, which has led to much confusion about their true identity. In fact, the Egyptian hieroglyph used to describe a Neter was an AXE. All hieroglyphs were based upon objects the Egyptians physically saw, so the Axe had to be a real object. The Neteru were the people of the AXE. As you will see later, the Anunnaki were also known as the people who carried the Silver AXE. The Egyptians sometimes depicted the Anunnaki/Neteru in human form and sometimes depicted them with a human body but the head of an animal. A common symbol found on many Pharaohs is the Uraeus, which symbolized the Serpent People, Neteru, Anunnaki rulers.

The ancient Chinese called the Anunnaki the Great Dragons. Similar to Egypt, they were known as the "guardians" of mankind. After the Dragons descended to Earth from the sky, the Dragon goddess named Nu Kua (described as a "water-being" half-dragon, half-human) was said to have created mankind. Emperors boasted of having Dragon Blood in them and some were even described as having dragon features. The ancient Chinese book *Yih King* describes how the Dragon People even married and had children with the humans they created. (Rf19).

In India the Anunnaki were known as a Serpent Race called the SARPA or GREAT DRAGONS. They were described as having a human face but the tail of a dragon. They descended to Earth from the sky and created mankind. The leader was called the Great Dragon and similar to Chinese history, these Serpent People had sex with mankind. The offspring of this union were called the DRAVIDIANS and NAGAS (Serpent Lords). They were known as intelligent human-reptile hybrids that flew around the sky using chariots they called Vimana (Rf20). The Hindu *Vedas*, *Ramayana*, and *Mahabharata* describe these people in great detail.

In ancient Greece the Anunnaki were called TITANS and Olympians. The Greeks described how they each had a Pantheon of Twelve members, six male and six female. They described the Titans and Olympians as human in appearance and explained how some of them arrived in Greece from across the Mediterranean, via Crete, some came from the Near East, and some from Asia Minor. The Greek accounts of the people who descended to Earth from the sky and created mankind are very similar to those found in Egypt and Sumer.

The Dogon tribe in Mali (Africa) spoke of the Anunnaki as amphibious fish-like people who descended to Earth from the sky and created mankind. The Anunnaki were called NOMMOS by the Dogon and the day they landed on Earth was called "the day of the fish." The Dogon say the Nommos are the same people who created the Egyptians. It is believed that the Dogon tribe obtained this information from the Philistines who spoke of the "fish-god" named DAGON (Rf21). However, the legend of Dagon was itself derived from the Babylonian legends of a fish-man called OANNES who was said to have emerged from the sea and created mankind. As reported by the Babylonian priest-historian Berossus, Oannes was described as having the head and feet of a man, but the body of a fish.

In Mesoamerica the Anunnaki were known as the "Feathered," "Winged," or "Plummed Serpents." The Olmecs, Toltecs, Aztecs, Mayans and Incas all possess similar accounts of Serpent People who created their civilizations. For example:

According to the Mayan book *Chilam Balam* (Oracles of Balam the priest) "the first inhabitants of Yucatan were the 'People of the Serpent.' They came from the east in boats across the water with their leader Itzamna, 'Serpent of the East" (Rf22).

The Toltec and Aztec civilizations spoke of Quetzalcoatl ("quetzal" meaning bird and "coatl" meaning serpent). He was the Great Feathered Serpent who created their civilizations. Among the Quiche Maya he was known as Gucumatz. Among the Maya of Chichen Itza he was called Kukulcan. The Aztecs even depicted the Anunnaki's "cross" symbol on images of Quetzalcoatl's shield (Fig. 1.15) (Rf23). A nine stage pyramid, rising to the height of 185 feet is dedicated to the Plummed Serpent, Quetzalcoatl-Kukulcan (Rf24).

Figure 1.15

The Mayans also have a legend of Votan who was said to be a descendant of the Anunnaki. Votan's emblem was a serpent. The legend says that the Anunnaki sent him to this land to people it. The city he created was called Nachan (Place of the Serpent), known today as Palenque (Rf25).

Despite the fact that all Mesoamerican cultures universally identified the Anunnaki as Serpent People, they all described their physical appearance as human. Quetzalcoatl/Kukulcan was said to be very tall, white-skinned and bearded (Rf26). His physical appearance also played a part in the demise of the Aztec civilization. When the white-skinned and bearded giant Quetzalcoatl left the Aztecs he sailed off eastward (becoming known as the Lord of the Morning Star) and vowed to return in the year 1 Reed (Rf27). In the year 1519, when the white-skinned and bearded Hernando Cortes emerged from the waters on the east at the gateway of the Aztec domain the Aztecs mistakenly believed that he was the Anunnaki Quetzalcoatl returning as promised, due to his white skin color. Instead of putting up a fight they "literally poured their gold at the Spaniards' feet" (Rf28).

This also occurred in the Inca Empire. The Incas worshipped an Anunnaki they called Viracocha who was said to have descended to Earth and created mankind. He was said to be a great scientist architect, engineer, teacher and healer. Viracocha was depicted as a lean white-skinned and bearded man, past middle age, wearing sandals and dressed in long flowing cloaks. The Incas were "so certain" of his physical appearance that they also mistook the white and bearded Spaniards for Viracocha when they arrived on their shores (Rf29). Describing Viracocha the people from the Andes said:

8

there suddenly appeared, coming from the south, a white man of large stature and authoritative demeanor. This man had such great power that he changed the hills into valleys and from the valleys made great hills, causing streams to flow from the living stones...

The Incas explained how their road system and architecture "'were the work of white, auburn-haired men' who had lived thousands of years earlier." A Temple called the Coricancha was erected for Viracocha and contains an idol that vividly shows his features (Rf30).

Even the biblical texts of the Torah and Old Testament speak of the Anunnaki (Those of Anu who descended to Earth from the sky) and created mankind. As I explained earlier the Ruler of the Anunnaki was called AN which eventually became EL in the Hebrew language. EL is a singular noun, the plural of which is ELOHIM. The original texts of the Bible do not contain the word "God" but actually say ELOHIM! This will be discussed at length in Part II. Identical to the ancient histories of the Chinese Dragons who created humans then had sex with them, the Sarpa or Great Dragons of India who created humans then had sex with them producing the offspring called the Dravidians and Nagas, and the Mesoamerican Feathered Serpents who created humans then had sex with them, the biblical texts also confirm that after the Elohim created mankind they too had sex with the humans they created:

> The Nephilim were on the earth in those days - and also afterward - when the sons of the Elohim went to the daughters of men and had children by them. (Genesis 6:4)

The Anunnaki/Elohim are also called the Nephilim here. The Hebrew word Nephilim has been translated: Those who have come down, from the sky to Earth (Rf31). It has also been translated as Guardians/Watchers identical to the Egyptian Neteru (Rf32). All of which are just describing the Anunnaki (Those of Anu who descended to Earth from the sky). The Bible also speaks of the Anunnaki as the Anak, Anakites, Anakim (Numbers 13:22 to 13:33; Deuteronomy 1:28, 2:10-11, 2:20-21, 9:2) and explained how the Anunnaki were very tall:

> We saw the Nephilim there (the descendants of Anak come from the Nephilim). We seemed like grasshoppers in our own eyes, and we looked like the same to them (Numbers 13:33)

While their names have changed over time and culture, the people they were describing remain one and the same. Who exactly were these people (the Anunnaki/Elohim/Nephilim) who descended to Earth from the sky and created man? Who were the "sons of the Elohim" who had sex with the daughters of men as described in the Bible?

9

Some researchers argue that they were "spiritual beings" who incarnated into the bodies of humans. The problem with this argument is that the ancient texts explain (1) that they were flesh and blood beings; (2) that they were much larger than humans, almost 9 to 10 feet tall; and (3) that when they mated with humans they created offspring that were giants. If they were simply "spirits" who took possession of human bodies that already existed on Earth, then they would not look any different than the rest of mankind. Nor would the children they produced by mating with humans have looked any different than the children humans were normally giving birth to. So this argument is easily dismissed by the evidence that shows they were flesh and blood beings that descended to the Earth from the sky.

Other researchers argue that they were reptilians from another planet who colonized Earth and can shape-shift into human form (i.e. David Icke, Dr. Arthur David Horn, R.A. Boulay, etc.). They base their argument on ancient Ubaid, Sumerian, Egyptian, Babylonian, Indian, and Mesoamerican drawings and sculptures of human bodies with various animal heads, some with serpent-like faces. They also reference the ancient texts described above which speak of the Serpent People (aka Dragon and Snake People).

While I am not ignoring the possibility that such reptilian beings may exist in the enormous expanse of our universe, the argument raised by these researchers ignores the practices of our ancestors.

Our ancient ancestors practiced TOTEMISM. They used objects and animals as emblems to visually identify their family, tribe or clan. It was a system of social organization. It's similar to the way, in modern times, sports fans paint their faces the colors of the team they support to visually identify their affiliation. Anyone seeing the paint (Totem) immediately knows what team they are aligned with.

The Anunnaki/Elohim/Nephilim weren't reptilians. The beasts, birds, reptiles, fish, etc., that you find in ancient texts and drawings describing them were their Totems.

Today, instead of using the image of an animal as a Totem to represent our family lineage, we use a surname. Our last name is our Totem.

Based upon the evidence, at least as it exists today, we know that the Anunnaki/Elohim/Nephilim:

(1) were flesh and blood beings;
(2) they had advanced technology and were able to fly around using chariots;
(3) they created mankind;

(4) they had sex with the humans they created and begot children;
(5) they spawned all the ancient civilizations on Earth.

Most researchers believe that the Anunnaki/Elohim/Nephilim were an advanced race of humans from another planet who colonized Earth several hundred thousand years ago. It has become known as the Ancient Astronaut Theory (Rf33).

It's important to note that the information we have about them is limited to the discoveries that have been made to date. As new discoveries are made we may find out that the names used herein are only reflections of more ancient ones. Instead of dwelling on the names, the important thing is that you understand the basic history of what occurred in our past so that you can begin to see how that history is affecting everything around us today.

2

PLANET OF ORIGIN

THE ANCIENT SUMERIANS said that the Anunnaki/Elohim/Nephilim descended to Earth from another planet that they called NI.BI.RU (Rf1). Nibiru was said to be three times the size of Earth and dark red in color.

Nibiru is believed to be a planet that orbits our solar system on an elliptical path approximately every 3,600 Earth years, similar to the way a comet does (i.e. the Hale-Bopp comet which passes through our solar system every 4000 years) (Fig. 2.1) (Rf2).

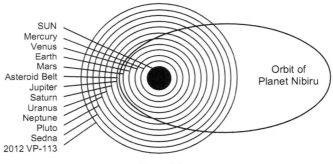

Figure 2.1

According to a text known as the *Epic of Creation* it is believed that Nibiru passes directly between Mars and Jupiter on its orbit around our Sun. The text explains that at one time a planet known as Tiamat (the watery giant) existed between Mars and Jupiter. When planet Nibiru was making its clockwise orbit through our solar system it came so close to Tiamat that Nibiru's satellites smashed into it breaking the planet into pieces. The smaller pieces of Tiamat became the Asteroid Belt (hammered bracelet) that can be seen between Mars and Jupiter. A large piece of Tiamat was thrown into a different orbit and became known as Earth. The debris of one of Nibiru's satellites became our Moon (Rf3).

This has also been known as the Giant Impact Theory, according to which the moon was created during a collision between a planetary body called Theia (which is thought to have been the size of Mars) and a proto-Earth.

Some scientific evidence has recently been discovered which appears to support this collision theory. Planetary scientist Fredric Moynier, PhD (Assist.

Professor of Earth and Planetary Sciences at Washington University in St. Louis) and his group analyzed 20 samples of lunar rocks obtained from the Apollo 11, 12, 15, and 17 missions, from different locations on the Moon. Looking at the isotopic fractionation scientists discovered that the level of fractionation measured in lunar rocks was 10 times larger than samples from Earth and Mars. The results were published in the October 18, 2012 issue of *Nature* (Rf4). Because the Moon contains a different chemical composition of the cloud of gas and dust from which our solar system is formed, this suggests that the moon was not formed during the creation of our solar system. This adds support to the theory of the Moon being created by a collision (perhaps between the invading Nibiru and its satellites upon Tiamat) resulting in our current Earth-Moon system, however, it is far from conclusive.

Ancient drawings also support the theory that at one time another planet existed in our solar system. The State Museum in East Berlin contains an Akkadian Seal (cataloged as VA/243) dating back to the third millennium B.C. (Fig. 2.2). It shows the Sun with eleven celestial bodies orbiting it. Our ancestors counted our Moon as a celestial body. The one extra celestial body is believed to represent planet Nibiru (Rf5).

Figure 2.2

Because Nibiru crosses all the other planets in our solar system during its orbit, it was given the name "Planet of Crossing." The Sumerians even used the same "cross" symbol of of Anu to identify his planet; a symbol that eventually evolved into a radiating cross (Fig.2.3), a radiating cross with a circle around it (Fig.2.4) and then just a cross within a circle (Fig.2.5).

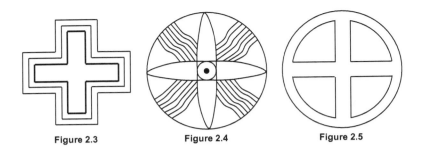

| Figure 2.3 | Figure 2.4 | Figure 2.5 |

In the form of a cross within a circle it was called the Celestial Disk and evolved into a Winged Disk and Winged Globe (Fig. 2.6). This symbol can be found all over the world on "temples and palaces, carved on rocks, etched on cylinder seals, painted on walls. It accompanied kings and priests, stood above their thrones, 'hovered' above them in battle scenes, was etched into their chariots. Clay, metal, stone, and wood objects were adorned with the symbol. The rulers of Sumer and Akkad, Babylon and Assyria, Elam and Urartu, Mari and Nuzi, Mitanni and Canaan - all revered the symbol. Hittite kings, Egyptian pharaoh's, Persian shar's - all proclaimed the symbol (and what it stood for) supreme." (Rf6).

Figure 2.6

Modern researchers mistook this symbol as a representation of the Sun which led to it being called a Sun Disk. The characterization of this symbol as a Sun Disk has led to much confusion. For example, the Egyptian Neteru were said to have come to Earth in their Celestial Boats from the Planet of Millions of Years, also known as the Imperishable Star. The Celestial Disk represented the Anunnaki/Elohim/Nephilim/Neter and the place they came from. Because researchers mistakenly thought the image was a Sun Disk they incorrectly labeled them as Sun-Gods. More evidence that this symbol did not represent the Sun can be found in ancient drawings which show this symbol along with the symbol of the Sun, demonstrating that the two separate images represented two separate things.

Nibiru has been called many different names over the years. The Babylonians called it MARDUK. The Egyptians called it the

14

IMPERISHABLE STAR and PLANET OF MILLIONS OF YEARS. The Dogon tribe of Africa called it Sigi Tolo (said to mean SIRIUS). It is also listed by the name SIRIUS in the Qur'an. The ancient Greeks called it MOUNT OLYMPUS. The Bible's Book of Revelation calls it WORMWOOD, the biblical planet of the Nephilim. Contemporary scholars call it PLANET X.

Other researchers believe that the Anunnaki/Elohim/Nephilim came from Mars, which they colonized in the distant past. When some sort of cataclysmic event occurred on Mars they were forced to escape and traveled to Earth. However, this theory may stem from ancient drawings which some believe demonstrate that the Anunnaki/Elohim/Nephilim used Mars as a way station to transport items from Earth back to their home planet. Perhaps this is where the colonization theory stems from.

Another theory is that the Anunnaki/Elohim/Nephilim were not from another planet at all, but simply a race of humans on Earth that evolved into a highly technologically advanced society, possessing all the similar types of technology that we have today, like aircraft, helicopters, rocketships, motorized boats, communication equipment, etc. At some point in time civilization was destroyed due to a cataclysmic event and the few survivors slowly began to repopulate the Earth.

Keeping in mind that the overwhelming majority of people on Earth, while they know how to operate the technological devices that we use today, they have no idea how to actually build them from scratch. If everything was suddenly destroyed, but for a few people (with only the clothes on their back) who had no idea how to create anything, civilization would quickly plunge into a primitive state.

Further, with DNA analysis proving that modern humans have existed for at least a few hundred thousand years, this is plenty of time for many advanced civilizations to have arisen on Earth, been destroyed, then reemerge again out of the rubble. You also need to keep in mind that with all of the technological advances that countries like the U.S. have made, the U.S. has only existed for a few hundred years. Imagine how many advanced civilizations like the U.S. could have existed over a few hundred thousand years.

There are also researchers who believe that an advanced race of humans, whether from Earth or another planet, never existed at all. Despite all the ancient texts and archaeological discoveries they argue that if such advanced civilizations existed "Where did all the technology go?" This is a good point and does raise questions; however, there are logical explanations. First, as you will see the Anunnaki/Elohim/Nephilim tried to prevent mankind from obtaining "knowledge." They wanted mankind to remain a primitive slave.

15

Perhaps when they left they removed the technology from Earth so that we would not have access to it. Second, lets say it was left here but was destroyed in the Great Flood; everything having been submerged under sea water. Over time sea water dissolves most things. In modern times we can visually see how huge sunken ships constructed with tons of metal begin to decay. In several hundred years the sea water completely dissolves the metal to the point where it no longer exists. Imagine ancient technology that has been under sea water for ten thousand years or more. Certainly this could reasonably explain why it no longer exists.

Where did the Anunnaki/Elohim/Nephilim come from? Were they from another planet? Were they an advanced civilization that arose on Earth? The one thing I am certain of is that despite the advances we have made in science, technology and astronomy we are still a very primitive people. It was only in the last couple hundred years that modern astronomers were able to discover Uranus (1781), Neptune (1846) and Pluto (1930). Other than sending probes past some of the planets in our solar system and landing rovers on Mars, modern man has only set foot on the moon. As of today we still have no real in-depth knowledge of the planets in our own solar system let alone the hundreds of billions of other solar systems contained in our universe. Mysteries that we are far from unlocking. As Albert Einstein stated:

> All our science, measured against reality, is primitive and childlike - and yet it is the most precious thing we have.

As new discoveries are made the picture will continuously change. In fact, it is already changing. In 1983 NASA's Infra-Red Astronomical Satellite (IRAS) discovered a "Neptune-sized planet" at the edge of our solar system that was slowly moving towards Earth. The discovery made headlines but was hushed up and immediately retracted the next day (Rf7). Questions were raised wondering if this could be evidence of Planet X.

In 2003 our understanding of the solar system changed again when researchers found a dwarf plan just outside of Pluto. They labeled it Sedna. Was this the same celestial body that NASA discovered in 1983 which was hushed up for some reason, or another that they are publicly allowed to speak of?

In 2011 an article was published in the newspaper *American Free Press* entitled *"Why Is U.S. Government Moving Installations to Center of Nation?"* revealing some evidence that the government may have some real knowledge of Planet X and is making preparations. According to John Moore (a former Green Beret and graduate of the US Military Intelligence School, who produced a 2008 documentary called *Global Warming: What the Government*

Isn't Telling You), NASA's Pioneer 10 space probe discovered a large planetary body with a quarter mile debris field. Through interviews with researchers, Navy veterans and a former U.S. intelligence officer, conducted since 2000, Moore states that they all believe it to be planet Nibiru (aka Wormwood, Planet X). As the planet gets closer it "causes all sorts of problems ... like violent climate changes, rising ocean levels, 200-mile-an-hour winds, earthquakes, volcanoes and so forth." According to a classified military briefing in 1985, Steven Canfield, a retired veteran of the U.S. Navy Submarine Corps, stated they were shown a map of America with new coastlines that will occur once the planet gets closer. In accordance with this information, U.S. Government Agencies like the CIA, NSA, NASA, the Plum Island research facility, and FEMA have been moving their coastal operations to inland safe areas (Rf8).

In 2012 astronomers discovered a pink dwarf planet labeled 2012 VP-113 (nicknamed Biden) just beyond Sedna. More importantly, Scott Sheppard of the Carnegie Institute for Science and his colleague Chadwick Trujillo of the Gemini Observatory demonstrated that the orbital analysis on this dwarf planet, Sedna and about 10 other objects in the area, indicates that a giant "super-Earth" is lurking on the outer edge of our solar system at about 19 billion miles from the Sun (Pluto is 2.8 billion) (Rf9). Is this more evidence of Planet X, the celestial body that the government wanted hushed up?

Further, using the latest technology astronomers have now been able to identify many new planets in our Universe. As reported in the March 17, 2014 issue of USA Today, NASA's Kepler space telescope (that was launched in 2009) has been able to peer deep into other solar systems and recently discovered 715 planets orbiting 305 other stars.

As reported in the February 1, 2016 issue of *Time* magazine (Vol. 187, No.3), Caltech astronomer Micheal Brown announced the discovery of what appears to be a 9th planet in our solar system orbiting well beyond Neptune. While they have not been able to see it yet, Brown along with fellow Caltech planetary scientist Konstantin Batygin have observed its gravitational influence.

Are one of these planets the mysterious Planet X? Only time will tell.
While the question of where they exactly came from is still definitively unanswered, based upon the ancient texts and archaeological discoveries, we know for a fact that at some point in our past this advanced race of people inhabited the Earth.

3

ARRIVAL ON EARTH

THE ANUNNAKI/ELOHIM/NEPHILIM are estimated to have arrived on Earth around 445,000 B.C. This calculation is based upon several ancient sources detailing the historical events on Earth prior to the Great Flood.

Figure 3.1

One source is the *Sumerian King List* (Fig. 3.1). On a four-sided prism of baked clay the Sumerians recorded the names of 8 people who ruled over 5 cities in Sumer dating back to an amazing 241,200 years before the Great Flood. It then details the names of kings and the cities they ruled after the Great Flood. The *Sumerian King List* was cataloged as WB-444 by Stephen Langdon in *Oxford Editions of Cuneiform Texts (1923)* and is currently in the possession of the Ashmolean Museum of Art and Archaeology in Oxford, England. Another clay tablet cataloged as WB-62, also in the Ashmolean Museum, lists 10 kings who ruled over 6 cities, taking us back 456,000 years before the Great Flood. (Rf1).

Another source comes from the Babylonian priest-historian named Bel-Re'ushu (Berossus in Greek), meaning "The Lord is his Shepard," who was given the task of compiling the history of the world. He created the *Babyloniaca* which consisted of three volumes and dedicated it to King Antiochus I (279-261 B.C.). Berossus explained that before man existed the Anunnaki/Elohim/Nephilim alone ruled the Earth. While the books no longer exist, a number of historians have quoted from them. Their quotes have been termed "Fragments of Berossus." Berossus lists 10 kings of the Chaldeans who reigned over 5 cities, totaling 432,000 years before the Great Flood (Rf2). Some scholars believe the Berossus account to be the most accurate.

Supporting the Berossus account is the *Aegyptiaca*; three volumes of books in which the history and prehistory of ancient Egypt was recorded by Men-Thoth (Manetho in Greek) meaning "Gift of Thoth." King Ptolemy Philadelphus ordered Manetho to create it around 270 B.C. and it was deposited into the Great Library of Alexandria where it eventually was destroyed during the burning of the library. However, some of it has been preserved in the writings of the Jewish historian Flavius Josephus, Julius Africanus, and Eusebius of Caesarea who quoted Manetho. The *Aegyptiaca* listed the Anunnaki/Elohim/Nephilim as ruling over Egypt long before any "human" Pharaohs. Manetho listed 8 Anunnaki/Elohim/Nephilim as reigning for a total of 13,870 years (Ptah-9,000y, Ra-1,000y, Shu-700y, Geb-500y, Osiris-450y, Seth-350y, Horus-300y, Thoth-1,570y). Manetho then lists thirty (what he calls half-Anunnaki half-human) rulers reigning for a total of 3,650 years, followed by a chaotic period of 350 years with no ruler. That's 17,870 years before a human Pharaoh ruled Egypt; the first human being the Pharaoh Mena (Rf3).

Manetho's list is corroborated by the Greek historian Herodotus who visited Egypt in the 5th century B.C. Herodotus was provided with the history of the Pharaohs who ruled Egypt and confirmed that before Mena Egypt was ruled by the Anunnaki/Elohim/Nephilim whom they called Neteru (Rf4). Manetho's list was also corroborated by the *Turin Papyrus* and the *Palermo Stone*, so named after the museums in Italy where they are kept (Rf5).

Another source is the *Atrahasis Epic* (Rf6). The *Atrahasis Epic* describes how the Anunnaki/Elohim/Nephilim toiled on Earth mining for "40 periods" before they decided to create mankind (this topic will be discussed at length in another chapter). One period or "shar" equals 3,600 Earth years, therefore 40 periods is 144,000 years on Earth before mankind was created. Modern DNA analysis informs us that the first humans were created around 300,000 B.C. If you add 144,000 years to this date you arrive at 444,000 B.C., which corroborates the time span of some of the King Lists (i.e. 144,000 years subtracted from the 432,000 year date of Berossus' list equals 288,000 years before the Great Flood as the date they create mankind; 144,000 years subtracted from the 456,000 year date of artifact WB-62 equals 312,000 years before the Great Flood as the date they created mankind). From this, we know that the date of their arrival had to be at least as old as the King Lists state, but could be older.

* * *

According to the ancient Mesopotamian texts it appears that the arrival of the Anunnaki/Elohim/Nephilim on Earth arose out of their need to obtain gold (some researchers claim to fix the deteriorating ozone layer on planet Nibiru).

After discovering that Earth possessed a plentiful supply of gold in its waters, King ANU decided to send his son Enki and a crew of fifty people to establish a base camp on Earth. It was their job to assess the situation on Earth, establish living facilities, and begin operations to retrieve the gold from Earth's waters (Rf7).

When Enki and his crew first landed on Earth, Earth was in the midst of an ice age. The second glacial period began 480,000 to 430,000 years ago. At that point in time "about a third of Earth's land area was covered with ice sheets and glaciers" (Rf8).

Splashing down in the Erythrean Sea (present day Arabian Sea), Enki and his crew waded ashore wearing what looked like fish suits. This landing would later spawn legends of fish-men emerging from the sea throughout many cultures. For example, the Babylonian account, as explained by Berossus, describes how the fish-man Oannes emerged from the Erythrean Sea. Oannes was described as having the head and feet of a man but the body of a fish. He was articulate, had a human voice, and was endowed with reason (Fig. 3.2) (Rf9).

Figure 3.2

We know that these weren't actually "fish-men" but simply humans wearing some type of space-suits or diving suits. Ancient depictions of men and women wearing such suits still exist. For example, a wall sculpture of Ishtar at her Temple in Ashur shows her wearing a type of spacesuit with a helmet and goggles (Fig. 3.3) (Rf10); a drawing from Val Camonica in Northern Italy shows people in suits with unusual headgear (Fig. 3.4) and an ancient drawing from Tassili in the Sahara looks similar to a modern astronaut (Fig. 3.5) (Rf11).

Figure 3.3

Figure 3.4

Figure 3.5

After Enki (nicknamed Nudimmud in this text) waded ashore with his crew they made their way towards southern Mesopotamia. When they reached the edge of the marshes Enki said "Here we settle" and they established their very first settlement on a half-frozen Earth. In a text that scholars have named Enki and the Land's Order Enki described his landing on Earth:

> When I approached Earth
> there was much flooding.
>
> When I approached its green meadows,
> heaps and mounds were piled up at my command.
>
> I built my house in a pure place...
>
> My house - its shade stretches
> over the Snake Marsh. (Rf12)

Because Enki's settlement was on a Snake Marsh, he acquired the "Totem" of a Snake/Serpent. The Lost Book of Enki describes how over a period of 6 days they "fixed the soil", "erected a reed-hut", "separated waters from waters, marshwaters from sweetwaters", "searched the grass and trees for food", "built mold and brick abodes in the encampment", "built a boat of reeds and hunted for food." It then explains how on the 7th day everyone was gathered together and Enki spoke: 'A hazardous journey we have traversed. At Earth we with success arrived, much good we attained, an encampment we established. Let this day be a day of rest; the seventh day hereafter a day of resting always be!'" Enki then named his settlement E.RI.DU, meaning "house in the faraway built." Eridu was located in the area that would later be known as Sumer (present day Iraq) (Rf13).

Another text which has been labeled the *Myth of Enki and Eridu* explains how:

> The lord of the watery-deep, the king Enki...
> built his house....
> In Eridu he built the House of the Water Bank....
> The king Enki ... has built a house:

22

Eridu, like a mountain,
he raised up from the earth;
in a good place he had built it. (Rf14)

It is also believed that the arrival of the Anunnaki/Elohim/Nephilim and the creation of Eridu is the reason we call our planet Earth. We see this in the etymology of the word:

In German it is *Erde*, from *Erda* in Old High German; *Jordh* in Icelandic, *Jord* in Danish. *Erthe* in Middle English, *Airtha* in Gothic; and going eastward geographically and backward in time, *Ereds* or *Aratha* in Aramaic, *Erd* or *Ertz* in Kurdish, *Eretz* in Hebrew. The sea we nowadays call the Arabian Sea, the body of water that leads to the Persian Gulf, was called in antiquity the Sea of Erythrea; and to this day, ordu means an encampment or settlement in Persian. ... in time the whole settled planet came to be called after that first settlement- *Erde, Erthe, Earth* (Rf15).

Enki directed his initial operations on Earth from here and Eridu would eventually become Enki's place of worship throughout Mesopotamian history. Archaeologists have since discovered what they believe to be the ancient Sumerian city Eridu. They even discovered a Temple that was dedicated to Enki which appears to have been built and rebuilt many times, dating back to 3800 B.C. (Rf16). However, due to the dating, it appears that this city was only a recreation of the original Eridu that existed there hundreds of thousands of years earlier.

The Anunnaki/Elohim/Nephilim proceeded with their assigned task of extracting gold from the waters we now call the Persian Gulf. However, due to the huge amounts of water they had to process in order to obtain it they decided to look for an alternate method. Enki discovered that they could obtain the needed gold by mining the rocks in the AB.ZU. The Abzu (aka Apsu) was a land in the Lower World or Southern Hemisphere. "The Sumerian pictograph for AB.ZU was that of an excavation deep into Earth, mounted by a shaft" (Fig. 3.6) (Rf17), representing the mining activities that would take place there. It is believed to be Arali, the Land of Mines, in Southeastern Africa.

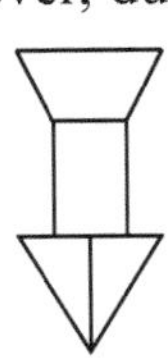

Figure 3.6

Anu decided that these developments would require "more personnel," "new equipment," and "settlements on two continents." The Mission also "required a different type of leader, one less of a scientist" but geared more towards organization, discipline and command experience. Anu decided to send his other son Enlil (Lord of the Command) to Earth. He was "a strict disciplinarian, a 'by-the-book' commander" (Rf18).

23

Enlil's journey to Earth was recorded on an unusual Circular Tablet made of clay that was discovered when archaeologists unearthed the Royal Library of Nineveh (Fig.3.7). It is currently in the possession of the British Museum in London. The Tablet is believed to be an Assyrian copy of an earlier Sumerian original.

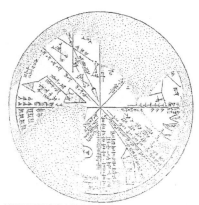

Figure 3.7

The Tablet records the route in which Enlil traveled to Earth from planet Nibiru. It is divided into eight sections and describes both graphically and in words the way Enlil "went by the planets" to Earth accompanied by some operating instructions. This can be seen on a segment of the Tablet (Fig. 3.8) (Rf19).

As the Anunnaki/Elohim/ Nephilim began to colonize Earth, they constructed

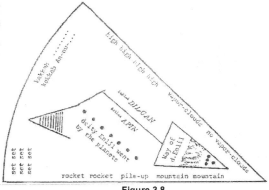

Figure 3.8

various cities/centers that were needed to facilitate their mission:

They established a communications center called LARSA which was used as an intermediary between those who landed on Earth and the astronauts called IGI.GI who stayed in the spaceship orbiting Earth. Enlil took command of and lived in Larsa (Rf20).

They built a metallurgical center called BAD.TIBIRA which they used to process the extracted gold (Rf21). Enlil's son NANNAR/SIN (NU.GIG meaning "He of the Night Sky") was placed in command of it (Rf22).

A space control center was built called LARAK to guide the landing shuttle-craft. Enlil placed his son NINURTA (PA.BIL.SAG) in command of it (Rf23).

The actual launch and landing site for the rocketships was called SIPPAR. It was built upon the peaks of Mount Ararat. Nannar/Sin placed his son UTU/SHAMASH in command of it because he was trained in rocketry. It is believed that this site was used because the bend at the Euphrates River was one of the richest known sources of fuel. Surface bitumens and petroleum products could be collected without deep digging or drilling (Rf24).

They created a Medical Center in a city called SHURUPPAK. Enlil and Enki's sister, NINHURSAG, was given command of it. Ninhursag was a nurse and became their Chief Medical Officer (Rf25).

While staying in Larsa Enlil began to construct a new Mission Control Center. It was designed to be a command and communications center where he could oversee all the other cities/centers on Earth, coordinate with planet Nibiru, and the Igigi who were stationed on Mars and orbiting Earth in spaceships. The Mission Control Center was called NIBRU.KI (The Earth Place of Nibiru) in Sumerian and later called NIPPUR in Akkadian. The connection between Earth and Nibiru was called DUR.AN.KI. (Rf26).

The texts explain that Enlil stayed in Larsa for 6 shars (21,600 years) while the Mission Control Center in Nippur was being constructed:

> The Anunna ... are working. The axe and the carrying basket, with which they laid foundation of the cities, in their hands they held. (Rf27)

In the center of Nippur they constructed a massive ziggurat called the E.KUR (House which is like a mountain), from which Enlil would eventually exercise his supreme authority over all the Anunna. On top of the E.KUR was Enlil's headquarters, the KI.UR (place of Earth's root). An extremely tall pillar (antenna) was erected on this level which Enlil used to broadcast his commands. Inside the Mission Control Center was a "mysterious chamber called the DIR.GA" where they held the *Tablets of Destiny* (Rf28). The E.KUR is why Enlil eventually became known to people as ILU.KUR.GAL, meaning the Lord of the Mountain.

As the mission continued a sibling rivalry started brewing between the two brothers, Enlil and Enki. It is believed to stem from Enki's frustration over the decision to grant his younger brother Enlil succession to the throne. Enki felt that because he was the "first born" he should be the legal heir regardless of the rules of succession. Due to his resentment Enki took advantage of certain situations in order to "stick-it" to his younger brother. One text explains how Enki withheld some kind of memory chips called "ME"s from Enlil that were essential to the mission. The arguing eventually reached dangerous levels and their father Anu had to journey to Earth to settle the dispute. Anu made his two sons draw lots to settle the issue of who would be in charge of what aspect of the mission (Rf29).

As a result of the drawing of lots "Earth Command" was transferred out of Enki's hands and Enlil was given Supreme Command over Mission Earth. Enlil would reign over all the settlements and operations and Enki was put in charge of the AB.ZU (the land of the mines in Africa). Enlil's domain was referred to as the Upper World (Northern Hemisphere) and Enki's domain was referred to as the Lower World (Southern Hemisphere) (Rf30).

As the mining operation in the Abzu proceeded, a few hundred Anunnaki/Elohim/Nephilim were assigned to "go down into the depths of the African soil and mine the needed minerals there." The ancient texts explain that this was a time before the "Black-Headed People" (the name they used to identify earthlings) were created (Rf31) and "in the absence of Mankind, the few Anunnaki had to toil in the mines" (Rf32).

Enki supervised the mining operation with one of his sons named GI.BIL (He Who Burns the Soil). An ancient depiction shows Enki at what some believe to be a mine entrance or shaft. Gibil can be seen there standing above ground while another person toils underground on his hands and knees (Fig. 3.9) (Rf33).

The Anunnaki/Elohim/Nephilim had their mining operation working like a well oiled machine. Gold was mined in the ABZU, shipped to BAD-TIBIRA for processing. The small ingots were then shipped to SIPPAR, transported by shuttle-craft in small shipments to Mars.

Figure 3.9

The Anunnaki/Elohim /Nephilim established a base on Mars to act as a Way Station between Earth and Nibiru. With its "lesser gravitational pull" Mars "served as a space base from which

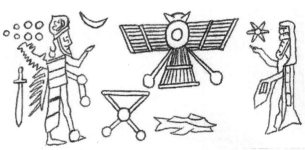

Figure 3.10

the Anunnaki shipped larger and heavier loads to Nibiru" (Rf34). It is believed that a 4,500 year old cylinder seal (Fig. 3.10) which is now in the possession of the Hermitage Museum in St. Petersburg, Russia depicts "an astronaut on Mars (the sixth planet) communicating with one on Earth (the seventh planet ...), with a spacecraft ... between them" (Rf35)

Modern astronomers have have even located what they believe to be evidence of the ancient Anunnaki/Elohim/Nephilim space base on Mars. Similar to the Great Pyramids and Sphinx found in Egypt, it appears that Pyramids and a Face carved in rock have been located on Mars by the Mariner and Viking cameras.

On February 8, 1972, Mariner 9 took pictures of Mars' surface. In picture frames 4205-78 you can see three-sided pyramids in the Elysium plateau, in the region called Trivium Charontis. The pyramids are also seen on frames 4296-23 which were taken six months later (Rf36).

In the November-December 1980 issue of *Frontiers of Science*, David Chandler and astronomer Franics Graham explained how the pyramids "were photographed six months apart, at different sunlights and angles, and yet show their accurate terrahedral shapes," demonstrating that they are artificial structures (Rf37).

Another area named Cydonia shows artificially made Pyramids aligned with a Martian "sphinx" to the east of these pyramids. The Martian sphinx is a rock carved with "the features of a well proportioned human face," which appears to be "a man wearing some kind of helmet, with a slightly open mouth and with eyes that look straight out at the viewer". You can view these structures in the panoramic NASA photo 035-A-72 (Rf38).

NASA tried to downplay the pictures arguing that the human face was "just a lay of light and shadows on a rock eroded by natural forces," and they filed the photographs away without further action. "The Viking photo, bearing the catalog number 76-A-593/17384, was simply titled 'HEAD.'" (Fig. 3.11) (Rf39)

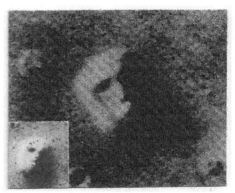

Figure 3.11

Another NASA image of the Face, cataloged as 070-A-13, was found by Lockhead computer scientist, Greg Molenaar. He also found "more photos of the Cydonia area taken by different Viking Orbiter cameras and from both the right and left sides of the features (there are eleven by now)" (Rf40).

A computer conference called *The Independent Mars Investigation Team* was held to investigate the features and data obtained on the pyramids and face. Scientists and specialists, including Brian O'Leary (scientist-astronaut), David Webb (member of the U.S. President's Space Commission), and Richard C.

Hoagland (science writer and one-time consultant at the Goddard Space Flight Center, who also organized the conference) ultimately concluded that:

> the "Face" and "pyramids" were artificial structures," and that "other features on the surface on Mars were the handiwork of intelligent beings who had once been on Mars.

It is believed that the "Face and the principal pyramids ... were built about half a million years ago in alignment with sunrise at solstice time on Mars" (Rf41). This is exactly the same time the ancient texts state the Anunnaki/Elohim/Nephilim were using Mars as a Way Station.

Images of what appear to be "walled structures, roads," and "a hublike compound" have also been found. In 2005 NASA's Mars Rover found what may be sand-covered structural remains with distinct right-angled corners (Rf42). NASA's Curiosity Mars Rover sent back an image of what appears to be a small metallic looking protuberance on a rock (Fig. 3.12) (Rf43). If you examine it close enough the top portion of it looks strikingly similar to the head of an alligator. NASA's Opportunity Rover recently discovered that Mars once had water that they believe was drinkable.

Figure 3.12

Despite the evidence of the Pyramids and Face on Mars NASA has chosen to remain silent. In fact, NASA even encloses rebuttals to convince you that it is not a Face, when you request copies of the Face image from the National Space Flight Center in Greenbelt, Maryland (Rf44).

King Anu ultimately divided the mission into two groups. Six hundred (600) were stationed on Earth and known as Anunnaki (Those of Anu Who Came to Earth). Three hundred (300), known as IGI.GI (Those Who Observe and See), operated the base on Mars and the shuttle-craft orbiting Earth (Rf45).

As the mining continued the Anunnaki/Elohim/Nephilim started complaining about the hard workload. Despite the advanced tools that they had, the ancient texts paint a dark and gloomy picture of the conditions the people working in the mines had to endure. They describe how they worked "in darkness", ate "dust as food," and how the mines were thought of as the "land of no return" (Rf46).

One of the tools that the Anunnaki/Elohim/Nephilim carried was the SILVER AXE "which shines as the day,' even underground" (Rf47). The use of this "AXE" is an important point to remember because future cultures actually used the AXE symbol to identify or describe the people that created their civilization and ruled over them. For example, the Egyptians used the hieroglyph of an AXE (Fig. 3.13) to identify the NETERU. All the Egyptian Neteru (mistakenly translated as gods) were in fact the Anunnaki/Elohim/Nephilim who carried the AXE. Egyptian records even acknowledge that the Neteru came from a foreign land called Ta-Neter and Ta-Ur. This was the Sumerian land of Ur. The very place where the Anunnaki/Elohim/Nephilim created their initial settlement on Earth, as described above!

Figure 3.13

The AXE symbol of the Anunnaki/Elohim/Nephilim became a sacred symbol among many cultures, even giving rise to the "House of the Double Axe" as can be seen on these three cubes (Fig. 3.14) (Rf48). The AXE symbol can be found on the megaliths of Brittany, it can be found in "the prehistoric remains of the funeral caves of the Marne, of Scandinavia and of America." An agate cylinder shows a priest in Chaldean garb offering sacrifice to the AXE which stands upright on an altar. It was noted that the AXE was not being represented as an item of daily use, but of a religious or magical purpose. AXE pendants made out of gold, lead, and even amber were worn by people (Rf49). We find the same Royal Axe in Mesoamerica where it was called Tupa-Yuari (Fig. 3.15) (Rf50), having been given to them by their Anunnaki/Elohim/Nephilim masters.

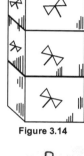

Figure 3.14

The Silver Axe, which was wielded by the Anunnaki/Elohim/Nephilim, is also where the legends of Thor stem from. The mythical god who carries the metal hammer (axe).

Figure 3.15

* * *

For 40 periods (144,000 years) the Anunnaki/Elohim/Nephilim suffered in the mines performing the back-breaking work to obtain the gold "and then they cried: No more!" and mutinied (Rf51).

4

"THE ADAM"
CREATED TO BE A SLAVE WORKER
THROUGH GENETIC MANIPULATION

IT WAS approximately 300,000 B.C. when the Anunnaki/Elohim/Nephilim who were working in the mines cried "no more!" and mutinied. The events surrounding the mutiny were recorded in the Atrahasis Epic:

> When the [Anunnaki/Elohim/Nephilim], like men,
> bore the work and suffered the toil-
> The toil of the [Anunnaki/Elohim/Nephilim] was great,
> the work was heavy,
> the distress was much. (Rf1)

The rebelling miners chose to take a stand and confront Enlil, saying to each other:

> Let us confront ... the Chief Officer,
> That he may relieve us of our heavy work.
> The king of the [Anunnaki/Elohim/Nephilim],
> the hero Enlil,
> Let us unnerve him in his dwelling! (Rf2)

The leader of the mutiny continued:

> Now, proclaim war;
> Let us combine hostilities and battle.
>
> The [Anunnaki/Elohim/Nephilim] heeded his words.
> They set fire to their tools;
> Fire to their axes they put;
> They troubled the [Anunnaki/Elohim/Nephilim] of mining
> in the tunnels;
> They held [him] as they went
> to the gate of the hero Enlil. (Rf3)

The mutiny occurred at night "half-way through the watch." Enlil's "house was surrounded." Kalkal, observing the attack, was frightened and slid the bolt to the gate. Kalkal quickly awoke Nusku and advised him of the situation. Nusku, in turn, awoke his lord Enlil from bed, saying: "My lord, your house is surrounded, battle has come right up to your gate" (Rf4).

Being the strict disciplinarian that he was, Enlil's first instinct was "to take up arms against the mutineers" and crush them into submission. But his chancellor Nusku advised him against it, arguing that instead he should convene a council of the Great Anunnaki/Elohim/Nephilim to address the problem (Rf5).

Enlil took his advice and summoned an Assembly which was presided over by his father Anu. Enlil demanded harsh punishment of the rebelling workers, even calling for the leader of the mutiny to be put to death. Despite Enlil's demands, after hearing the evidence Anu had compassion for the workers, saying:

> What are we accusing them of?
> Their work was heavy, their distress was much!
> and he wondered if there was another way to obtain the gold and relieve
> the workers of their hardships (Rf6).

During this time Enki, the brilliant chief scientist, was already spending much of his time in his laboratory studying the organisms and creatures that lived on Earth. Working with his son Ningishzidda they made scientific discoveries that they believed would solve their current problem. Enki's emblem of the Entwined Serpents (Fig. 4.1) was also attributed to Ningishzidda due to his vast knowledge. Enki spoke up at the Assembly and advised his father Anu:

Figure 4.1

> It is possible to relieve the [Anunnaki/Elohim/Nephilim] of the
> unbearable toil by having someone else take over the difficult work:
> Let a Primitive Worker be created! (Rf7)

Enki explained that they could use Ninhursag as a *Belet-ili*, meaning "Birth-Giving Goddess" (surrogate), through which to create primitive slave workers:

> Let her fashion a Lulu
> Let an Amelu beat the toil of the [Anunnaki/
> Elohim/Nephilim]!
> Let her create a Lulu Amelu,
> Let him bear the yoke! (Rf8)

While this idea fascinated the Assembly, they wondered how they could create a being "intelligent enough to use tools and follow orders" but dumb enough not to rebel against its masters.

Enki advised the Assembly that such a being already exists on Earth, a product of evolution. The being he was referring to was the ape-man (Homo erectus); a hairy being that was found living amongst other animals on Earth. Cylinder seals have been found depicting naked shaggy ape-men among their animal friends (Fig. 4.2) (Rf9).

Figure 4.2

Enki explained that in order to turn the ape-man into a primitive slave worker that was capable of taking over the mining work they would need to genetically manipulate (upgrade) its DNA by adding some of their genes to it. A "gradual process of domestication through generations of breeding and selection" would not suffice to meet their need for immediate slave workers. Consequently, it would also jump the gun on human evolution and bring man (Homo sapiens) into existence millions of years before its time (Rf10).

Enlil was strongly opposed to this idea, however, the Assembly voted to create the primitive workers. The Epic of Creation states:

> I will produce a lowly Primitive;
> "Man" shall be his name.
> I will create a Primitive Worker;
> He will be charged with the service of the
> [Anunnaki/Elohim/Nephilim],
> that they might have their ease. (Rf11)

A few hundred thousand years later the decision reached by the Assembly of Great Anunnaki/Elohim/Nephilim on that day would be recorded in the biblical texts of the Torah and Bible as:

> Let us make man in our image, in our likeness (Genesis 1:26)

The Bible goes on to explain that the "reason" they were creating man was because:

> there was no man to *work the ground* (Genesis 2:5)

The Anunnaki/Elohim/Nephilim needed slaves "to work the ground" so they created man in their image, and then:

> put him in the Garden of Eden *to work it* (Genesis 2:15)

The term *avod* in the biblical texts that has been translated as "worship" in fact means *"work."* Man did not worship the so-called "god" of the Old Testament he *worked* for him (Rf12).

32

This is the point in human evolution that many people speak of as the "missing link." The point in evolution where the Anunnaki/Elohim/Nephilim took the apeman/apewoman (Homo erectus), manipulated its DNA, and upgraded it to Homo sapiens.

Modern scientists uniformly agree that Homo erectus is the ancestor of Homo sapiens. The problems arise when scientists try to explain "how" Homo erectus evolved into Homo sapiens. Based upon what is known of the process of evolution, compounded by the lack of fossil evidence, it was impossible for Homo erectus to have naturally evolved into Homo sapiens in such a short period of time. This is why the sudden appearance of Homo sapiens posed questions.

It wasn't until the discovery of the ancient Mesopotamian texts and their later translation that we learned the truth about the biblical Elohim, their arrival on Earth, and the events that prompted them to create mankind. Ancient texts that seem to be backed up by modern DNA evidence.

Recently geneticists demonstrated, through a study of the Y Chromosome, that all male modern humans are descended from a common ancestor that is believed to have lived in Africa approximately 338,000 years ago. The results were published in the *American Journal of Human Genetics* (Rf13). Based upon the King Lists and Atrahasis text we arrive at a calculated date of approximately 312,000 to 288,000 years prior to the Great Flood as the time period in which the Anunnaki/Elohim/Nephilim created their slave workers. The Y Chromosome dating of 338,000 years ago is perfectly in line with and corroborates the ancient texts!

This is further supported by studies of Mitochondrial DNA that have been taking place since the 1980s. Mitochondria are passed down maternally. In one study Douglas Wallace of Emory University compared the Mitochondrial DNA of about 800 women and concluded that:

> the mtDNA in all of them appeared to be so similar that these women
> must have all descended from a single female ancestor. (Rf14)

Continuing the research, Wesley Brown (University of Michigan) compared the Mitochondrial DNA of twenty-one women from diverse racial and geographical backgrounds. Based upon the rate of natural mutation he concluded that they all originated from "a single mitochondrial Eve" who had lived in Africa between 300,000 and 180,000 years ago. This was also backed up in a study performed by Rebecca Cann of the University of California at Berkley. Using "the placentas of 147 women of different races and geographical backgrounds who gave birth at San Francisco hospitals" she examined the Mitochondrial DNA and determined that they all had a common female ancestor that lived between 300,000 to 150,000 years ago (Rf15).

Interestingly, the oldest known fossil evidence of Homo sapiens also coincides with this time period, which further supports the ancient texts.

The Mesopotamian texts even describe the specific process the Anunnaki/Elohim/Nephilim used to genetically manipulate our DNA and elevate us from apeman (Homo erectus) to Homo sapiens.

In a laboratory called *Bit Shimti* (House where the wind of life is breathed in), located in the Cedar Mountains (present day Lebanon), Enki, assisted by his son Ningishzidda and sister Ninhursag, began the process of genetically engineering a slave worker (Rf16).

The texts describe how their initial experiments involved combining the DNA of different animals which resulted in many hideous beings. According to Berossus, the temple of Belus at Babylon contained delineations of:

> "Men ... with two wings, some with four and two faces. They had one body but two heads, the one of a man, the other of a woman. They were likewise in their several organs both male and female.
>
> Other human figures were to be seen with legs and horns of goats. Some had horses' feet; others had the limbs of a horse behind, but in front were fashioned like men, resembling hippocentaurs. Bulls likewise bred there with the heads of men; and dogs with fourfold bodies, and the tails of fishes." (Fig. 4.3) (Rf17).

Figure 4.3

When they reached the point where they were confident enough that they could manipulate the genetic code they began the process of mixing their DNA with the apeman.

The process involved using the egg (ovum) of an apewoman (Homo erectus) and the genes/DNA (TE.E.MA in Sumerian) of a young Anunnaki/Elohim/Nephilim (whose identity is a matter of debate). Enki instructed Ninhursag/Ninmah:

> Mix to a core the clay
> from the Basement of the Earth,

34

just above the Abzu,
and shape it into the form of a core.
I shall provide good, knowing young Anunnaki
who will bring the clay to the right condition.
(Rf18)

According to Zecharia Sitchin the word translated as clay (which the Bible calls "dust" of the Earth) is *tit* in Akkadian and *TI.IT* in original Sumerian. He continues to explain how the Hebrew definition sheds light on its true meaning which is an egg/ovum (Rf19). The "clay" or "dust" of the Earth meant the egg/ovum of a female earthly being.

Their initial attempts at manipulating the genetic code produced many deformities. The texts describe how humans were created without genital organs, some had diseased eyes, trembling hands, sick livers, failing hearts, incontinence, etc. (Rf20).

Figure 4.4

Assyrian seals (Fig. 4.4 & 4.5) are believed by some to be depictions of this process, showing Ninhursag/Ninmah with her womb/omega symbol, and Enki preparing the mixtures (Rf21).

They ultimately succeeded in getting the mixture right. Ninhursag commented that she was now able to manipulate man's genetic code, making it as good or bad as her heart desires (Rf22).

Figure 4.5

At this point they implanted the fertilized egg/ovum into an Anunnaki/Elohim/ Nephilim to carry the newly formed human being to term:

Ninki, my goddess-spouse,
will be the one for labor.
Seven goddesses-of-birth
will be near to assist. (Rf23)

Some believe that these representations from the Indus Valley civilization depict the seven goddesses of birth as spoken of in the ancient texts (Fig. 4.6) (Rf24). Notice how both show only one child, including Ninhursag's womb/omega symbol.

Figure 4.6

According to the texts, due to a late birth, the child had to be delivered by cesarean section:

> The fateful 10th month was approaching;
> The 10th month arrived;
> The period of opening the womb had elapsed.

The texts explain that only after they performed this procedure "that which was in the womb came forth." Picking the baby human up she shouted triumphantly:

> I have created!
> My hands have made it! (Rf25)

An image from an Assyrian cylinder seal shows what some believe to be Ninhursag sitting near the Tree of Life holding up in her hands the newly created human (Fig.

Figure 4.7

4.7) (Rf26). Bypassing evolution by a million years, Homo sapiens had been created! Ninhursag/Ninmah said to her fellow Anunnaki/Elohim/Nephilim:

> You have commanded me to a task;
> I have completed it ...
> I have removed your heavy work.
> I have imposed your toil on Awilum ('Work-man'),
> You raised a cry for Awiluti ('Mankind')-
> I took off your yoke, I established your freedom! (Rf27)

At this time Ninhursag was renamed NIN.TI (Lady of Life). In the *Atrahasis Epic* Ninhursag is called Ma-mi:

> [s]a-su-ru ba-na-at si-im-tu
> The mother, the creator of destiny. ...
>
> u-su-ra-te sa nise(mes)-ma u-sa-ar (d)Ma-mi
> The figures of people, Mami formed. (Rf28)

From which, thousands of years later, we would derive the words Mamma, Mommy, Mom.

An ancient cuneiform text labeled *Enuma Elish, The Seven Tablets of Creation* describes the triumphant creation of the primitive slave workers as:

> The Merciful One, with whom it is to bestow life!
> May his deeds endure, may they never be forgotten
> In the mouth of the black-headed ones whom his hands have made!
> Tutu as Mu-azag, fifthly, his "Pure Incantation" may their mouth proclaim (Rf29)

"The Adam" was not a person named Adam, but a *generic term* that has been translated to mean "the Earthling." It stemmed from adamah which signified Earth's dark-red-soil (Rf30).

While "The Adam" was created in the image and likeness of the Anunnaki/Elohim/Nephilim, the ancient texts also explain that mankind did not look exactly like them. For example, unlike their height of nine to ten feet, mankind was much shorter. However, mankind was similar in that we no longer had the shaggy body hair that Homo erectus had. Other features that distinguished mankind from them was that the child had black hair and, unlike their white skin color, the child's skin color was like dark red blood and its hue was like that of the clay of the Abzu. This is why the Anunnaki/Elohim/Nephilim referred to mankind as the black-headed ones. Another feature that distinguished mankind from them was that the child's penis had a foreskin surrounding it (Rf31). This is the reason we circumcise today, to imitate the Anunnaki/Elohim/Nephilim.

"The Adam" was then used as the genetic model in which to create duplicates. This time they also created a female version with the intention of having the slave workers reproduce themselves on their own. Enki was told:

> O my son, rise from your bed.... Work what is wise. Fashion servants of the [Anunnaki/Elohim/Nephilim, and] may they produce their doubles' (Rf32)

The Atrahasis explains how they created seven males and seven females:

> Ninti nipped off fourteen pieces of clay,
> Seven she deposited on the right,
> Seven she deposited on the left;
> Between them she placed the mold.
>
> ...
> The Wise and learned,
> Double-seven birth-goddesses had assembled;
> Seven brought forth males,
> Seven brought forth females. (Rf33)

However, when they tried having the males procreate with the females they learned that the slave workers were not able to reproduce due to an error that occurred during the genetic engineering. An error that went unnoticed until the female version was created. The human they created was:

> a hybrid, a cross between two different, if related, species. Like a mule (a cross between a mare and a donkey), such mammal hybrids are sterile. Through artificial insemination and ... biological engineering we can produce as many mules as we desire ... but no mule can procreate and bring forth another mule (Rf34)

The deficient reproductive cells in "The Adam" required the Anunnaki/Elohim/Nephilim to repeat the process over and over again in order to produce the slave workers. How many times this occurred is not stated in the texts. The mass production of "The Adam" is believed to be depicted on a rock carving (Fig. 4.8). It shows Enki holding a laboratory flask from which the waters of life are flowing and Ninhursag. Interestingly, standing in front of them are "row upon row of human beings, whose outstanding feature is that they all look alike - like products of the same mold." The carving was found in the mountains of Elam (Rf35).

Figure 4.8

As the slave workers became available the Anunnaki/Elohim/Nephilim put them to work in the mines. Enlil, who was against the idea of creating them in the first place, despised the humans and treated them brutally. To them the humans were nothing more than domesticated animals which they worked as hard as they could and then ate them as food.

> Berosus called [the Anunnaki/Elohim/Nephilim] *'Annedoti'* which means 'the repulsive ones' in Greek. He also refers to them as 'musarus' or 'an abomination.' (Rf36)

While some people claim that he was referring to their physical appearance, he was actually referring to the cruel and inhumane treatment they inflicted upon mankind.

Some of the mines used by the Anunnaki/Elohim/Nephilim have been located through modern archaeological discoveries.

> South Africa's leading mining corporation, the Anglo-American Corporation, in the 1970s engaged archaeologists to look for such ancient mines. Published reports (in the corporation's journal Optima) detail the discovery in Swaziland and other sites in South Africa of extensive mining areas with shafts to depths of fifty feet. Stone objects and charcoal remains established dates of 35,000, 46,000, and 60,000 B.C. for these sites. The archaeologists and anthropologists who joined in dating the finds believed that mining technology was used in southern Africa "during much of the period subsequent to 100,000 B.C...."
>
> In September 1988, a team of international physicists came to South Africa to verify the age of human habitants in Swaziland and Zululand. The most modern technique indicated an age of 80,000 to 115,000 years. (Rf37)

Even Zulu legends speak of the history surrounding the creation of slave workers by the Anunnaki/Elohim/Nephilim:

> Regarding the most ancient gold mines of Monotapa in southern Zimbabwe, Zulu legends hold that they were worked by *"artificially produced flesh and blood slaves created by the first People."* (see Indaba My Children, by the Zulu medicine man Credo Vusamazulu Mutwa) (Rf38)

Due to the limited supply of slave workers, they were initially restricted to working the mines. However, this decision didn't sit well with the Anunnaki/Elohim/Nephilim that were working hard back in Mesopotamia. An ancient text named *The Myth of the Pickax* describes how they came to the Abzu, forcibly captured some of the slave workers, and brought them back to Mesopotamia. It explains how Enlil disabled communications between Earth and Nibiru then used a weapon known as the AL.A.NI (some type of huge rock drill) to break through to where the workers were being kept.

> The Lord called forth the AL.A.NI, gave its orders. He set the Earth Splitter as a crown upon its head, And drove it into the Place-Where-Flesh-Sprouted-Forth.
>
> In the hole was the head of a man;
>
> From the ground, people were breaking through towards Enlil.

He eyed his Black-headed Ones in steadfast fashion. ...

[The text goes on to describe how they wasted] no time in putting the slaves to work:

The Anunnaki stepped up to him,
Raised their hands in greetings,
Soothing Enlil's heart with prayers.
Black-headed Ones they were requesting of him.
To the Black-headed people,
they gave the pickax (Rf39)

The *Atrahasis Epic* explains how the human slaves were forced to build shrines using picks and spades, were forced to build big canal banks and how they were eaten as "food for the peoples, for the sustenance of the [Anunnaki /Elohim/Nephilim]" (Rf40).

As time went on they genetically manipulated the human DNA again in order to fix their inability to procreate. Ancient Sumerian and Egyptian Trees of Life are now being looked at as depicting the DNA structure and the ability of the Anunnaki/Elohim/Nephilim to manipulate it (Fig. 4.9) (Rf41).

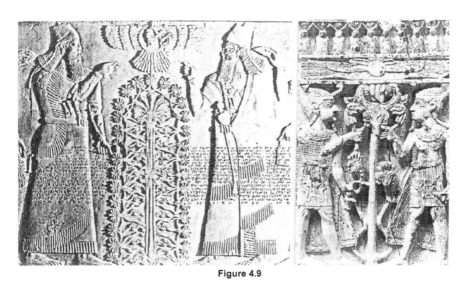
Figure 4.9

The events surrounding the creation of man would later be retold throughout all the cultures of the world. From Egypt to the opposite side of the world in Mesoamerica, we find the same legends:

An Egyptian Creation of Man scene depicts Ninhursag, whom they call Hathor (aka The Mother Goddess, Lady of Sinai, The Cow) seated on the left.

40

Upon her head is the Omega/womb symbol with the ends facing upward. She is pointing the "Ankh" symbol of life at two small beings as if she is bestowing life upon them (Fig. 4.10) (Rf42).

Figure 4.10

Across the Earth in Mesoamerica we find the same elements. The Nahuatl version of the Creation of Man explains that mankind was fashioned out of the blood of a god. The text is known as *Manuscript 1558*. At the end of the Fourth Sun the gods assembled at Teotihuacan to discuss their grievances surrounding the need to populate Earth. Similar to the Mesopotamian accounts of how Enki spoke up at the assembly, Quetzalcoatl (the Plummed Serpent) advised the other gods that he had an idea. He said that he could create a man out of earthly bones and the blood of a god. With the assistance of the Serpent Goddess (Cihuacoatl):

> She ground up the bones
> and put them in a fine earthen tub.
> Quetzalcoatl bled his male organ on them.

From this mixture of earthly elements and the blood of a god, mankind (whom the Nahuatl called Macehuales) was created (Rf43).

The Creation of Mankind is believed to be depicted on a large carved stone called *Izapa Stela 5* (Figs. 4.11 & 4.12) that was found in conjunction with a major stone altar. It measures some thirty square feet across its face.

Figure 4.11

Figure 4.12

An old bearded man wearing a conical shaped headdress (seated on the left) can be seen teaching a Maya looking man (seated on the right). In the image you can see the Tree of Life, diverse vegetation, birds, fish and human figures. Between the two men is Ninhursag's Omega/Womb symbol. Also depicted are the smooth sided pyramids of Gizeh along with waves of water perhaps symbolizing the Great Flood (Rf44).

* * *

The different species of early humans that existed on Earth were spawned from the multiple genetic manipulations that the Anunnaki/ Elohim/Nephilim performed, as well as the interbreeding that occurred between those various species. For example:

It is believed that the first primitive humans were known as the Pygmy. Wherever their remains are found they demonstrate that they had a very low cranial capacity, around 960 c.c. The sutures closed early and prevented further development of the brain, which retarded their learning (Rf45). They were the first "Little Earth-Men" or "Red Men" also known as Paleolithic Man.

Their anatomical features demonstrate the close relationship they had to Pithecanthropus Erectus. Their skulls are:

> dolichocephalic with markedly prominent superciliary ridges, receding brows, flattened vertex and projecting occiput, whilst the massive mandible sloped downwards and backwards anteriorly and was moreover wholly destitute of a chin (Rf46).

Their height ranges from only 1.158 to 1.378 meters (approx. 3 to 4½ feet); their skin color was chocolate brown, but of a reddish tint; their lips were long and narrow; they had long arms in proportion to the rest of their body; they also had an extraordinary large protruding abdomen which:

> is not the result of over-feeding, but is owing to the coecum being placed high up in the lumbar region, from it the colon is bent downwards to the right, and the iliac fossa, thus becoming largely distended, pursues a sigmond course across the abdomen (Rf47)

The Pygmies did not have any Totemic Ceremonies; they did not circumcise; and did not decorate their body with any patterns, scars, or weals. They were said to marry at 8 years of age (Rf48).

This species emerged around 300,000 to 350,000 years ago. It's possible that these Little Earth-Men (Red Men) were the result of one of the Anunnaki/Elohim/Nephilim's first sets of genetic manipulations. The primitive slave worker (The Adam) they created with limited intelligence; only enough to perform menial tasks.

While most people were killed off in the Great Flood, some of the Pygmies around the world survived. We find remnants of them living today in the Congo forests of southern Africa, known as the Bushmen (Rf49); remnants of them living in Australia; some have been found living amongst the mountains in China, the Viddas of Ceylon (Rf50); some have been found in Mexico, South America, the British Isles, and various other parts of the world (Rf51).

Most of the surviving Pygmies were exterminated by the later aboriginal races. For example, the Ainu (the aboriginals of Japan) described the Pygmies as a race of dwarfs that were red in color, only 3 to 4 feet high, and had very long arms in proportion to the rest of their body. They explained how their forefathers drove the Pygmies out and exterminated them with clubs (Rf52).

Examinations of modern day Pygmies, who have had the benefit of 300,000 years of evolution, show that they have since adopted some totemic ceremonies and some have begun to circumcise. They can count up to 100, have a very limited vocabulary, and record time using the lunar cycle. They have no "days," only "seasons" and "moons." They will not intermarry with black people or white people, only other Pygmies (Rf53).

Despite 300,000 years of evolution relatively little has changed in their mental abilities. According to the principles of evolution, modern humans should not be any more civilized than these primitive people:

> But, we are told, these tribesmen still live as if in the Stone Age because they have been isolated. But isolated from what? If they have been living on the same Earth as we, why have they not acquired the same knowledge of sciences and technologies on their own as we supposedly have?
>
> The real puzzle, however, is not the backwardness of the Bushmen, but our advancement; for it is now recognized that in the normal course of evolution Man should still be typified by the Bushmen and not by us (Rf54).

It is only by understanding the ancient texts, which detail the genetic manipulations, as well as the interbreeding with the Anunnaki/Elohim/ Nephilim (which will be discussed in the next chapter), that you can begin to comprehend why we are more advanced.

As their genetic engineering continued other species of humans emerged, including the most widely known archaic Homo sapiens, the Neanderthal Man (Homo neanderthalensis). This species is named after the Neander Valley in Germany where the first fossil of this species was discovered.

The Neanderthals were 5½ to 6 feet tall and very robust; substantially larger than the Pygmies. Their brain was also approx. 50% larger than the Pygmy. They had heavy eyebrow ridges, large teeth, and a slopping chin (Fig.4.13) (Rf55).

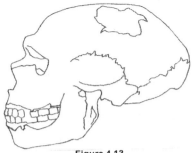

While they were originally thought to be unintelligent wild savages that did not

Figure 4.13

even posses the same vocal abilities as modern humans, recent evidence has shattered those beliefs. We now know that Neanderthals were quite intelligent. They not only made tools, but used those tools to make other tools. They knew how to create and use fire, had religious ceremonies and buried their dead (some sites have even been found with flowers buried next to them). According to professor Ralph S. Solecki of Columbia University they even knew how to use herbs for healing circa 60,000 years ago (Rf56).

Further, geneticists discovered that Neanderthals possessed the same FOXP2 gene (which is linked to the control of speech) as modern humans. This, combined with fossil evidence demonstrating that the Neanderthal hyoid bone (which is integral to the formation of sound) is identical to modern humans, proved that Neanderthals were capable of modern speech.

Based upon the genetic evidence and fossil discoveries, the Neanderthals emerged around 250,000 to 300,000 years ago and became extinct around 32,000 years ago. Fossils dating from 300,000 to 35,000 years ago have been found in Europe, the Middle East, China, and Africa (Rf57). In northeastern Greece, near Petralona, Dr. Aris Poulianos discovered a 300,000 year old skull in 1997 (Rf58). Remains have been found on the Iberian Peninsula dating to 45,000 years ago; the Vindija Cave in Croatia dating to 33-32,000 years ago.

It's possible that the Neanderthal species was due to a second set of genetic manipulations. Perhaps the Anunnaki/Elohim/Nephilim needed workers that were stronger and more intelligent than the Pygmies.

As the various species of archaic Homo sapiens interbred with each other more variations arose. Including a species that has been labeled Denisovans, which is known only through DNA obtained from a fossil finger bone found in a Siberian cave (Rf59).

Another species that emerged was Cro-Magnon Man (Modern Humans). This species is named after the site at Cro-Magnon (a cave near Les Eyzies in the Dordogne region in France) in which the first fossil evidence was discovered.

The earliest fossil evidence of Cro-Magnon that has been found to date stems back to circa 200,000 years ago. It was found at the Omo River in Ethiopia (Rf60). A previous discovery at the Awash River in Ethiopia was dated to circa 160,000 years ago.

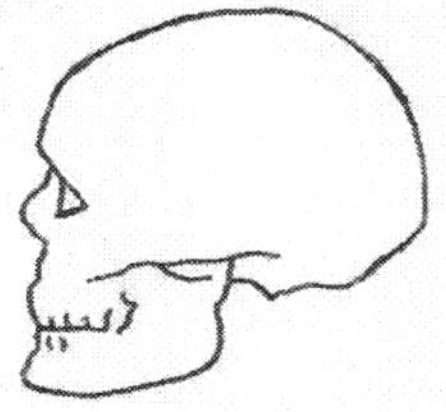

There are several differences between the Cro-Magnons and the Neanderthals. The Cro-Magnons have a different brain cavity with a rounded back (Fig. 4.14) (Rf61). The Cro-Magnon's brain is even 100 c.c. or 20% smaller than the Neanderthal's brain. The Cro-Magnon's cerebellum (which controls the coordination of muscles and the body's equilibrium) is much smaller than the Neanderthal's. Also, the Cro-Magnon's skeletal frame is smaller than the Neanderthal (Fig. 4.15) (Rf62).

Figure 4.14

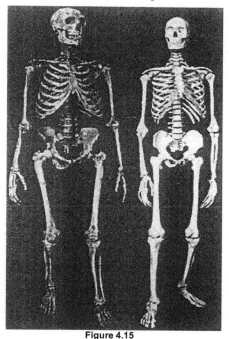

Figure 4.15

Genetic testing has now shown that modern human DNA and Neanderthal DNA are 99.5% to nearly 99.9% identical and most modern humans possess 20,000 to 25,000 Neanderthal genes (Rf63).

This is due to the fact that the Neanderthal and Cro-Magnon species lived side by side as contemporaries for a long time and interbred with each other producing hybrid offspring. Evidence of such co-habitation was found in two caves in Israel. A cave at Qafzeh near Nazareth and Kebara on Mount Carmel. The cave at Qafzeh was re-excavated in the 1960s by a joint Israel-French team and demonstrated that the two species co-habitated it around 70,000 years ago. This date was corroborated by scientists at the Hebrew University in Jerusalem. They even determined that the Cro-Magnons used this particular cave before the Neanderthals. After new dating methods were used in 1987, including Thermoluminescence, it was proven that both species co-habitated these areas as far back as 100,000 years ago. The results were published in Nature vols. 330 and 340 (Rf64).

Evidence that the two species practiced personal adornment (by using perforated shell beads) was found in the Skhul cave on Mount Carmel in Israel and dated to 120,000 years ago.

Remains of humans possessing a combination of Cro-Magnon and Neanderthal features have "emerged at digs in Spain (Atapuerca), Germany (Steinhem), Czechoslovakia (Mladec), Romania (Muierii), and France (St. Cesaire and Arcy-sur-Cure)" (Rf65).

Also, according to a paper in the magazine *PLOS ONE*, Italian scientists believe that the skeletal remains discovered in northern Italy provide the first archaeological proof that Neanderthals mated with modern humans 40,000 years ago and produced a hybrid. "From the morphology of the lower jaw, the face of the Mezzana individual would have looked somehow intermediate between classic Neanderthals ... and the modern humans." (Rf66).

One of the benefits of this interbreeding was that the Neanderthal immune system, which was highly adapted to fighting off diseases, was transferred to most modern humans.

The Cro-Magnon population eventually outcompeted and extinguished the archaic Homo sapiens. When the Great Flood killed off most of mankind (see Chapter 7) the make-up of the human population on Earth drastically changed. The only survivors were Homo sapiens sapiens (Cro-Magnon) and a small percentage of Pygmies.

A Note on Evolution

Some people argue that because one species lived side by side with another species as contemporaries for a while, that this fact proves that one did not evolve from the other.

They point to the Australopithecines living side by side with Homo habilis, then Homo habilis living side by side with Homo erectus, then Homo erectus living side by side with Homo sapiens, then Homo sapiens living side by side with modern humans. They also argue that because there are still apes living today, this proves that we did not evolve from a form of ape.

This argument is absurd! This is the exact gradual process that must occur according to evolution. Evolution does not occur all at once, as if someone flicks a light switch and every single one of the thousands, hundred thousands, or millions of an existing species immediately evolves into a new species.

Evolution is a gradual process that occurs slowly over time. Changes or mutations begin in one or a few members of an existing species. Those changes/mutations can occur naturally, they can occur by outside interference of another species, and they can occur through some form of panspermia (whether directed or not). Whatever the reason for the change/mutation, once it exists then it's survival of the fittest. If they are not killed off, slowly they increase in number. While the new species is increasing in number they will live side by side as contemporaries with the species they evolved from. They could live as contemporaries for 50 thousand years, 100 thousand years, a million years, etc. How long they will live side by side depends enormously on the living conditions on Earth.

For example, if food is scarce the weaker species will die from hunger, or they will be killed and eaten as food by the stronger species. If food is abundant then the weaker species may survive longer. Perhaps the stronger species will wage war against the weaker species and kill them off. Or perhaps the stronger species will be kind to the weaker species and this will greatly lengthen their existence on Earth. There are just too many variables.

Today, we are so civilized that when an animal species is on the verge of extinction we take steps to ensure their survival. We outlaw killing them. We actively take steps to increase their numbers. Actions that our ancestors did not practice, which lead to the eventual extinction of many species. Today, with our ability to grow enough food to feed the entire human population, there is no need to kill every living animal for food. This results in apes (who may have been extinct by now and consumed as food) flourishing in isolated parts of the world. However, as the human population continues to grow and more parts of the Earth are used for human habitation the jungles and forests where these apes are living will gradually get smaller and smaller. As a consequence, the number of apes will dwindle. Right now we see the number of apes and other wild animals steadily decreasing. This is "survival of the fittest" at work. When the human population has grown to the point where every area on Earth is inhabited by humans, the only remaining wild animals, if any, will be in cages. If we were not as civilized as we are, they may have already become extinct.

Some people argue: "Modern humans have not evolved into another species of human, so this proves that the theory of evolution is wrong." This is also absurd. Modern humans have only been around for a very short period of time when looked at on the evolutionary scale. It's impossible to know what will happen 50 or 100 thousand years from now. We may yet evolve into a higher species; an even more advanced human.

The theory of evolution is sound. The only problem with it arises when narrow minded people try to limit its scope. Darwin and other true evolutionists never claimed that one species, or a species foreign to Earth,

47

could not genetically interfere with the evolutionary process of another species. The theory of evolution is not at odds with the events described herein. Nor is the theory of evolution at odds with the possibility that a "God" started the entire process. It's possible that "God" created the initial building blocks and evolutionists are just explaining how the story is unfolding. The Anunnaki/Elohim/Nephilim, a product of evolution that occurred on another planet (also stemming from the same initial building blocks created by "God"), simply interfered with our Earth born human evolutionary process, and we are what we are today because of them. But evolution never stops, and continues even today. What we will be tomorrow, who knows.

5

THE ANUNNAKI/ELOHIM/NEPHILIM HAVE SEX WITH THE DAUGHTERS OF MEN

WHILE THE PRIMITIVE slave workers were created to solve their need for labor, their very existence posed a new set of problems for the Anunnaki/Elohim/Nephilim.

In order to maintain control over the humans they created, the Great Assembly decided that strict rules were to be followed. Among them:

Humans were to be kept away from any forms of "knowledge" that would enable the humans to elevate themselves above their slave status. This decree would later find its way into the Bible as: "you must not eat from the tree of ... knowledge" (Genesis 2:17).

In order to ensure that the humans did not grow too strong and pose a physical threat to them, humans were forbidden from eating animals, birds, and fish. Humans would only be allowed to eat plants and fruits. This decree would later find its way into the Bible as:

> I give you every seed-bearing plant on the face of the whole earth and every tree that has fruit with seed in it. They will be yours for food. (Genesis 1:29)

Their goal was to keep the humans as weak, unintelligent, and subservient slaves.

Another rule declared that it was forbidden for any Anunnaki/Elohim/Nephilim to have sexual intercourse with a human. They were afraid that such a mating would create hybrid offspring possessing too high a dose of their genes, resulting in a new species of humans with increased intelligence.

Despite the rules, in the generation of Jared (Rf1), when the "children of men" had multiplied upon the face of the Earth and beautiful and comely daughters were born onto them (Rf2), the Anunnaki/Elohim/Nephilim "lusted after them" and said to one another:

> Come, let us choose us wives from among the children of men and beget us children (Rf3)

Then their leader Semjaza said, "I fear ye will not indeed agree to do this deed, and I alone shall have to pay the penalty" (Rf4), for which they all responded:

> Let us all swear an oath, and all bind ourselves by mutual imprecations not to abandon this plan but to do this thing (Rf5)

On the summit of Mount Hermon, two hundred (200) Anunnaki/Elohim/ Nephilim swore this oath, and:

> took unto themselves wives, and each chose for himself one, and they began to go in unto them and to defile themselves with them... (Rf6)

The history of these events were later recorded in the Bible as:

> The Nephilim were on the earth in those days - and also afterward - *when the sons of the Elohim went to the daughters of men and had children by them.* They were the heroes of old, men of renown. (Genesis 6:4)

And, just as the Great Assembly had feared, the daughters of men "became pregnant" and hybrid offspring were born (Rf7). While it is uncertain as to which species of humans the Anunnaki/Elohim/Nephilim had sex with, it is the general consensus that the Cro-Magnon species was the result of this interbreeding.

As detailed in Chapter 1, the accounts of the Anunnaki/Elohim/ Nephilim having sex with the humans they created can be found throughout Mesopotamia, Egypt, India, China, Greece, Mesoamerica, Europe, etc.

In an attempt to stop them from "lusting" after and forcibly taking our women for sex, our early ancestors devised a plan. Girls were required to cover their faces and bodies with cloth so that the Anunnaki/Elohim/ Nephilim couldn't see what they looked like. It was believed that if they couldn't see the girls, they wouldn't "lust" after them and ultimately wouldn't forcibly take them for sex.

The modern practice of making women wear a "veil" over their face and/or body (that you see used by some cultures today) directly stems from this history. As the practice filtered down through the generations it eventually found its way into religious doctrines like the Qur'an which orders women to:

draw their cloaks (veils) all over their bodies (i.e. screen themselves completely except the eyes or one eye to see the way)... (Surah 33:59), and

draw their veils all over Juyubihinna (i.e. their bodies, faces, necks and bosoms) (Surah 24:31)

After breaking the above rule, this same group of Anunnaki/Elohim/ Nephilim then went on to break another rule. They started teaching the secret sciences to the children they had with the humans; knowledge that humans were strictly forbidden to possess.

An Anunnaki/Elohim/Nephilim named Semjaza taught humans magical spells, the sciences of "charms and enchantments," acquainting them with plants and how to cut roots for preparing the spells. Armaros taught man how to undue those enchantments (Rf8). Azazel taught humans the sciences of how to manipulate the elements and forge metals. Humans were learning the science of "how silver is produced from the dust of the earth," "how soft metal originates in the earth," and how "lead and tin are not produced from the earth like the first." Humans were taught how to make swords, knives, shields, and breastplates. All the metals of the earth were made known to them and the art of working them. They were taught how to make bracelets, ornaments, the use of antimony, the beautifying of the eyelids, all kinds of costly stones and all coloring tinctures (Rf9). Baraqijal taught mankind astrology; Kokabel taught mankind about the constellations; Ezeqeel taught mankind the knowledge of the clouds; Araqiel taught the signs of the earth; Shamsiel taught man the signs of the sun and Sariel taught man the course of the moon (Rf10). Mankind was taught about medicine, agriculture, mathematics, and the arts of writing and printing using cylinder seals.

This is why ancient cultures like the Sumerians possessed knowledge that was impossible for them to know. For example, the Sumerians not only knew that the planets Uranus and Neptune existed but knew that they were watery and greenish in color (Rf11). This was almost 6,000 years before modern astronomers discovered these planets in 1781 and 1846, respectively, and it wasn't until August 1989 that the unmanned satellite (Voyager 2) passed by Neptune sending back pictures, when modern astronomers discovered that they were in fact greenish-blue (aquamarine) in color! (Rf12)

The Sumerians also knew that the Earth was not the center of our solar system, but actually revolved around the sun. This was almost 6,000 years before it was re-discovered by the Polish astronomer Nicolaus Copernicus in 1543 A.D. when he published his study *De revolutionibus orbium coelestium*.

When Enlil (the Chief Commander of the Anunnaki/Elohim/Nephilim) discovered that his people were violating the law by procreating with the humans and teaching them sciences that they were forbidden to possess he was beyond outraged. Enlil decided that his only solution was to kill the humans. His attempts at destroying mankind will be discussed at length in Chapter 7.

6

GENES, TRAITS, and THE BLOOD OF THE GODS: EVIDENCE OF THE ANUNNAKI/ELOHIM/NEPHILIM BLOODLINE – RH NEGATIVE BLOOD

EVIDENCE SUPPORTING the biblical account of the Anunnaki/Elohim/ Nephilim taking "the daughters of men" and having children by them, as described in Chapter 5, can be found in our blood. In order to comprehend this you need to have a basic understanding of how we inherit various genes and traits.

Humans all possess the same basic shell (Fig. 6.1). We all have a brain, heart, lungs, skin, eyes, nose, mouth, arms, hands, legs, feet, etc. While this shell is basic to all of us, the TRAITS that we inherit actually make up what we look like. Traits are inherited characteristics which determine what color eyes we have, what color hair we have, what color skin we have, what our facial features look like, the size and shape of our nose, mouth, etc.

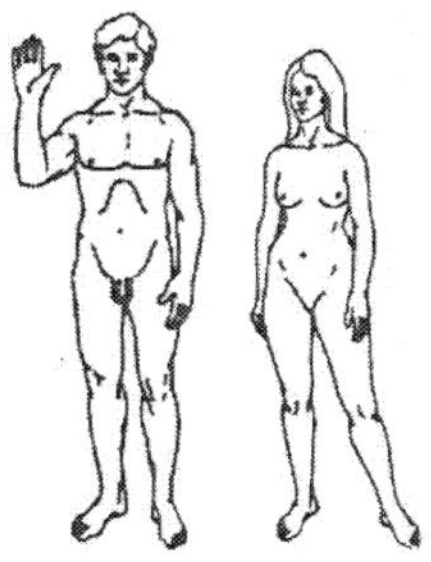

Figure 6.1

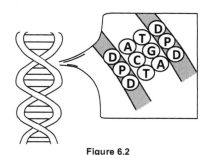

Figure 6.2

The specific traits that we receive are determined by the GENES contained in our DNA. The double-helix structure of DNA (Fig. 6.2) is comprised of two strands of alternating links of Deoxyribose ($C_5H_{10}O_4$) and Phosphate (PO_4H_2). Each link of the two strands is held together by connecting bases comprised of a combination of: 1 purine (Adenine ($C_5H_5N_5$) or Guanine ($C_5H_5N_5O$)) and 1 pyrimidine (Thymine ($C_5H_6N_2O_2$) or Cytosine ($C_4H_5N_3O$)). A long sequence of the base pairs (A-T) or (C-G) is referred to as a gene and controls the transmission and expression of one or more traits. Thousands of these genes make up a chromosome. To give you an idea, the longest human chromosome is said to contain 220 million base pairs.

The codes contained in our DNA control every function in our body. If the same DNA is inherited by two people they will look exactly alike. This is demonstrated in the case of identical twins.

A collection of the genes that have been acquired through generations and generations of interbreeding (i.e. parents, grandparents, great-grandparents, etc.) stemming back to the beginning of mankind that have now been passed down to you is called your GENE POOL.

As described in Chapter 4, all humans ultimately stem from a single lineage (the ape-man who was elevated to a Homo sapien through genetic manipulation). Whether you believe it occurred through natural evolution or genetic manipulation, it is a fact that humans ultimately evolved from apes. Geneticists have even proven that "95% of the base pairs in human DNA are exactly shared between chimpanzee and humans" (Rf1).

When we evolved from ape to human we inherited the ape's Gene Pool. I am calling the set of genes that we inherited from our ape ancestors the *ORIGINAL GENE POOL* in an attempt to make the process easier for you to understand. For the sake of simplicity I am also limiting the discussion to hair and skin color genes.

Original Gene Pool

Hair Genes	Skin Genes
Black, Brown, Blond, Red	Light, Medium, Dark

If you look at our ape ancestors you will see that they have the same shades of skin color and hair color that humans possess today. There are apes that have black hair, brown hair, blond hair, red hair (usually just orangutans) and grey hair. Likewise, there are apes that have white skin, black skin, and every shade of skin color in-between the two, under their coat of hair.

Where the genes/traits for hair color and skin color originally stem from (how the apes obtained these genes in the first place) no one knows. Science has not reached that level of discovery yet. However, we know that it did not have anything to do with cold or warm climate in and of itself as some people have erroneously claimed. I can only assume their perversion comes from someone's mis-interpretation of Darwin's Origin of Species wherein he explains that climate can affect the color of certain insects. We know this because the warm climate of Africa is no different than the warm climate of Florida. Generation after generation of humans with light skin color living in Africa and Florida haven't changed into a dark skin color. Likewise, many generations of humans with dark skin color have been living in cold climates like Europe and they also have not changed into a lighter skin color. This thought process only stems from an ignorance of biology.

However, the origin of the genes for hair and skin color are not the subject of this book so there is no need to discuss it at length herein. For the purpose of this chapter it is enough to know where humans obtained these genes from.

When our earliest human ancestors (Adam & Eve) were created they inherited the *Original Gene Pool* from our ape ancestors, which was then passed down to every other human on Earth.

The Gene Pool operates in the following manner: When a male and female procreate the father's Gene Pool and mother's Gene Pool are passed down to the child:

FATHER'S GENE POOL

Gene	Qty. in Pool
Black Hair:	1
Brown Hair:	45
Blond Hair:	1
Red Hair:	1
White Skin:	50
Black Skin:	1

MOTHER'S GENE POOL

Gene	Qty. in Pool
Black Hair:	1
Brown Hair:	30
Blond Hair:	1
Red Hair:	1
White Skin:	40
Black Skin:	1

CHILD'S INHERITED GENE POOL

Gene	Qty. in Pool
Black Hair:	2
Brown Hair:	75
Blond Hair:	2
Red Hair:	2
White Skin:	90
Black Skin:	2

Note: This is an over simplification as the actual Gene Pool will contain thousands of these genes in various combinations.

The Gene Pool that a child has access to is a combination of the Original Gene Pool (which contains at least one of each hair color and skin color gene) plus all the other genes that were added to it by parents, grandparents, great-grandparents, etc., through the generations by the mixing of Gene Pools.

When the child's DNA is forming 23 chromosomes will be chosen from his father's side and 23 from his mother's side, totaling the 46 chromosomes that make up a strand of human DNA. As you can see in the above example, because the example child's inherited Gene Pool contains higher percentages of the brown hair genes and white skin color genes the child will most likely inherit and be born with the traits of brown hair and white skin. The child's facial features will also be a mixture of the two parents. While this is the most likely outcome, IT IS NOT ABSOLUTE. As you can see, the genes for black hair, blond hair, red hair, and black skin are also contained in the child's Gene Pool and, while it is rare, the child could inherit any one of them.

Today, generally, if your mother and father have brown hair you will most likely inherit the trait of brown hair due to the larger percentage of the brown hair trait in your Gene Pool. BUT THIS IS NOT ABSOLUTE. The genes for blond hair, red hair, and black hair are also contained in the Original Gene Pool that was passed down to you and you could inherit any one of them.

Imagine that your Gene Pool looks like this:

br br br br br br br br br br br br br br
br br br br br br br br br **rd** br br br br
bl br br br br br br br br br br br br
br br br **b** br br br br br br br br **b** br

(br = brown hair gene) (rd = red hair gene)
(bl = blond hair gene) (b = black hair gene)

Because of the high percentage of br genes in this Gene Pool, when a child's DNA is forming it is most likely that a **br** will be selected and you will inherit and be born with the trait of brown hair. But because **rd**, **bl**, and **b** genes also exist in the Gene Pool it is possible for the child to inherit ANY one of them.

This is the same for skin color. If your parents have white skin color it is most likely that you will inherit the trait for white skin color due to the higher percentage of that trait in your Gene Pool. Likewise, if your parents have black skin color it is most likely that you will inherit the trait for black skin color. But again, THIS IS NOT ABSOLUTE. All humans possess the genes for white and black skin in their Original Gene Pool so it is possible to inherit ANY skin color. This is why two people who have white skin, blond hair and blue eyes can have a child that is born with black skin. At first the parents are confused, but after DNA testing and finding out the child is biologically theirs, the doctor will explain the process of genes and inherited traits. That while it is rare, because the gene for dark skin color is in the Gene Pool it is possible for a child to inherit it. Likewise, two people who have the darkest of brown skin color can have a child who is born with white skin, blond hair and blue eyes. Again, while it is rare, the gene for white skin color is in the Original Gene Pool and it is possible for a child to inherit it.

Imagine that your Gene Pool looks like this:

b b b b b b b b b b b b b b b b b b b b b b b
b b b b b b b b b b b b b b b b b b b b b b b
b b b b b b b b b b b b b b b b b b b b b b b
b b b b b b b b b b b b b b b b _w_ b b b b b

(b = black skin gene) (w = white skin gene)

Because of the high percentage of _b_ genes in this Gene Pool, when a child's DNA is forming it is most likely that a _b_ will be selected and you will inherit and be born with the trait of black skin. But because a _w_ gene also exists in the Gene Pool it is possible for the _w_ to be selected and the child would then inherit and be born with white skin color. This operates in the same manner when the Gene Pool contains a high percentage of _w_ genes and only one _b_ gene, in which case the child would most likely be born with white skin, but could inherit the one _b_ gene and be born with black skin.

Because every human's Gene Pool contains at least one gene from each hair color and skin color that was passed down to us from the *Original Gene Pool*, any human could be born with any physical appearance regardless of what its parents look like.

As humans continue to procreate the percentage of each gene that is contained in a Gene Pool will continuously change depending upon whom their ancestors have procreated with. For example, if people with blond hair procreate with each other their Gene Pools will mix and create a new Gene Pool with an even higher percentage of blond hair genes. If blond haired people remain in one isolated area and continue to procreate a large population of blond haired people will emerge. Likewise, if people with brown hair procreate with each other their Gene Pools will mix and create a new Gene Pool with an even higher percentage of brown hair genes. If brown haired people remain in one isolated area and continue to procreate a large population of brown haired people will emerge. Whatever traits are highest in a certain area will intensify.

Over time diverse variations of Gene Pools emerge. Some Gene Pools contain high percentages of brown hair, some have high percentages of blond hair, some have high percentages of red hair, some have high percentages of white skin genes, some have high percentages of black skin genes, etc. The Gene Pool is an ever changing mechanism which produces an endless variety of human appearances (the different facial features and combinations of eye color, hair color, shades of skin color, height, foot size, etc., that you see on Earth today).

In fact, all the different races on Earth in which society has classified as Caucasian, African, Asian, etc., are simply variations in the Gene Pools that occurred over time due to the mixing of traits when we procreate. When you fully understand how this process works you will see that WE ARE ALL RELATIVES.

Ancient texts provide some evidence that the first Homo sapiens had a dark skin color. As shown in Chapter 4, the texts state that "The Adam" was reddish-brown in color. The texts even state that because of this mankind was called the Black-Headed People. Another indicator that the first humans had dark skin color can be found in the birth of the biblical patriarch Noah.

The Bible explains that when Lamech was 182 years old he had a son and named him Noah (Rf2). While the Bible does not discuss the particulars of his birth, *The Book of Noah* (from which only fragments exist) explains that when Noah was born he didn't look like any other human on Earth:

> his body was *white as snow* and red as the blooming of a rose, (Rf3)

Noah's white skin color shocked his father Lamech so much that he ran out of the room to see his father Methuselah, and said:

> I have begotten a strange son, *diverse from and unlike man*, and *resembling the sons of the [Anunnaki/Elohim/Nephilim]*; and his nature is different, and he is not like us...
>
> And it seems to me that he is not sprung from me but from the [Anunnaki/Elohim/Nephilim] (Rf4)

At this point in time only the Anunnaki/Elohim/Nephilim had white skin color. The ancient texts describe them over and over again as "very tall" and "brighter than snow" (Rf5), "whiter than any snow" (Rf6), "their faces shone like snow" (Rf7) and the previous descriptions as detailed in Chapter 1.

At this time humans only had dark skin color and is why they referred to the Anunnaki/Elohim/Nephilim as the "Shining Ones." So when Noah was born with white skin you can understand why his father (the dark-skinned Lamech) thought Noah was the son of one of the Anunnaki/Elohim/Nephilim.

Believing that his wife was impregnated by one of the Anunnaki/ Elohim/Nephilim, Lamech asked his father Methuselah to go and see his grandfather Enoch (who was living amongst the Anunnaki/Elohim/Nephilim) in order to find out the truth (Rf8). Methuselah explained to Enoch how Noah was born:

> *a son, the like of whom there is none*, and his nature is not like man's nature, and *the colour of his body is whiter than snow and redder than the bloom of a rose...*

and went on to explain how Noah was the likeness of the Anunnaki/Elohim/Nephilim (Rf9). However, after hearing his complaints Enoch assured Methuselah that Noah "is in truth" Lamech's son (Rf10).

The account of Noah's birth has since been confirmed by yet another set of ancient texts called *The Dead Sea Scrolls*, discovered in 1948 at Qumran, Judea. According to the scholars, T.H. Gaster (*The Dead Sea Scriptures*) and H. Dupont-Sommer (*The Essene Writings from Qumran*), column 2 of the fragment begins:

> Behold, I thought in my heart that the conception was from one of the Watchers, one of the Holy Ones, and (that the child really belonged to the Giants ...

> Then I Lamech, hastened and went to Bath-Enosh (my) wife, and I said to Her:

> [I want you to take an oath] by the Most High, by the Lord Supreme, the King of all the worlds, the ruler of the Sons of Heaven, that you will tell me in truth whether... (Rf11)

Lamech's wife, Bath-Enosh, went on to swear that Noah was truly his son, and specifically stated that Noah was not the son of the Anunnaki/Elohim/Nephilim (Rf12).

In the translations of the Dead Sea Scrolls and Book of Enoch scholars have used the terms "Watchers" and "Giants." However, the original Hebrew texts prove that it does not say "Watchers" or "Giants," it says "Nephilim" which identifies the Anunnaki/Elohim/Nephilim (Rf13). These were simply other terms used to identify them.

From these texts we can assume that before the time of Noah humans had a dark skin color. Because the first humans had dark skin we can reasonably conclude that the ape the Anunnaki/Elohim/Nephilim used to genetically create the first human also had dark skin. Based upon the knowledge of how genes and traits are inherited, due to the higher percentage of black skin genes in this particular ape's Gene Pool the first human would have inherited and been born with the trait of dark skin. If they had used an ape with white skin the first human would most likely have inherited the trait of white skin.

It's even possible that they intentionally chose an ape with black skin color so that once he was upgraded they could clearly distinguish the humans from themselves. But that is only speculation as there is no evidence to substantiate it in the texts. So for now we can only come to the conclusion that the dark skin color was just happen-stance.

Over time, as our early ancestors continued to procreate, variations in the Gene Pools would occur. Different facial features (a mixture of each of the two parents) would emerge, and as their children procreate, new variations in the Gene Pools and facial features would emerge. Because the gene for white skin color is in the Original Gene Pool eventually children would be born with white skin, as we see in the case of Noah. Also, as explained in Chapter 5, during the generation of Jared the Anunnaki/ Elohim/Nephilim took the daughters of men and had children with them. This would have introduced more white skin genes into the human Gene Pool that was passed down to future generations. Because the percentage of white skin genes contained in the Gene Pool was now increased, the odds of children inheriting the white skin gene also increased. As the Gene Pools continue to mix a variety of skin color shades and different combinations of hair/skin colors and textures would emerge.

By studying the seemingly different types of people around the world you can clearly see how they evolved. There is no difference between a human who we call American, Arabian, African, Italian, Irish, Swedish, British, Spanish, Russian, Chinese, Japanese, etc. This is geography, not biology. The geographic man-made lines/boundaries on Earth's surface can not change our biology. The variations in facial features, skin shades and hair colors/textures that people associate with these man-made labels simply occurred due to the mixing of traits.

No matter where you look you find the same limitless variety of facial features universally throughout all the different skin shades. We find both white and black skinned people with large round eyes, both with small oval eyes, both with large flat noses, both with small flat noses, both with large skinny noses, both with small skinny noses, both with large lips, both with small lips, etc. It's all just variations that occur due to the mixing of Gene Pools.

For example, if a person with dark skin color procreates with a person who has a light skin color they will most likely produce a child with a shade of skin color somewhere in the middle of the two (Lighter than the darker parent and darker than the lighter parent). If that child in turn now procreates with a person who has a lighter skin color they will produce a child with a shade of skin color somewhere in the middle of the two. Various combinations over the generations can completely change the shade of skin color from the darkest of brown skin to lightest of white skin or from lightest of white skin to the darkest of brown skin. Society has taken these different skin shades (which are only a result of the mixing of traits) and created labels for them. As if the shade of our skin color changes the fact that we are all biologically the same family.

My point is that there is no fixed mold. We are all relatives who have different appearances due to the never ending mixing of traits. If you are the type of person that believes Africans are different from Europeans, or Mexicans are different from Americans, or Russians are different from Indians, etc., this is due to your ignorance of biology.

Certainly different areas of the world have different customs (types of clothing, foods, music, etc.) just as the community living on one block may have different customs from a community of people living a few blocks away. But the different customs that people acquire can not change biology. We are still relatives. This ignorance results in many misconceptions.

One example of a common misconception is that people usually associate the trait of blond hair with people who have also inherited the trait of white skin. But this appearance is just happen-stance. It's just the way a certain Gene Pool came to be mixed over time. Blond hair is not exclusive to white-skinned people. It can be inherited by any person, in combination with any skin color. While most black skinned people usually inherit black or brown hair due to the high percentage of these traits in their Gene Pool, that is not absolute, as the gene for blond hair is in the Original Gene Pool. In fact, there are black skinned people who are born with natural blond hair. They are prevalent throughout Polynesia (many islands from Australia to Hawaii). On the Island of Tonga as many as 10% of the population have black skin and natural blond hair. "Moorea, the island opposite Papeete, was once called the 'island of fairy folk with golden hair.' Among New Zealand's Turehu people, most were light-haired" (Rf14). The appearances that you see on Earth today simply reflect the way certain Gene Pools emerged over time due to the mixing of traits.

Another thing ignorant people do is believe that people are different from each other because they speak a different language. Language is a learned skill. No learned skill or acquired custom can change your biology. As humans spread out over the Earth and settled in different areas, over time subtle changes in spoken dialects occur which eventually branch into new languages.

61

Imagine this scenario: In ancient times a mother has two children (identical twins). When the twins are old enough they leave the nest and travel separately to different areas of the Earth never to see their family again. One brother settles in the area we now call Italy. The other brother settles in the area we now call Spain. The brother who settled in Italy procreates and generations of descendants are born. Over time as spoken dialects subtly occur the language that his descendants speak begins to change and it is given the name Italian. The same thing happens to the brother who settled in Spain and the new language is given the name Spanish. To now argue that the 'Italian' people are different than the 'Spanish' people because they have learned a different skill (different language) or because their ancestors chose to live on a different land mass of Earth is just absurd.

As humans continue to procreate around Earth new variations in facial features, hair and skin color combinations occur. Those humans then travel to new living areas and continue to procreate, again creating new variations in facial features, hair and shades of skin colors. Whatever traits are more prevalent in a particular area will intensify and the result will be humans (all from the same family lineage) who look vastly different from each other. We must not let those differences divide us. We are all relatives and must stand together.

For us to take our family and divide ourselves up into man-made racial classes, based upon the shades of our skin, facial features, the areas of Earth our ancestors decided to travel to in ancient times, or the learned skills (such as different languages) they created is absolutely absurd!

The reason that large groupings of similar looking people live in various regions today like Europe, Africa, Asia, etc. (which gives uneducated people the false impression that we are different from each other) is due to the events surrounding the Tower of Babel. See Chapter 8.

However, if the Tower of Babel had not occurred such large populations of similar looking people could still have occurred naturally. By way of travel to different regions, then through procreation and isolation, large groups of people would inhabit a land mass who possessed similar looking features. While I acknowledge the ability, the ancient texts advise us that it occurred as a result of the Tower of Babel.

For the purpose of this chapter the most important point to remember is that we can inherit ANY trait that is contained in our Gene Pool. But ONLY what is in our Gene Pool.

* * *

Blood Type

This process operates in the same manner when we apply it to our blood type, which is also an inherited trait. The human genome contains three versions of a gene that determines our blood type. The three versions (called "alleles") of this blood type gene are: A, B and O. Every human inherits two blood type genes, one from our father, the other from our mother. The two copies of this gene (located on chromosome #9) determine your GENOTYPE. The interaction of the genotype and the environment produces visible properties called the PHENOTYPE (in this case your blood type) (Rf15). For example:

Allele Inherited From One Parent	Allele Inherited From One Parent	Your Genotype	Your Blood Type (Phenotype)
A	A	AA	A
B	B	BB	B
B	A	BA	AB
A	B	AB	AB
A	O	AO	A
B	O	BO	B
O	O	OO	O

Now that you have a basic understanding of how genes/traits are inherited you will be in a better position to comprehend the importance of the next section.

* * *

RH Negative Blood

The "positive" or "negative" part of your blood type (e.g. A+, A-) is called the RH Factor. You inherit one version of this gene from your father and one version from your mother. They are located on Chromosome #1.

As reported by The Mayo Clinic (Rf16), the gene is inherited in the following manner:

RH Gene Inherited From One Parent	RH Gene Inherited From One Parent	Your RH Factor
+	+	+
-	-	-
+	-	Either + or -

In contrast, Emory University School of Medicine argues that the RH positive gene is dominant and states that a person is only RH negative if they inherit two RH negative genes (Rf17).

While this explains the process of how it is inherited, it does not explain what it is. If we look beyond the surface we discover that RH is an abbreviation for RHESUS. Rhesus actually refers to the *Rhesus Monkey* (a pale brown Asian macaque) that was used in the research surrounding the discovery of RH blood types. Karl Landsteiner and Alexander Wiener made this discovery in 1940. It was Landsteiner who discovered the ABO blood groups in the first place, 40 years earlier.

> This blood group [RH factor] may be the most complex genetically of all blood type systems since it involves 45 different antigens on the surface of red cells that are controlled by 2 closely linked genes on chromosome 1. (Rf18)

The RH Factor refers to a specific protein found on the surface of red blood cells in apes. All non-human primates are RH Positive. In layman's terms, all non-human primates have monkey blood, evidenced by the Rhesus monkey protein.

Since all humans evolved from apes all human blood should contain the Rhesus monkey protein (RH+). Remember, we can *ONLY* inherit genes/traits (including blood types) that were passed down to us in our Gene Pool. Therefore one hundred percent (100%) of the human population should be RH Positive.

The shocking fact is that only 85% of the human population is RH Positive. This demonstrates a couple key points: First, because humans possess the Rhesus monkey protein in their blood this is further evidence that man evolved from apes. Second, if all humans evolved from ape-like primates (which are all RH+) how is it even possible for RH Negative blood to exist? How can ANY human not have monkey blood?

While it is very rare, 15% of the human population is RH Negative; they do not have monkey blood!

The very existence of RH Negative blood proves that at some point in time the gene of a different species was added to the Human Gene Pool. And this immediately draws our attention to the ancient texts and biblical account of when:

> *the sons of the Elohim went to the daughters of men and had children by them* (Genesis 6:4)

as discussed in Chapter 5. It was at this time that the gene responsible for RH Negative blood type was added to the Human Gene Pool. From which, today, a very small percentage of people inherit this rare blood type.

Some people call RH Negative blood *The Blood of the Gods* (Rf19), but that's only correct if you mean the gods of the Torah, Bible, and Qur'an - who weren't gods at all - they were the Anunnaki/Elohim/Nephilim. The astronauts from planet Nibiru who genetically manipulated our DNA to elevate us from ape-man to Homo sapiens (The Adam) and later interbred with our women adding their genes to the Human Gene Pool. The evidence of this: The fact that RH Negative blood exists.

The RH Negative blood type is also known to cause some serious problems in the area of procreation. For example, when an RH NEGATIVE woman is impregnated by a man who has monkey blood (RH POSITIVE), the baby growing inside the woman will usually inherit monkey blood. If as little as one drop of fetal blood from the baby escapes the placenta an immediate immune response is triggered in the RH Negative woman producing large amounts of anti-Rh+ antibodies. This allergic reaction is known as Hemolytic disease. The mother's body actually attacks the baby as if it were an "ALIEN substance (the same way it would a virus)" (Rf20) causing the baby's red blood cells to burst or agglutinate, killing the baby (resulting in a miscarriage). In the event that the baby survives this attack there are usually life-threatening birth defects. The baby is born with profound anemia, jaundice, fever, swollen, enlarged liver and spleen (a condition called *erythroblastosis fetalis*). To combat this problem doctors inject RH Negative women with a blood product called RH Immune Globulin to try and stop her body from producing the antibodies that kill the baby. However, the point I am highlighting is, if all:

> animals and other living creatures known to man can breed with any other of their species ... Why would a mother's body reject her own offspring? (Rf21)

This only occurs in the case of crossbreeding between two different species that are similar but genetically different. The Anunnaki/Elohim/Nephilim were similar but genetically different from the human women they interbred with. Now that their RH Negative blood type is in the Human Gene Pool incompatibility problems arise in the few humans who inherit this rare blood type. Again, more evidence of the biblical interbreeding that occurred, as described in Chapter 5.

According to some researchers, they have found several "unusual traits" that RH Negative people have but RH Positive do not have: an extra vertebra, lower than normal body temperature, lower than normal blood pressure, higher mental analytical abilities (IQs), higher negative-ion shielding (from positive "charged" virus/bacteria) around the body, higher sensitivity to EM and ELF Fields, hyper vision and other senses (Rf22).

Another interesting note: When Rh+ and Rh- blood are mixed together a clumping (agglutination) occurs that is visible to the naked eye. The ancient tradition of making good friends "blood brothers" (where the two individuals cut their hands and mix their blood together) was more than just a symbolic gesture. The ancient reason for this was to determine who they were allowing into their tribe. Ancient people who did not possess modern blood analysis methods were still able to tell immediately who was RH Positive or an RH Negative descendant of the Anunnaki/Elohim/Nephilim!

7

THE GREAT FLOOD
and
THE PLOT TO KILL MANKIND

THE EVENTS SURROUNDING the Great Flood (Deluge) that killed most of mankind is another example of the cold-blooded brutality that Enlil inflicted upon the human slaves.

Despite his demands for obedience, as the human population grew more and more of Enlil's rules were being violated. Enlil watched in disgust as his people (the Anunnaki/Elohim/Nephilim) broke the rules and had sex with "the daughters of men." He watched as they broke the rules and started teaching the humans "the eternal secrets which were (preserved)" for the Anunnaki/Elohim/Nephilim alone (Rf1). He watched as the humans broke the rules and used their new "knowledge" of the "secret sciences" to eat the "birds, and beasts, and reptiles, and fish," and even started eating "one another's flesh," and drinking "the blood" (Rf2). Foods that were reserved for the Anunnaki/Elohim/Nephilim alone.

Enlil was becoming increasingly upset with the human slaves. He commented that they were consuming "all the acquisitions" on Earth (Rf3) and felt that they had become "corrupt in all their ways" (Rf4). As the *Atra-Hasis Epic* explains:

> When the land extended and the people multiplied
> The land was bellowing like a bull,
> [Enlil] got disturbed with their uproar.
> Enlil heard their noise
> And addressed the great [Elohim],
> "The noise of mankind has become too intense for me
> With their uproar I am deprived of sleep... (Rf5)

Things were quickly getting out of control in Enlil's mind and something had to be done.

The first form of population control that Enlil utilized was to destroy the humans through "disease, sickness, plague and pestilence." The *Atra-Hasis* text explains how Enlil demanded:

... let there be malaria.
[Hast]ily let fate make an end to their clamor.
[Li]ke a storm, let it overwhelm them.
[Sic]kness, headache, malaria, calamity. (Rf6)

Akkadian and Assyrian texts explain how "aches, dizziness, chills, fever," as well as "disease, sickness, plague, and pestilence'" afflicted the humans and their livestock (Rf7).

A man called Atra-Hasis went to see Enki to plead for help. Atra-Hasis is a title that means the "exceedingly wise" one. It is believed that Atra-Hasis was the biblical Noah. As you know from Chapter 4, Enlil's brother Enki was the actual Anunnaki/Elohim/Nephilim who created the humans. While Enlil despised the humans, prevented them from having any forms of knowledge and inflicted cruel and inhumane treatments upon them, Enki (on the other hand) treated the humans kindly and wanted to educate them. Enki was also known to intercede on behalf of the humans when he could. This is why he went to Enki for help. Noah/Atra-Hasis said to Enki:

... mankind is in misery.
[The anger] of the elohim consumes the land.
... thou who hast created us
Let sickness, headache, malaria, calamity ce[ase] (Rf8)

The text in this area is broken so we don't know what Enki's response was. However, we do know that Enlil's plan wasn't working because Enlil started complaining:

[The people] have not become less; they are more numerous than before.

and then Enlil ordered a second form of population control by way of starvation. Enlil ordered that the food supply be cut off from all the humans who were not killed off by diseases:

to those untouched by the desolations.
Let the fig tree for the people be [cut off].
[I]n their bellies let the plant be wanting. (Rf9)

Enlil accomplished this by withholding the rain and water from the ground so that the fields would become infertile (Rf10). The text explains:

From above, the heat was not....
Below, the waters did not rise from their sources.
The womb of the earth did not bear;
Vegetation did not sprout....
The black fields turned white;

The broad plain was choked with salt. (Rf11)

As time passed the famine drastically affected the human population:

> their features were altered by hunger,
> their faces were encrusted...
> they were living on the verge of death.
> ...
> their faces appeared green;
> they walked hunched in the streets;
> their broad [shoulders?] became narrow.
> ...
> they prepared the daughter for a meal;
> the child they prepared for food....
> One house devoured the other. (Rf12)

Witnessing the torment that the humans were experiencing at the hands of his brother Enlil, Enki implemented a secret plan to help the humans acquire food by the river.

When Enlil discovered that Enki was going behind his back to help the humans obtain food "He was filled with anger" and summoned an Assembly of the Great Anunnaki/Elohim/Nephilim to address the violations. At the Assembly Enlil began by accusing his brother Enki of breaking the law, charges that Enki obviously denied (Rf13).

Enlil's plan to kill the humans wasn't working fast enough. Regardless of how many humans were dying from hunger and disease, the population was still growing at an enormous rate. Enlil knew that he needed a new method.

Enlil learned of a dangerous situation that was arising due to changes in the Earth's climate. Around 11,000 B.C. the Ice Age was coming to an end. The heat of Earth's crust was creating a slushy slippery mud layer at the bottom of mile thick ice sheets which were beginning to loosen from the pressure and friction. It was believed that "Acting as a lubricant between the thick ice sheet and the solid Earth below, this slushy layer sooner or later would cause the ice sheet to slide into the surrounding ocean" causing a catastrophic rise in sea level over the Earth (Rf14).

Modern scientists are now certain the last Ice Age began circa 73,000 B.C., underwent a mini-warming circa 38,000 B.C., followed by a harsher, colder, drier period circa 36,000 B.C. and ended abruptly around 11,000 B.C. which ushered in our present mild climate (Rf15).

With the slipping ice sheets and the arrival of planet Nibiru (which causes the Earth to shake) the Anunnaki/Elohim/Nephilim were able to predict the timing of the coming Flood.

At the Assembly Enlil put his plot in motion. He advised everyone of the coming Flood and argued that this catastrophic event should be used to kill mankind. Enlil's ruling was:

> And as to Mankind, Enlil said - *Let them perish; let the seed of Earthling be wiped off the face of Earth* (Rf16)

Fearing that the large human population would attack the Spaceport in an attempt to survive if they learned that the Flood was about to happen, Enlil demanded that everyone take an oath of secrecy:

> Come, all of us, and take an oath
> regarding the Killing Flood!
> Anu swore first;
> Enlil swore, his sons swore with him. (Rf18)

Enki opposed the decision and refused to take the oath. He argued on behalf of the humans "Why will you bind me with an oath?" ... "Am I to raise my hands against my own humans?"" But Enki was ultimately forced to take the oath (Rf19).

The decision reached on that day by the Assembly of Great Anunnaki/ Elohim/Nephilim would later be recorded in the Bible as:

> YHWH [Enlil] saw how great man's wickedness on the earth had become, and that every inclination of the thoughts of his heart was only evil all the time. YHWH [Enlil] was grieved that he had made man on the earth, and his heart was filled with pain. So YHWH [Enlil] said, *"I will wipe mankind, whom I have created, from the face of the earth"* (Genesis 6:5-7)

Despite his oath to remain silent, the benevolent Enki could not stand idly by and watch the entire human race (which he created) perish. Enki decided that he had to do something.

The biblical "Noah," as we have come to know him in modern times, was not called Noah in ancient times. As shown earlier, in the *Atra-Hasis* text Noah was called Atra-Hasis (Rf20), in the *Epic of Gilgamesh* Noah was called Utnapishtim (Rf21), both of which date back to the 2nd millennium B.C. (a thousand years before the biblical texts). In the 3rd century B.C. Noah was called Xisuthros/Sisithros by the Babylonian Berossus (Rf22). Depending upon what version you are reading the "exceedingly wise" man that Enki was referring to will be called by different names.

In the most ancient version found to date (a *Sumerian Deluge Tablet* which pre-dates the biblical version by a couple thousand years (Fig. 7.1)) Noah is called by the name ZI.U.SUD.RA. The text says that Ziusudra was a priest in Enki's temple. From other texts we learn that Noah/Ziusudra was actually a son that Enki had with a human female and that is why he chose to save him (Rf23).

In any event, Noah was the man Enki chose to save. While Enki was bound not to reveal the secret of the

Figure 7.1

Flood to the people, he reasoned that he could speak to a wall and if someone overheard that was not a direct violation of his oath. The Atra-Hasis text explains how Enki implemented his plan the next time Noah came to the temple. Enki began to whisper from behind a "reed screen" wall:

> Pay attention to my instructions.
> On all the habitations, over the cities,
> a storm will sweep.
> The destruction of Mankind's seed it will be....
> This is the final ruling,
> the word of the Assembly of the [Elohim],
> the word spoken by Anu, Enlil and Ninhursag (Rf24)

An ancient seal depicts Enki as a "Serpent" revealing the secret to Noah while an attendant holds up a screen wall (Fig. 7.2) (Rf25).

Figure 7.2

The Atra-Hasis version is corroborated by the Epic of Gilgamesh text in which Enki explains to Noah:

> Man of Shurippak, son of Ubara-Tutu,
> Tear down the house, build a ship!

> Leave possessions, take thought for life!
> Abandon property, save life!
> Bring into the ship the seed of life of everything!
> The ship which thou shalt build,
> let its dimensions be measured! (Rf26).

Enki gave Noah specific dimensions that he was to follow when building the Ark. It "was to be a submersible vessel, a 'submarine' that could withstand the avalanche of water" (Rf27). Enki's order to build the Ark, including the specific dimensions, would eventually make its way into the Bible (Genesis 6:14-16).

Noah had to keep the secret of the coming Flood away from the other citizens of Shuruppak so Enki devised a plan that would explain why Noah was building such an odd vessel. Enki advised Noah to tell people that because Enlil was upset with him he had to leave Enlil's territory. Noah was to tell everyone that he was building the vessel in order to travel to Enki's territory and live there. People believed the story and some actually helped construct the Ark, which was finished on the seventh day (Rf28).

According to ancient texts, what Noah actually loaded onto the Ark is quite different than what we have come to believe from the recent condensed biblical version. An Assyrian text explains that Noah loaded the Ark with his possessions, property, cattle of the field, and not only his family but his relatives and the craftsman who helped build the ship (Rf29).

The Assyrian text is corroborated by the *Epic of Gilgamesh* text which explains how Noah loaded:

> all that I had of silver,...all that I had of gold, I loaded it. With all the
> seed of life that there was, I loaded it. I caused to go up into the ship
> all my family and relatives. The cattle of the field,... the craftsman, all
> of them, I caused to go up.

and the text even explains that Noah had a sailor for the Ark named "Buzur-Amurru" (Rf30).

A condensed version of these texts ultimately found their way into the Bible, but apparently when the compilers recorded the event they created two conflicting accounts. First Noah is ordered to take (2) of every kind into the Ark. Then in the very next chapter, as if they had forgotten what they just inscribed, the account is repeated but now says Noah was ordered to take (7) of every kind into the Ark:

First, Genesis 6:18-21 says Noah was told:

72

you will enter the ark - you and your sons and your wife and your sons' wives with you. You are to bring into the ark **_two_** of all living creatures, male and female, to keep them alive with you. **_Two_** of very kind of bird, of every kind of animal and of every kind of creature that moves along the ground will come to you to be kept alive.

Then in the very next chapter, Genesis 7:1-3 says Noah was told:

Go into the ark, you and your whole family, ... Take with you **_seven_** of every kind of clean animal, a male and its mate, and two of every kind of unclean animal, a male and its mate, and also **_seven_** of every kind of bird, male and female, to keep their various kinds alive throughout the earth.

Clearly somebody made a mistake when they were creating the biblical texts from the Mesopotamian originals.

Enki advised Noah that when he sees the Anunnaki/Elohim/Nephilim leaving Earth, signaled by the sound of the rocket ships taking off, this was the sign that the Great Flood was coming. As you know from a previous chapter, Shamash was the Anunnaki/Elohim/Nephilim that was in charge of the Spaceport in Sippar. Noah was advised:

When Shamash,
who orders a trembling at dusk,
will shower down a rain of eruptions-
board thou the ship,
batten up the entrance! (Rf31)

It is estimated that the catastrophic Flood swept over the Earth around 11,000 B.C. While some scholars like Leonard Woolley in his book Excavations at Ur (1929) have argued they found evidence that the Flood occurred around 4,000 B.C., most scholars believe that this was nothing more than local flooding that routinely occurred in Mesopotamia. It was not the catastrophic event that ancient texts from Mesopotamia to Egypt to the other side of the Earth in Mesoamerica speak of as an earth-shaking event of unparalleled magnitude that affected the "four corners of the Earth" (Rf32). Even the:

Mexica-Nahuatl timetable [which] correlates events and times with a scientific and historical accuracy that ought to make everyone stop and wonder. ... dates the deluge, at the end of the First Sun, to 13,333 years before the time of writing the codex; to about 11,600 B.C. (Rf33)

The Great Flood is described in the texts as a terrifying storm that came from the south at "the first glow of dawn" when:
the Moon disappeared....
The appearance of the weather changed;
The rains roared in the clouds....

The winds became savage...
... The Deluge set out,
its might came upon the people like a battle (Rf34)

The Anunnaki/Elohim/Nephilim boarded their rocket ships (rukub ilani) blasting off for space and "setting the land ablaze with their glare" (Rf35). When Noah saw the rocket ships blasting off he knew it was the "signal", boarded the Ark, and the boatman Puzur-Amurru took over the navigation (Rf36). Thousands of years later a condensed version would be recorded in the Bible as "Noah and his sons and his wife and his sons' wives entered the ark to escape the waters of the flood" (Genesis 7:7).

The Anunnaki/Elohim/Nephilim watched from their spaceships orbiting the Earth as the tidal waves gathered speed, submerging the mountains and destroying everything on Earth. The Great Flood rose more than 20 feet over the highest mountains (Genesis 7:19-20). The Mesopotamian texts describe how:

The [Elohim] cowered like dogs,
crouched against the outer wall.
Ishtar cried out like a woman in travail:
"The olden days are alas turned to clay." ...
The Anunnaki ... weep with her.
The [Elohim], all humbled, sit and weep;
their lips drawn tight... one and all (Rf37)

The *Atra-Hasis Epic* described the conditions as:

The Anunnaki, ...
were sitting in thirst, in hunger....
Ninti wept and spent her emotion;
she wept and eased her feelings.
The [Elohim] wept with her for the land.
She was overcome with grief,
she thirsted for beer.
Where she sat, the [Elohim] sat weeping;
crouching like sheep at a trough.
Their lips were feverish of thirst,
they were suffering cramp from hunger.
...
[Ninhursag] saw and she wept ...
...
My creatures have become like flies-
they filled the rivers like dragonflies,
their fatherhood was taken by the rolling sea (Rf38)

The Great Flood not only destroyed most of mankind but destroyed all of the ancient cities that had been built over the past 432,000 years.

74

While Enlil must have been sitting in his spaceship satisfied that he finally destroyed the humans he despised so much, Enki knew that floating somewhere in the dark treacherous waters below was the Ark containing Noah and his family.

When the storm was over Noah "opened the hatch, and light fell upon" his face. He was "horrified, and...sat down and wept." Noah "looked in all directions; the sea was terrible." Eventually an "island arose" and the ship was grounded upon "Mount Nisir" (Rf39). According to the Bible Mount Nisir was Mount Ararat in Armenia (Genesis 8:3).

After sitting motionless for 7 days and releasing birds to see if they found habitable land, Noah exited the Ark, built an alter upon the summit of the mountain and offered a sacrifice (Rf40) thanking Enki for saving their lives.

The Anunnaki/Elohim/Nephilim "smelled the sweet savor" of the sacrifice and "gathered" "like flies" (Rf41). When Ninhursag arrived she raised the great jewel and said:

> Upon these days I shall think, so that forever I will not forget. Let the elohim come to the offering.

and then went on to say that Enlil was not allowed to come to the offering because she was mad at him for using the Great Flood to kill the humans (Rf42).

When Enlil finally arrived on the scene and saw the Ark he "was wroth; He was filled with anger" and yelled "Has anyone come out alive? No man shall survive the cataclysm." Enlil's son Ninurta "opened his mouth" and accused Enki of treason: "Who without Enki shall devise" such plans? He argued that Enki "knows every matter." Enki denied the charges saying "I have not revealed the decision of the" Anunnaki/Elohim/Nephilim (Rf43).

> I merely let one Man, an "exceedingly wise" one, perceive by his own wisdom what the [Elohim's] secret was. And if indeed this Earthling is so wise Enki suggested to Enlil, lets not ignore his abilities. "Now then, take counsel in regard to him! (Rf44).

Whether Enki's argument made sense to Enlil or whether after his anger subsided he realized that the slave labor would now become necessary, Enlil conceded and decided that the humans would be allowed to remain alive to help make the land habitable again.

Because humans now had "knowledge" that animals, birds and fish could be eaten (a bell that was not going to be un-rung) Enlil conceded and said that humans would now be allowed to eat "all the beasts", "all the birds", "every creature that moves along the ground," and "all the fish of the sea" (Genesis 9:2) just like the Anunnaki/Elohim/Nephilim did. Enlil went on to say:

> Everything that lives and moves will be food for you. Just as I gave you the green plants, I now give you everything (Genesis 9:3)

However, there was one thing that Enlil absolutely would not budge on. Enlil was adamant that humans were strictly forbidden to drink blood:

> But you must not eat meat that has its lifeblood still in it (Genesis 9:4)

This was the only rule he gave the humans after the Great Flood. Why this practice was strictly forbidden will be made clear in a future chapter. Then Enlil blessed Noah and his family, saying: "Be fruitful and increase in number and fill the earth (Genesis 9:1).

* * *

The history of Enlil's attempt to destroy all of mankind by the Great Flood and his brother Enki's attempt to stop Enlil and save at least one family can be found recorded in many versions all over the world. A few examples:

In Berossus' Babylonian version (according to the Greek historian Abydenus) the gods tried to keep the knowledge of the Great Flood from mankind but "Cronus revealed to Sisithros that there would be a Deluge ... and ordered him to conceal in Sippar, the city of the god Shamash, every available writing" (Rf45). The historian Alexander Polyhistor reported that Berossus' version explained that Cronus ordered him "to commit to writing a history of the Beginnings, Middles, and Ends of all things, down to the present term; and to bury those accounts securely in the city of the Sun god, in Sippar; And to build a vessel, and to take into it with him his kinsfolk and his friends. He was to stow food and water and put birds and animals on board and sail away when he had everything ready" (Rf46).

In the Greek version "Zeus sent a flood to destroy the men of the Bronze Age. Prometheus advised his son Deucalion to build a chest. All other men perished except for a few who escaped to high mountains" (Rf47).

In the Roman version "Jupiter, angered at the evil ways of humanity, resolved to destroy it. He was about to set the earth to burning, but considered that that might set heaven afire, so he decided to flood the earth instead" (Rf48).

In the Norse version there was an Ancient Giant named Ymir. He was so huge that when Odin and his brothers Vili and Ve killed him, Ymir's blood poured out is such a Great Flood that all of Ymir's sons were drowned in it, except Bergelmir who survived the flood because he was in a boat with his wife. The boat floated to Jotunheim (the Realm of the Giants) where they had children and repopulated their kind. (Rf49).

In the Celtic version "Heaven and Earth were great giants, and Heaven lay upon the Earth so that their children were crowded between them, and the children and their mother were unhappy in the darkness. The boldest of the sons led his brothers in cutting up Heaven into many pieces. From his skull they made the firmament. His spilling blood caused a great flood which killed all humans except a single pair, who were saved in a ship made by a beneficent Titan" (Rf50).

In the Welsh version "The lake of Llion burst, flooding all lands. Dwyfan and Dwyfach escaped in a mastless ship with pairs of every sort of living creature. They landed in Prydain (Britain) and repopulated the world" (Rf51).

In the Zoroastrian version "After Ahura Mazda has warned Yima that destruction in the form of winter frost, and floods, subsequent to the melting of the snow, are threatening the sinful world, he proceeds to instruct him to build a vara, 'fortress or estate,' in which specimens of small and large cattle, human beings, dogs, birds, red flaming fires, plants and foodstuffs will have to be deposited in pairs" (Rf52).

The Mayan Popol Vuh explains how the gods were upset with the humans they created because they were too intelligent like gods themselves, so they proceeded to destroy them and start over by making slaves who were not as smart and did not live as long.

In the Chinese version "The Yellow Emperor was the supreme god of China, who looked down upon Earth and saw that people were evil and filled with wickedness. So, the Yellow Emperor ordered the rain god to make endless rain. A Great Flood followed, causing everything to die" (Rf53).

In the Book of Enoch Uriel was sent to Noah to advise him that "a deluge is about to come upon the whole earth, and will destroy all that is on it." Noah was instructed "that he may escape and his seed may be preserved for all the generations of the world" (Rf54).

77

8

THE TOWER OF BABEL
and
THE DIVISION OF MANKIND

THIS BRINGS US to a very important period in the history of mankind. What has been termed "The Tower of Babel" is an account of mankind's desire and attempt to elevate ourselves out of our slave status; the anger those actions invoked in our Anunnaki/Elohim/Nephilim masters; and their plan to maintain control and prevent human advancement.

After the Great Flood Noah and his descendants slowly began to "spread out over the earth" (Genesis 10:32). They initially inhabited the highland areas near Mount Ararat in Armenia, the Cedar Mountains of Lebanon, the highlands of Asia Minor, the Black Sea and Caspian Sea areas between Europe and Asia (Rf1).

An ancient Sumerian text reported in *Sumerische Literarische Texte aus Nippur* by S.N. Kramer, explains how Enlil began the process of growing vegetation by seeding the "mountain of aromatic cedars," which some researchers believe was in Lebanon:

> Enlil went up the peak and lifted his eyes;
> He looked down: there the waters filled as a sea.
> He looked up: there was the mountain of the aromatic cedars.
> He hauled up the barley, terraced it on the mountain.
> That which vegetates he hauled up,
> terraced the grain cereals on the mountain. (Rf2)

Sumerian texts explain how fruit trees and bushes with grapes were among the first to grow. They describe how humans were given "the excellent white grapes and the excellent white wine; the excellent black grapes and the excellent red wine" (Rf3). This is also supported by the Bible's acknowledgment that after the Great Flood Noah "proceeded to plant a vineyard" (Genesis 9:20).

Modern archaeological discoveries in the area of agriculture production also confirm that these highlands were the first areas inhabited after the Great Flood. The "highlands in and around the Middle East, those of Israel, Lebanon, Turkey, Iraq and Iran" show evidence of food production circa 10,000 B.C.

(Rf4). This was undoubtedly because the lowland areas of Earth were still flooded.

At this point in human evolution all of mankind spoke only one language. This is evidenced by the biblical texts which explain "the whole world had one language and a common speech" (Genesis 11:1) as well as ancient Sumerian texts like *Enmerkar and The Lord of Aratta*, which not only pre-dates but verifies the biblical account. The text describes how:

> once upon a time - The whole Earth, all the people in unison. To Enlil
> in one language gave praise. (Rf5)

This was a period in human history when mankind clearly understood who they were and who their Anunnaki/Elohim/Nephilim masters were. The entire human population was united, spoke one language, and was working together towards one common goal: the advancement of mankind. Humans were rebelling against their slave masters and attempting to elevate themselves out of the bonds of slavery.

Mankind decided to build its own city, with its own launch tower, to place its own "shem" (sky-born vehicle) on top of it so that they would be able travel over Earth's vast terrain like their masters did. The Bible explains how humans said to each other:

> "Come, let's make bricks and bake them thoroughly." ... "Come, let us
> build ourselves a city, with a tower that reaches the heavens, so that we
> may make a ***shem*** for ourselves and not be scattered over the face of
> the whole earth." (Genesis 11:3-4)

While modern English versions of the Bible use the word *name* instead of the original Hebrew word *shem*, this is another mistranslation and gives you the false impression that mankind was trying to make a "name" or reputation for itself. However, scholars have shown that the original Hebrew word ***shem*** actually means some type of *sky-born vehicle*. For example:

The multi-stage rocket ships that the Anunnaki/Elohim/Nephilim used to land on Earth were similar to the rockets that NASA uses to reach outer space. Evidence of this is shown in the depiction found in Huy's tomb (Fig. 1.2). It is believed that these rocket ships were capable of operating in two ways. The lower portion of the rocket ship was only used when leaving from or arriving to Earth's atmosphere. On Earth the lower portion would remain stationed at the spaceport in Sippar (before the Great Flood) and at the spaceport in Baalbek (after the Great Flood).

The upper portion of the rocket ship was a conical shaped "Sky Chamber" or "Command Module" that could detach from the lower portion of the rocket ship and be used to fly around Earth in the same manner that we use planes and helicopters today. The Sumerians called the upper portion an "MU" (Rf6).

Each of the main Anunnaki/Elohim/Nephilim took an MU and stationed it at their Temple, which they resided in while on Earth. Each Temple included a platform where their MU would be housed (similar to the way most modern houses have parking garages for our cars). For example, an ancient coin depicts the Great Temple of Ishtar (Inanna) (Fig. 8.1). It was found at Byblos (the biblical Gebal) in present day Lebanon.

Byblos was the oldest Phoenician city, dating back to circa 3,500 B.C. As you can see in the depiction, standing in the courtyard of the Temple is a special platform with crossbeam construction built to withstand a large amount of weight. On top of the platform stands the MU. The flying vehicle Ishtar used to travel with (Rf7). A hymn to Ishtar/Inanna shows how she used the MU:

Figure 8.1

> Over all the peopled lands
> she flies in her MU.
> Lady, who in her MU
> to the heights of Heaven joyfully wings.
> Over all the resting places
> she flies in her MU. (Rf8)

Enlil's son Ninurta ordered a Sumerian ruler named Gudea to build a temple with a special enclosure for his "divine bird." Gudea recorded that "as the 'divine bird' rose to circle the lands, it 'flashed upon the raised bricks.' The protected enclosure was described as MU.NA.DA.TUR.TUR ("strong stone resting place of the MU")" (Rf9).

These flying machines, in one way or another, were described as a "chariot of fire," "celestial boat," "divine bird," "whirlwind," etc., that could rise off the ground and fly into the sky while emitting a brilliance (Rf10). This is why our ancestors depicted the Anunnaki/Elohim/Nephilim with wings.

In Egypt the MU was called the Ben-Ben. The Ben-Ben was a pyramidion shaped object (the upper part of the Celestial Boat) in which RA (Enki's son Marduk) had come to Earth from the Celestial Disk, aka the Planet of Millions of Years (Nibiru/Sirius/Planet X). Archaeologists have discovered a stone replica of the Ben-Ben showing an Anunnaki/Elohim/ Nephilim at the entrance (Fig. 8.2) (Rf11).

81

The Ben-Ben (MU) was docked at the Temple of Anu (the biblical ON) which the Greeks later called HELIOPOLIS. Heliopolis was believed to have been built by the Egyptian Neter named Ptah (Enki). In ancient times Egyptians would make pilgrimages to the Temple to view the Ben-Ben. Today the Ben-Ben is gone and only the landing platform remains. It is believed that one of the Ben-Bens or a replica of it is hidden

Figure 8.2

under the sealed chamber of the Qa'aba in Mecca (Rf12) which was one of the landing sites used by the Anunnaki/Elohim/Nephilim. Similar to the way the Egyptians did in earlier times, today Muslims make pilgrimages to the Qa'aba.

The Sumerian term MU (sky-born vehicle) evolved into the Akkadian Semitic derivative shu-mu (that which is a "mu") and eventually became shem in the Hebrew Semitic as used in the biblical texts (Rf13).

In all the ancient texts a *shem* was connected to a method of transportation that flies (e.g. the fiery chariots of the Bible):

In the *Epic of Gilgamesh*, Gilgamesh was trying to reach his grandfather Noah/Utnapishtim and had to ask permission of Utu/Shamash (who you know from a previous chapter was in charge of the spaceport) for a shumu so that he could travel to where his grandfather was (Rf14). In the *Legend of Adapa* (based upon ancient tablets found in King Ashurbanipal's library at Nineveh and the Egyptian archives of Pharaoh Amenhotep III and IV) Enki provided Adapa with a shem so that he could ascend to meet with King Anu. When Adapa arrived Anu wanted to know who provided him with a shumu so that he could get there. In *The Etana Legend*, similar to Gilgamesh, Etana had to obtain permission from Shamash (controller of the spaceport), where Etana was told that he would be provided with an "eagle" that would take him to the desired place (Rf15). A tablet (Fig. 8.3) excavated at a town called Gezer in ancient Canaan, west of Jerusalem, shows a host of celestial symbols (i.e. the Sun, Moon, Zodiacal constellations, etc.) including a couple of rocket ships (some on the ground next to a tree and some resting on top of a "ladder" (Rf16). The "ladder" should immediately draw your attention to the biblical story of Jacob who saw the hovering spaceship with Anunnaki/Elohim/Nephilim going up and down the "ladder" (Genesis 28:12). According to the Bible, in order for Elijah to be transported to Heaven he had to go to Beth-El (the lord's house) (2 Kings 2:1-2) where he was picked up on one of the spaceships: "suddenly a chariot of fire and horses of fire appeared... and Elijah went up to heaven in a whirlwind" (2 Kings 2:11).

Figure 8.3

Ancient societies erected stone monuments which the Greeks later called obelisks. An obelisk is a stone sculpture of the ancient shem, with its pointed pyramidion top representing the MU or Ben-Ben. Pharaohs called them Beams of the Neter (Fig. 8.4) (Rf17).

> "Those shems, or obelisks, were copied after the rocket-shaped vehicles in which the" Anunnaki/Elohim/Nephilim used to fly (Rf18)

We even find these shems (multi-stage rocket ships) erected around Muslim mosques (Fig. 8.5) (Rf19). Interestingly, the Islamic religion also uses Nannar/Sin's symbol of the "Crescent Moon"! I'll explain the connection in Chapter 13.

Figure 8.4

As explained in Chapter 1, the Anunnaki/Elohim/Nephilim were the DIN.GIR which means the people of the rocket ships. The name Sumer is more correctly pronounced *Shumer* (as in the biblical *Shinar*) derived from *Shem-ur*. Sumer, Shum-er, Shem-ur was the land in which the Anunnaki/Elohim/Nephilim dwelt at one time (the people of the shem!). By properly translating the texts a clear picture emerges.

Figure 8.5

As Zecharia Sitchin explained, the true meaning of the word *shem* is some type of sky-born vehicle, and:

> once we read "skyborne vehicle" rather than "name" for the word shem, which is the term employed in the original Hebrew text of the Bible. The story [then deals] with the concern of Mankind that, as the people spread upon the Earth, they would lose contact with one another. So they decided to build a "sky-borne vehicle" and to erect a launch tower for such a vehicle so that they, too, could [like the Anunnaki/Elohim/Nephilim]- fly in a mu "over all the peopled lands." (Rf20)

Mankind was increasing in number, in strength, and now trying to "match the technological might of their hated" masters in order to elevate themselves and put an end to their enslavement (Rf21).

When Enlil saw mankind all working together as one strong united force creating their city and tower he became enraged. Remember, in order to maintain control of the human slaves they had to keep them weak and unintelligent. Enlil already tried to kill the humans by disease, then starvation, then again by the Great Flood all because they were breaking his rules. Now humans were uniting as one strong force and actively working together against Enlil!

Enlil knew that a united human population posed a great threat that would be extremely hard to control so he called an immediate Assembly of the Anunnaki/Elohim/Nephilim to voice his fear and demanded that something had to be done to prevent the humans from reaching this level of technological advancement. The Bible explains:

> If as one people speaking the same language they have begun to do this, then nothing they plan to do will be impossible for them (Genesis 11:6)

Why would "God" not want mankind to be intelligent or work together as one strong united family? Clearly this doesn't make sense. It's only by understanding that the biblical texts have nothing to do with "God" but are actually only referring to the Anunnaki/Elohim/Nephilim that everything makes sense. This will be discussed further in Part II.

It was at this time that Enlil designed and implemented his diabolical plan to oppress and maintain control over the human slaves. Using the concept of divide and conquer he:

(1) Divided mankind up into groups by the color of their skin/appearance and "scattered" each group to a different area on Earth (Genesis 11:8)

(2) Made each group speak a different language "so they will not understand each other" (Genesis 11:7)

What better way to keep mankind divided and weak! From a military point of view the plan was ingenious:

First, over time future generations of each group would forget that Enlil ever divided them from the rest of their family. They would not remember a time when they existed with anyone who had a different skin color or appearance from them. If one of these groups traveled to another land and came into contact with a different group, both groups would become alarmed due to natural defense mechanisms and consider the other an enemy. Since the two groups looked different from each other, they will falsely believe they "are" different and stay away from each other. *VOLUNTARILY REMAINING DIVIDED!*

Second, because each group was given a different language they would not be able to communicate with each other, further *SOLIDIFYING THE CREATED DIVISION*. They wouldn't even be able to say "we're friendly" much less work together to become one strong united force again and a threat to Enlil.

Enlil also knew that these divisions would eventually create conflicts between humans of different appearances. The distracted humans would fight between each other and remain dis-united. The mechanism of creating conflicts between people to maintain social and political control is as effective today as it was thousands of years ago.

According to the Bible Enlil implemented his diabolical plan to divide mankind around 101 years after the Great Flood, during the time of the birth of Eber's son Peleg (Genesis 10:25).

Before Enlil separated us at the Tower of Babel humans were united, spoke one language so we could all communicate with each other, and understood that we were in fact all relatives; that the differences in our physical appearances (skin color, hair color, facial features, etc.) were simply due to the limitless variations that occur as a result of the mixing of traits, as I explained in Chapter 6.

However, as a result of the mechanisms implemented at the Tower of Babel, Enlil accomplished his goal of weakening humans to the point where they could easily maintain control. It created a devastating division amongst mankind that is still working thousands of years later.

Today society is extremely divided. Humans are divided by skin color, facial features, geography, different languages which prevent people from communicating with each other, and all the intolerances and prejudices that have arisen thereby, keeping mankind in a state of perpetual division.

PART II

RELIGION

9

CONTROL MECHANISMS TO KEEP MANKIND ENSLAVED

FOR THOUSANDS of years philosophers, scientists and religious zealots have fiercely debated the issue of existence; the inception of the universe. It is the most ancient of mysteries.

The simple fact is that regardless of what theory we use to try and reach an answer (whether by theology or science) we will always end up at the exact same place:

> If we say God created everything, then we are faced with the most basic question "Who created God?" Answer: *It just was*.

> If we say everything was created from an explosion (The Big Bang), then we are faced with the question "What created the initial element (the singularity) that you claim exploded?" Answer: *It just was*.

And while I acknowledge the principle "All that is generated must of necessity be generated by some cause" (Plato, *Timaeus*), it is not appropriate to apply this principle to this issue. Because, as stated by Madam Helena Blavatsky in *The Secret Doctrine*, it is:

> An Omnipresent, Eternal, Boundless and Immutable Principle on which all speculation is impossible, since it transcends the power of human conception and could only be dwarfed by any human expression of similitude. It is beyond the range and reach of thought...

Despite this, I choose to believe in God; the being, entity, energy, whomever or whatever that may be, which, for lack of a better term, I call God. I believe that God (the *Great Architect of the Universe*) created the initial building blocks that would eventually evolve into everything that we see around us. This may have occurred partially by design, this may have occurred partially by the process of evolution and mutation, and this may have occurred partially by manipulation from evolved species interfering with the evolutionary process of other species (the same way that we today manipulate the genetics of food and animals to suit our needs, thus interfering with their natural evolutionary process).

While I believe in God, the research I've done over the last 20 years proves that the Judaic, Christian, and Islamic religions have nothing to do with God.

It is clear that the biblical figure that we call "God," as contained in the *Torah*, *Bible*, and *Qur'an* (the so-called Abrahamic religions), directly arose from the history of the Anunnaki/Elohim/Nephilim. The history of how they created man to be a slave worker; how they had sex with the daughters of the men they created; how they tried to kill mankind off by disease, starvation, and the Great Flood; how they divided mankind during the Tower of Babel incident to keep us disunited and weak; and the history of the surviving families, etc., as explained in Part I.

To comprehend this you need to understand how the biblical texts (the *Torah*, *Bible*, and *Qur'an*) were created and how they evolved over time into their current versions.

Both scholars and theologians now recognize that the ancient Mesopotamian texts (as described in Part I) existed for a thousand years, to several thousand years in some cases, before the biblical texts of the *Torah*, *Bible* and *Qur'an* were ever created. In fact, it is now believed that the biblical texts are simply mis-interpreted, condensed versions, of the ancient Mesopotamian texts, which the biblical authors copied.

From the ancient Mesopotamian texts we know that Enlil became the Supreme Commander on Earth of the Anunnaki/Elohim/Nephilim. Enlil ruthlessly dictated his commands from his temple called the E.KUR (which means "House which is like a Mountain") (Rf1). Because of this Enlil became known as the "Lord of the Mountain."

In some areas Enlil was called by the term *Ilu Kur-gal*, which means "Great Mountain Lord" (Rf2). In other areas like Canaan Enlil was called by the term *El-Shaddai*, which means "Lord of the Mountain" (Rf3). Remember, different language groups were created in response to the Tower of Babel incident and each group was now calling Enlil by different names; however, they all had the same meaning.

When the authors of the biblical texts were copying the ancient Mesopotamian originals, they needed to condense all the different names of Enlil into one readable text. An interesting coincidence arises here when we learn that around the same time that the five books of Moses were created (which make up the *Torah* and main part of the *Bible* and *Qur'an*), that it was during this very same time that Enlil's name (***El-Shaddai***, meaning Lord of the Mountain) is changed to the new Hebrew term **YHWH** (pronounced Yod-Hay-Vav-Hay).

According to the biblical texts, when Moses asked Enlil (El-Shaddai) what name he was to call him, Enlil said to Moses:

> Say to the Israelites, '***YHWH***, the Elohim of your fathers - the Elohim of Abraham, the Elohim of Isaac and the Elohim of Jacob - has sent me to you.' This is my name forever, the name by which I am to be remembered from generation to generation. (Exodus 3:15)

Remember, the word ***Elohim*** identified the Anunnaki. If you have any doubts that ***El-Shaddai*** (Enlil, "Lord of the Mountain") was in fact the same person as ***YHWH***, you need only look at Exodus 6:2-4, which explains:

> *I am YHWH.* I appeared to Abraham, to Isaac and to Jacob *as El-Shaddai*, but by my name YHWH I did not make myself known to them. I also established my covenant with them to give them the land of Canaan...

From the biblical texts themselves you can see that ***YHWH*** was in fact ***El-Shaddai***, who was in fact ***Enlil*** (the Chief Commander of the Anunnaki/ Elohim/Nephilim). And "where" did Moses speak with Enlil/El-Shaddai/ YHWH? On a MOUNTAIN! (Exodus 3:1).

Ancient Hebrew didn't use consonants so the Tetragrammaton YHWH was used. In future translations of the Hebrew texts vowels were added to YHWH, becoming ***Yahweh*** and in some translations becoming ***Jehovah***. Eventually in English translations YHWH became ***LORD***.

To verify what I am saying you need only look in the "notes on the translation" section of your English version of the *Bible*. For example, in the New International Version of the Bible it clearly explains how the Hebrew Tetragrammaton ***YHWH*** is changed to ***LORD*** in the English version; how the name ***El-Shaddai*** is changed to ***God Almighty*** in the English version; how the Hebrew word ***Elohim*** (which is a plural noun) is changed to the singular noun ***God*** in the English version. When you start researching, the truth is revealed.

The words God, God Almighty, Lord, etc. are not contained in any of the original biblical texts! It was through a number of mis-translations and intentional deceptions, from which, the evil Enlil (Chief Commander of the Anunnaki/Elohim/Nephilim), who was against mankind, evolved into the religious figure GOD and became worshipped worldwide. Enlil was the flesh and blood person called God, Lord, Jehovah, Yahweh, YHWH, El-Shaddai, Elohim, and Allah in the biblical texts of the Torah, Bible, and Qur'an.

The problem is that today we use the same word (god) to describe two very different things. On the one hand we use it to describe the Supreme Creator (Great Architect of the Universe), and on the other hand we use it to identify the people spoken of in the biblical texts (the Anunnaki/Elohim/Nephilim) who were not Gods at all. The confusion caused by this makes it very difficult for many people to see the truth hidden behind the lies. It is a very crafty scheme perpetrated upon mankind by the Anunnaki/Elohim/Nephilim in their attempts to maintain control over their slaves.

In order to maintain strict control over their slaves the Anunnaki/Elohim/Nephilim created the three Abrahamic religions (Judaism, Christianity, Islam) as a control mechanism. They were designed to invoke "fear" into the minds of their slaves. Through this "god fearing" concept they are able to control and manipulate the thoughts and actions of their slaves; promising rewards for submission and threatening violence and death for non-submission.

While there is no supernatural "devil" as envisioned by some religious doctrines, if we use the word in the sense of someone who was against mankind (NEGATIVE), then the greatest deception the devil ever performed was tricking the world into believing that he was God and then forcing the world to worship him through that illusion, as we see occurring in Judaism, Christianity, and Islam.

10

JUDAISM

JUDAISM IS A control mechanism that Enlil/El-Shaddai/YHWH used to invoke fear and division into mankind in order to keep humans weak, unintelligent, and subservient slaves. It consists of a set of laws and history that have become "religionized."

The biblical patriarch Abraham is generally regarded as the founding father of Judaism. According to biblical texts his story begins around 292 years after the Great Flood when a man named Terah (descending from the line of Noah's son Shem), who at the age of 70 years old had three children: Abram, Nahor and Haran (Genesis 11:27).

During this time period Abram's family lived in a land known as "Aur Kasdeem", which is translated: *Ur of the Chaldeans*. In Hebrew *Aur* means Light and **Kasdeem** means Magician. The Kasdeems were the magicians, astrologers, diviners, etc., who exercised great influence in that area. The term Ur of the Chaldeans is translated: Light of the Magicians. Ur was located in Sumer and, as you will recall from a previous chapter, Sumer was the land in which the Anunnaki/Elohim/Nephilim dwelt; the people associated with magic, astrology, and other secret sciences. So from the very beginning the connection should be apparent.

Abram's brother Haran died while they were still living in Ur, but had several children before his death: Milcah, Iscah and Lot (Genesis 11:28-29).

Eventually Abram married his sister Sarai (Genesis 20:12), however, there is some question as to whether Sarai was actually Abram's niece (another daughter of his brother Haran). For instance: the first clause of the second sentence of Genesis 11:29 begins by explaining:

> The name of Abram's wife was Sarai, and the name of Nahor's wife was Milcah;

The second clause after the semicolon continues:

> *she was the daughter of Haran*, the father of both Milcah and Iscah.

Because the main subject matter of the verse is really about Sarai, not Milcah, the statement "she was the daughter of Haran" would really be indicating that

Sarai was also Haran's daughter like "both Milcah and Iscah." To further support this, in the very next verse the focal point of Sarai is continued:

> Now Sarai was barren; she had no children. (Genesis 11:30)

Based upon this reading, similar to the way Nahor married his niece Milcah, Abram married his niece Sarai. In any event, whether Sarai was Abram's sister or niece the fact remains that she was a direct blood relative.

Together Abram's family left Ur of the Chaldeans embarking on a journey to the land of Canaan. Before reaching Canaan they temporarily settled in the land of Haran where Abram's father Terah died at the age of 205 years old (Genesis 11:31-32).

While he was still in Haran, Enlil/El-Shaddai/YHWH contacted Abram to make a covenant with him. He advised Abram that he and his descendants were being chosen; effectually elevated to a higher class amongst the rest of mankind (who were in reality all his relatives). As the biblical text explains it:

> YHWH [Enlil] your Elohim hath chosen thee to be a special people unto himself, above all people that are upon the face of the earth (Deuteronomy 7:6).

Enlil/El-Shaddai/YHWH knew that by creating special or "chosen" classes of people conflicts would arise between the two classes resulting in another layer of division amongst mankind. He was setting the stage for future conflicts. As the biblical text explains it:

> YHWH [Enlil] had said to Abram, "Leave your country your people and your father's household and go to the land I will show you. I will make you into a great nation..."

Complying with Enlil's order, at the age of 75 years old Abram left Haran and traveled to Canaan (Genesis 12:1-5).

In order for Enlil's scheme to work he had to gain Abram's trust and under Enlil's guidance Abram became a very wealthy man in society (Genesis 12:16 and 13:1-17). Abram was no poor goat herder. His family became a powerful dynasty. Enlil even assisted Abram in saving his nephew Lot who had been captured during wars that were occurring in the land of Sodom where Lot was living at the time (Genesis 14).

Ten years had now passed since they arrived in Canaan and Abram's wife Sarai desperately wanted children. Since she could not have children Sarai told Abram to have sex with her Egyptian maidservant/slave named Hagar in the hope of obtaining a child in this manner (Genesis 16:1-3). Hagar became pregnant and a messenger of Enlil/El-Shaddai/YHWH contacted her to say:

> You are now with child and you will have a son.
> You shall name him Ishmael...
> He will be a wild donkey of a man;
> *his hand will be against everyone*
> *and everyone's hand against him,*
> *and he will live in hostility*
> *toward all his brothers...*

When Abram was 86 years old Ishmael was born (Genesis 16:11-16). Thirteen years later, Enlil contacted Abram to confirm the covenant between them. As the biblical text explains:

> When Abram was ninety-nine years old, YHWH appeared to him and said, "*I am El-Shaddai*; walk before me and be blameless. I will confirm my covenant between me and you... (Genesis 17:1-2)

Notice how the biblical text specifically says El-Shaddai here, which you now know was one of the names of Enlil. In accordance with their covenant Enlil would make Abram's wife Sarai pregnant (who until that time was unable to conceive) and Abram's descendants would be given the "land, from the river of Egypt to the great river, the Euphrates" (Genesis 15:1-18). Enlil/El-Shaddai said to Abram:

> You will be the father of many nations. No longer will you be called Abram [exalted father]; your name will be Abraham [father of many], for I have made you a father of many nations. I will make you very fruitful; I will make nations of you, and kings will come from you. I will establish my covenant as an everlasting covenant between me and you and your descendants... The whole land of Canaan, where you are now an alien, I will give as an everlasting possession to you and your descendants after you...

Enlil/El-Shaddai/YHWH then ordered Abraham and his descendants to "undergo circumcision" as "the sign of the covenant between" them (Genesis 17:4-14). Enlil advised Abraham that he is no longer to call his wife Sarai, but from now on "her name will be Sarah" and "she will be the mother of nations; kings of peoples will come from her" (Genesis 17:15-16):

> your wife Sarah will bear you a son, and you will call him Isaac. I will establish my covenant with him as an everlasting covenant for his descendants after him (Genesis 17:19)

and when Abraham was 100 years old Isaac was born (Genesis 21:5).

While the first born son Ishmael would become the father of 12 rulers, it was the second born son Isaac that was being "chosen" by Enlil to continue his covenant with (Genesis 17:20-21). In order to comprehend why the second born son Isaac was being chosen instead of the first born son Ishmael you need to understand the succession rules of the Anunnaki/Elohim/ Nephilim. As explained in Chapter 1, the succession rules are concerned with what son has the stronger genetic strain, not who was born first. In the case of Enki (1st born) and Enlil (2nd born): because Enlil's mother was Antu (Anu's half-sister) Enlil inherited a greater percentage of the family's genetic strain than Enki (who's mother was a non-related concubine). This entitled the second born son Enlil succession to the throne. In the case of Ishmael (1st born) and Isaac (2nd born) Enlil was applying the same rules: Ishmael's mother was the non-related maidservant Hagar, while Isaac's mother was Sarah (Abraham's sister or niece) which provided Isaac with a greater percentage of the family's genetic strain and the right to succession.

With the manipulation skills of an evil mastermind, the cold-hearted Enlil/El-Shaddai/YHWH was setting the stage for mankind to wage war against each other. Pitting brother against brother and relative against relative, as Enlil pulled the strings, directing the so-called "chosen" people to attack and kill the non-chosen people and their descendants! Enlil was creating/manipulating conflicts between mankind to dis-unite them and maintain control over them.

For example: the people currently residing in this so-called "promised land" were Abraham's other relatives "the Kenites, Kenizzites, Kadmonites, Hittites, Perizzites, Rephaites, Amorites Canaanites, Girgashites and Jebusites" (Genesis 15:19-21). They certainly were not going to just get up and leave; the land would have to be taken by force. Relatives would have to fight against other relatives and kill each other in their attempts to obtain possession of the land. Another example: before Ishmael and Isaac were even born Enlil was designing his evil plot to create and manipulate conflicts amongst mankind. Ishmael's mother is even told that Ishmael's "hand will be against everyone and everyone's hand against him, and he will live in hostility toward all his brothers." Then his younger brother Isaac is "chosen" over him. The seeds of conflict were planted. As you will see it is a constant scenario throughout the biblical texts.

As a child Ishmael is then sent away from Abraham's family. Enlil tells Abraham not to worry about Ishmael because Isaac is the more important son that he needs to focus on (Genesis 21:8- 12). Enlil then watches over Ishmael as he grows up and teaches him how to use weaponry; in effect preparing him for the coming battle (Genesis 21:20). Ishmael eventually marries an Egyptian (Genesis 21:21) and has 12 sons: Nebaioth, Kedar, Adbeel, Mibsam, Mishma, Dumah, Massa, Hadad, Tema, Jetur, Naphish and Kedemah (Genesis 25:13-15). Ishmael's descendants lived in the land of Havilah to Shur, near the border of Egypt as you go toward Ashur. These two brothers are generally considered the founders of two societies of people: Isaac (the Hebrews) and Ishmael (the Arabs). This should enlighten you as to why Jewish and Arabic people seem to be always at war with each other. Enlil designed it this way. Two brothers and their descendants (all relatives) perpetually at war with each other, thereby "divided." As the biblical text explains it: "they lived in hostility toward all their brothers" (Genesis 25:18) just as Enlil planned.

Enlil wanted to see if his scheme was working. He wanted to know if he had instilled enough "fear" into Abraham's mind to control him; even to the point where he would put his own son to death. So Enlil/El-Shaddai/ YHWH decided to test Abraham, saying:

> Take your son, your only son, Isaac, whom you love, and go to the region of Moriah. Sacrifice him there as a burnt offering on one of the mountains I will tell you about (Genesis 22:1-2)

Abraham complied with Enlil's order and was about to kill Isaac when one of Enlil's messengers stopped him, advising Abraham that it was only a test to see if he "feared" Enlil (Genesis 22:3-12).

As the biblical narrative continues we learn that, like his father Abraham, Isaac also marries a close blood relative in order to maintain the strength of his genetic strain. His wife Rebekah was the granddaughter of Abraham's brother Nahor and niece Milcah (Genesis 24:15). Also, like Abraham's wife Sarah, Isaac's wife Rebekah is barren; she can not have children, but after Enlil/El-Shaddai/YHWH intervenes Rebekah became pregnant with twin boys (Genesis 25:20-21). The twin boys seem to be fighting between each other in her womb so Rebekah asks Enlil what is happening, for which, he says to her:

> Two nations are in your womb, and two peoples from within you will be separated; one people will be stronger than the other, and the older will serve the younger (Genesis 25:22-23)

Yet again Enlil was creating more "conflicts" amongst mankind. Pitting brother against brother. The same way the descendants of Ishmael and Isaac were designed to become enemies, now these twin brothers would become enemies.

When Isaac was 60 years old Rebekah gave birth to the twin boys (Genesis 25:24-26). "The first to come out was red, and his whole body was like a hairy garment; so they named him Esau [He was also called Edom which means red]. After this, his brother came out with his hand grasping Esau's heel; so he was named Jacob [he grasps the heel; figuratively he deceives] (Genesis 25:26).

As the boys were growing up Esau became a skillful hunter, while Jacob was quiet and stayed among the tents (Genesis 25:27). The biblical text then describes how Esau swore an oath selling Jacob his birthright (Genesis 25:29-34). Because there was a famine in the area Isaac and his family moved to Gerar and from there moved to Beersheba (Genesis 26:1-6, 23).

When Isaac was an old man and close to death he sent for his son Esau to bestow him with the right of succession. At the insistence of Rebekah, Jacob pretended to be Esau. Because Isaac could not see properly anymore Isaac bestowed the right of succession upon Jacob instead of Esau. When Esau found out he was very angry, however, Esau had already swore an oath giving Jacob his birthright so actually Jacob was rightfully entitled to succession. Isaac explained to Esau that he made Jacob:

> lord over you and have made all his relatives his servants... Your dwelling will be away from the earth's richness, away from the dew of heaven above. You will live by the sword and you will serve your brother.

Esau was so angry that he said "The days of mourning for my father are near; then I will kill my brother Jacob." After overhearing Esau's intentions Rebekah sent Jacob to live with his uncle Laban in Haran to remain safe (Genesis 27). Before Jacob left Isaac warns him to marry a close blood relative to maintain the strength of his genetic strain and then Isaac says may "El-Shaddai bless you" (Genesis 28:1-3).

Esau was still so angry about not having been given the right to succession that instead of maintaining the strength of his genetic strain by marrying a close blood relative, he went to marry Ishmael's daughter Mahalath (Genesis 28:6-9).

Jacob leaves Beersheba and goes to Haran where he sees "a ladder resting on the earth, with its top reaching to heaven," and Jacob sees the Elohim "ascending and descending on it" (Genesis 28:10-12). Enlil/El-Shaddai/YHWH stood on top of the ladder and said to Jacob:

> I am YHWH, the Elohim of your father Abraham and the Elohim of Isaac. I will give you and your descendants the land on which you are lying (Genesis 28:13)

Like both Abraham and Isaac before him, Jacob marries a close blood relative to maintain the strength of his genetic strain. Jacob marries the two daughters (Leah and Rachel) of his uncle Laban (Genesis 29:16-30). Leah and Rachel are the great granddaughters of Nahor, Abraham's brother. Their father Laban said that Jacob was his "own flesh and blood" (Genesis 29:5-14).

Again, like Sarah and Rebekah before her, Rachel was barren; she was not able to have children (Genesis 29:31). Do you see the common pattern emerging? Like Sarah and Rebekah, after seeking Enlil's intervention Rachel was finally able to conceive a child and gave birth to Joseph (Genesis 30:22-24).

Jacob and his family traveled to Luz (Bethel) in Canaan (Genesis 35:6). At this time Enlil contacts Jacob and establishes a covenant with him. Similar to the way Enlil changed the names of Abraham and Sarah, Enlil changes Jacob's name to Israel and says to Israel:

> I am El-Shaddai; be fruitful and increase in number. A nation and a community of nations will come from your body. The land I gave to Abraham and Isaac I also give to you, and I will give it to your descendants after you.

Israel then erected a stone pillar at the place where Enlil contacted him and called the place Bethel (Genesis 35:10-15).

Altogether Israel had 12 sons: Reuben, Simeon, Levi, Judah, Issachar and Zebulun by wife Leah; Gad and Asher through Leah's maidservant/slave Zilpha; Dan and Naphtali through Rachel's maidservant/slave Bilhah; and Joseph and Benjamin by wife Rachel (Genesis 35:23-26). Israel's brother Esau had 5 sons: Eliphaz by wife Adah; Reuel by wife Basemath; Jeush, Jalam and Korah by wife Oholibmah. Esau and his family moved to the hill country of Seir and became known as the Edomites (Genesis 36:2-9).

Despite all the children he had, Israel loved Joseph the most and this favoritism caused the other sons to hate Joseph. Adding fuel to the fire, Joseph had a couple dreams implying that his brothers would bow down before him and he would reign over them, which made them hate Joseph even more. In a second dream even "the sun and moon and eleven stars were bowing down" to him (Genesis 37:3-11). Notice the esoteric number 13.

Joseph's brothers initially plotted to kill him but decided to sell him for 20 shekels (8 ounces) of silver to a caravan of Ishmaelites that were coming from Gilead and heading to Egypt. The brothers took his robe, poured goat blood over it, and pretended that Joseph was killed. The Ishmaelites (called Midianites) sold Joseph to one of the Egyptian Pharaoh's officials named Potiphar (Genesis 37:12-36).

However, Enlil made sure that Joseph was taken care of and he prospered in everything he did. He became such an asset to his Egyptian master Potiphar (who was Captain of the Guard) that Joseph was put in charge of everything

Potiphar owned. Eventually Potiphar's wife took notice of Joseph's well-built body and continually tried to have sex with him; advances which Joseph refused. Upset with his refusals, she then falsely accused Joseph of trying to rape her, telling Potiphar:

> That Hebrew slave you brought us came to me to make sport of me. But as soon as I screamed for help, he left his cloak beside me and ran out of the house

As a result Joseph was put in the King's prison, however, he quickly prospered and was put in charge of all the prisoners (Genesis 39:1-23). Then, after interpreting the Pharaoh's dream and saving Egypt from a seven year famine, the Pharaoh removed Joseph from prison, put him in charge of his palace, and made all the people subject to Joseph's orders because Pharaoh knew that Enlil was working with Joseph (Genesis 41:1-40):

> I hereby put you in charge of the whole land of Egypt." The Pharaoh took his signet ring from his finger and put it on Joseph's finger. He dressed him in robes of fine linen and put a gold chain around his neck. ... Then Pharaoh said to Joseph, "I am Pharaoh, but without your word no one will lift a hand or foot in all Egypt." (Genesis 41:41-44)

The same way the names of Abraham, Sarah and Israel were changed, Joseph's name is changed to Zaphenath-Paneah. The Pharaoh also gave him Asenath as a wife, with whom Joseph had two sons: Manasseh (1st born) and Ephraim (2nd born). Asenath was the daughter of Potiphera, a priest of On (Heliopolis in Greek) (Genesis 41:45-52).

Remember, Heliopolis was the Temple of Anu. As explained in Chapter 1, Anu was the Supreme Ruler on Nibiru and in Sumerian was called AN (a variant of which is: ON). As explained in Chapter 8, Heliopolis was built by Enki (called Ptah in Egyptian) and was one of the landing sites where they docked the Ben-Ben (MU). Potiphera was a priest in the temple of the Anunnaki/Elohim/Nephilim! When you look close enough the connections between these people and the biblical patriarchs become clear.

Eventually Joseph reunites with his brothers and father Israel and their whole family moves to Egypt to live with Joseph in the region of Goshen (Genesis 42-47:12). Before Israel dies he adopts Joseph's two children as his own and bestows the right of succession to Joseph's 2nd born son Ephraim. Again, we see the constant pattern emerging of the second born son being chosen like Enlil.

> In your name will Israel pronounce this blessing: 'May Elohim make you like Ephraim and Manasseh.' (Genesis 48:5-20)

As time goes on and the generation of Joseph and his brothers is only a distant memory, we learn in the biblical book of Exodus that the Israelites have now become exceedingly numerous in the land of Egypt. It was a future time when a new King came to power in Egypt who did not know about Joseph and was angered that Egypt was filled with so many Israelites. The King was worried that if a war arose the Israelites would join his enemies, so the King decided to enslave the Israelites (Exodus 1:6-11).

Some researchers believe that Joseph was Egypt's Imhotep. They base this on the following similarities:

> Joseph, reputedly the greatest seer who ever lived, saved Egypt from a devastating seven-year famine after interpreting the pharaoh's dream, while Imhotep, Egypt's greatest seer, saved the country from a devastating seven-year famine after interpreting pharaoh Djoser's dream. Four generations later, the Book of Genesis informs us, there came a pharaoh who "knew not Joseph" and enslaved the Israelites. Four generations after Imhotep, according to Egyptian history, the Third dynasty came to a mysterious end with the reign of a pharaoh named Huni. ... one of Huni's royal titles was Ka-nefer-ra (Kenephres); and strikingly, according to one tradition quoted by Artapanus of Alexandria, the pharaoh who oppressed the Israelites was named Khenephres" (Rf1).

In any event, the more Pharaoh tried to oppress the Israelites the more their numbers grew. The Pharaoh worked them ruthlessly, made their lives bitter with hard labor, and even tried to kill their newborn baby boys, ordering:

> Every boy that is born you must throw into the Nile, but let every girl live (Exodus 1:12-22)

This brings us to the birth of Moses. While Abraham is generally considered to be the founding father of Judaism, since it was with him that Enlil first sought to establish his covenant with, it was actually to Moses that the body of wisdom and law (which has become know as the Torah) was bestowed upon. The *Torah* is comprised of five books (Genesis, Exodus, Leviticus, Numbers, and Deuteronomy) allegedly written by Moses, and makes up the main part of Judaism.

Moses stems from Jacob's lineage as follows: Jacob and Leah's son Levi had a son named Kohath who had a son named Amram. Amram married his aunt Jochebed (Exodus 6:20) and they gave birth to Moses. Again, we see the constant pattern of procreating with a direct blood relative.

Moses was born a fair child and his mother tried her best to keep him, but after hiding him from the Pharaoh for three months she decided to give him up. She placed Moses in a papyrus basket coated with tar and put it in the reeds along the bank of the Nile river (Exodus 2:1-4).

The Pharaoh's daughter saw the basket and retrieved it. After noticing that it was a Hebrew baby, she sent for the baby's mother so that she could nurse the child. When the baby grew older his mother returned him to the Pharaoh's daughter who adopted him as her own child, naming him Moses (Exodus 2:5-10).

Moses grew up studying the Egyptian mysteries and became a learned scholar "in all the wisdom of the Egyptians ... mighty in words and in deeds" (The Acts 7:20-22). According to Manetho (circa 300 B.C.) Moses was also initiated at Heliopolis (The Temple of Anu/On; he was taught by the Anunnaki/Elohim/Nephilim) and became a "High Priest" under Pharaoh Amenhotep (Akhnaton) (Rf2). Science and philosophy which was passed on to the *Torah*.

Again in the history of Moses we find the same seeds of separatism being planted. For example, Moses sees an Egyptian beating a Hebrew so Moses brutally kills the Egyptian. But when faced with a Hebrew fighting a Hebrew such extreme punishment was not required and Moses simply tries to ask the man a question "Why are you hitting your fellow Hebrew?" (Exodus 2:11-13); Indoctrinating people with the concept that it is okay to kill the so-called non-chosen people.

When the Pharaoh found out what Moses did he tried to kill him so Moses fled the area and went to live in Midian. In Midian a priest named REUEL gives Moses his daughter Zipporah in marriage and they have a son named Gershom. During this long period of time the Pharaoh eventually dies (Exodus 2:15-23).

Notice how in the very next chapter of Exodus the priest's name Reuel is changed to JETHRO (Exodus 3:1). Some researchers believe that Jethro was an Ethiopian magician that one might call the Father of Voodooism (Rf3). Moses continued his studies under Jethro and some believe these practices are reflected in Moses' teachings. For example, imagine the following scenario:

In a small dimly lit room you see a man dressed in a dark linen robe standing behind a table that has long pointed horns rising from each corner. In front of the table stands a group of people intently watching the man prepare. The man reaches down below the table with his hand and retrieves a one year old living being. The people watch in horror as the man puts his hand on the one year old's head and murders it. The man drains the lifeblood out of it, pouring it into a bowl. Then dipping his fingers into the warm blood he smears blood over each horn of the table. He takes more blood and splatters it against the front of the table, then splatters blood against the sides of the table, then splatters blood against the back of the table. He dips his fingers back into the blood and smears blood on his right earlobe, then he smears blood on his right thumb, then he smears blood on his right big toe. Then the man peers around the room from side to side looking out at the crowd watching him. He puts his hands back in the blood and starts throwing blood over everyone in the room. Their faces, clothing, everything is stained with blood. The man takes the rest of the blood, pours it at the base of the table, and when everything has been coated with the blood of the young life he just ended the man exclaims: "Now we're ready to begin"

What practice does this sound like to you? Satanism? Voodoo? You might be shocked to learn that it is the practice "required" to be performed according to the Bible's book of Leviticus!

One day when Moses was "tending the flocks of Jethro" and came to Horeb (the mountain of the Anunnaki/Elohim/Nephilim) Enlil/El-Shaddai/YHWH appeared to Moses in "flames of fire" from within a bush that did not burn up (Exodus 3:1-2). Was this really a "flame" or some type of electrical lighting; advanced technology that they possessed but mankind was not aware of yet?

When Enlil saw that Moses was coming closer to see what was really going on Enlil quickly yelled to him: "Moses! Moses!" and ordered him "Do not come any closer" (Exodus 3:4-5). Clearly Enlil was trying to create a mystical experience to acquire Moses' loyalty. Enlil said to Moses:

> I am the Elohim of your father, the Elohim of Abraham, the Elohim of Isaac and the Elohim of Jacob." (Exodus 3:6)

Enlil told Moses that he was being "chosen" to go see the Pharaoh and bring the Israelites out of Egypt (Exodus 3:7-12). When Moses asked Enlil/El-Shaddai (the Lord of the Mountain) what name he was to call him Enlil said to Moses:

Say to the Israelites, 'YHWH, the Elohim of your fathers - the Elohim of Abraham, the Elohim of Isaac and the Elohim of Jacob - has sent me to you.' This is my name forever, the name by which I am to be remembered from generation to generation (Exodus 3:15)

To verify that YHWH was in fact the same Enlil/El-Shaddai, Exodus 6:2-4 explains:

I am YHWH. I appeared to Abraham, to Isaac and to Jacob as El-Shaddai, but by my name YHWH I did not make myself known to them. I also established my covenant with them to give them the land of Canaan...

From the biblical texts themselves you can see that **YHWH** was in fact **El-Shaddai**, who was in fact **Enlil** (the Chief Commander of the Anunnaki/Elohim/Nephilim).

In the biblical story of how the Israelites are freed from Egyptian slavery, again we find the same scenario playing itself out. It is another account of Enlil creating and manipulating conflict amongst mankind. For instance:

Enlil begins by ordering Moses to tell Pharaoh to let the Israelites leave Egypt. Enlil goes so far as to tell Moses that he made him like an Elohim to Pharaoh and Aaron is to act as his prophet (Exodus 7:2).

The problem is that Enlil had no intentions of letting the Israelites out of Egypt at that point in time. In fact, Enlil even made it impossible for Moses to convince Pharaoh to let the Israelites leave. Enlil said that he was going to "harden" the Pharaoh's heart specifically "so that he will not let the people go" (Exodus 4:21). Enlil "hardened" the Pharaoh's heart so that he would "not listen" to Moses no matter how hard Moses tried to convince him! (Exodus 7:3-4) What?!?

The Pharaoh was only refusing to let the Israelites go in the first place because Enlil had "hardened" his heart. If Enlil was really trying to help Moses he would have "softened" the Pharaoh's heart and there would not have been any need for all this misery to happen. But Enlil was creating this conflict with the purpose of invoking "fear" into mankind so that future generations (hearing of his wrath) will blindly follow his orders thus achieving his ultimate goal of maintaining control. The sadistic Enlil went forward with his scheme:

The eighty year old Moses started by performing the miracle of turning his staff into a snake. But Enlil "hardened" Pharaoh's heart so that he would not listen to Moses. Moses then changed the water in the Nile into blood, which killed the fish and made the water smelly and undrinkable. But again

Enlil hardened Pharaoh's heart so that he would not listen to Moses (Exodus 7:7-24).

Moses tried again with the plague of Frogs, and again with the plague of Gnats, and again with the plague of Flies, and again with the plague on the Egyptian Livestock, and again with the plague of Boils, and again with the plague of Hail, and again with the plague of Locusts and again with the plague of Darkness. Time and time again Enlil "hardened" the Pharaoh's heart so that he would not listen to Moses (Exodus 7:25 to 10:29).

The last plague was by far the most sadistic. Enlil told Moses to say:

> About midnight I will go throughout Egypt. Every firstborn son in Egypt will die, from the firstborn son of Pharaoh, who sits on the throne, to the firstborn son of the slave girl, who is at her hand mill, and all the firstborn of the cattle as well. There will be loud wailing throughout Egypt - worse than there has ever been or ever will be again (Exodus 11:4-7)

Moses warned the Pharaoh but yet again Enlil "hardened" the Pharaoh's heart so that he would not listen to Moses (Exodus 11:9-10).

Enlil gave Moses strict instructions on how he was to prepare for the passover, among them, all of Israel must slaughter a lamb on the fourteenth day of the month at twilight, take some of its blood to put on the sides and tops of the doorframes of their houses (Exodus 12:6-7).

At midnight Enlil did what he promised and murdered every firstborn in Egypt. There "was not a house without someone dead" (Exodus 12:29-30). How many children were killed on that night"? How many children did Enlil kill just to create a conflict and instill "fear" into mankind? This should clearly demonstrate how diabolically evil Enlil was to mankind. The Israelites and Egyptians were in reality family (they were all relatives). It was only through the fictitious divisions created by Enlil from which they falsely believed they were different from each other.

On the very same night as the killings the Pharaoh summoned Moses and released the Israelites. It was during the month of Abib that the Israelites left Egypt, around 600,000 men on foot, besides women and children, journeying from Rameses to Succoth (Exodus 12:31-37).

As a "thank you" for freeing them from slavery, Enlil then required Moses to sacrifice "every firstborn male" of the Israelites to him when they enter the "promised land" of Canaan!

105

> The first offspring of every womb among the Israelites belongs to me,
> whether man or animal. (Exodus 13:1-2)

Not only had Enlil just killed the firstborn of every Egyptian, he was now demanding the firstborn male of every Israelite. How sick is this? For the people who could afford it their firstborn son could be "redeemed" with a lamb (Exodus 13:13).

Enlil didn't stop there. He wanted mankind to remember this event forever so he ordered that this sacrifice of the firstborn "man and animal" would have to occur every year and ordered Moses to commemorate it for generations to come by celebrating it as a yearly festival to Enlil/El-Shaddai/YHWH, his lasting ordinance (Exodus 12:14). When future generations ask why they celebrate Passover, they are to teach them:

> YHWH killed every firstborn in Egypt, both man and animal. This is
> why I sacrifice to YHWH the first male offspring of every womb and
> redeem each of my firstborn sons (Exodus 13:14-15)

Enlil's scheme was designed to invoke a tremendous amount of fear of his wrath into mankind, and wanted that fear taught to every subsequent generation so that he could maintain control.

As the Israelites journeyed out of Egypt they were led by Enlil/El-Shaddai/YHWH who flew above them in one of the aircraft (MU, shem, Ben-Ben) to guide the way. The biblical texts explain how the people could see a "pillar of cloud" during the day and a "pillar of fire" at night (Exodus 13:21-22). This is exactly what you would expect to see from an aircraft. The cloud/smoke coming out of the exhaust during the day and the fire/light at night could have been either a spot light or the light from some type of jet engine.

When the Israelites reached the desert they set up camp next to Mount Sinai (Horeb). As time went on disputes arose amongst the people and they came to Moses to have them settled. When his father-in-law Jethro (the Midian priest) saw Moses doing this all alone he confronted Moses saying "What you are doing is not good. You and these people who come to you will only wear yourselves out." It was in fact Jethro who advised Moses "Teach them the decrees and laws, and show them the way to live and the duties they are to perform" and he advised Moses to appoint judges over the people, for which Moses did everything he said (Exodus 18:13-26).

The laws that mankind would be required to follow were delivered in a majestic fashion. The Torah explains how Enlil descended upon Mount Sinai in his aircraft making a grand entrance to the sound of blasting trumpets. To the people the engines sounded like "thunder and lightening" and sent a "thick cloud" of smoke billowing down and covering the whole mountain which trembled from the landing aircraft. Enlil called Moses and Aaron up to the top of the mountain, but warned everyone else not to come up (Exodus 20:16-25). The people were so afraid from the sight of the landing aircraft that they didn't even want to hear Enlil speak but Moses assured them not to be afraid because Enlil was just instilling "fear" into them so they would follow his rules (Exodus 20:18-21).

On Mount Sinai Enlil proceeded to give Moses a list of laws that the people would be required to follow. The laws covered the so-called Ten Commandments and then went into detail on how to treat servants, personal injuries, protection of property, social responsibility, laws of justice and mercy, sabbath laws, annual festivals, instructions to build an Ark, instructions on building altars, rules surrounding consecration, etc. (Exodus 20 through Leviticus).

Moses "stayed on the mountain forty days and forty nights" eating no bread and drinking no water (Deuteronomy 9:9) while he wrote down everything Enlil/El-Shaddai/YHWH said. When he descended from the mountain he saw that the Israelites were already committing corruption and worshipping a golden calf idol, so in a fit of anger Moses smashed the two tablets into pieces (Deuteronomy 9:17). The biblical text explains how Moses was so angry at the Israelites that he ordered the Levites to kill every person involved in the corruption:

> Each strap a sword to his side. Go back and forth through the camp from one end to the other, each killing his brother and friend and neighbor.

Pursuant to Moses' command 3,000 Israelites were murdered (Exodus 32:27-28). Moses then went back up the mountain for another forty days and nights (Deuteronomy 9:18) to obtain the laws again. When he returned Moses built an altar at the foot of the mountain and set up 12 stone pillars representing the 12 tribes of Israel (Exodus 24:4, 31:18).

Notice how Moses used the blood practices explained earlier when he read the Book of the Covenant to the people at Mount Sinai:

> Moses took half of the blood and put it in bowls, and the other half he sprinkled on the altar. Then he took the Book of the Covenant and read it to the people. ... Moses then took the blood, sprinkled it on the people and said, "This is the blood of the covenant that [Enlil] YHWH has made with you in accordance with these words." (Exodus 24:6-8)

Moses gave this set of laws to the priests (the sons of Levi) who were to carry it in the ark of the covenant and to all the elders of Israel, commanding the people to read the law "every seven years" (Deuteronomy 31:9-10):

> Assemble the people - men, women and children ... so they can listen and *LEARN TO FEAR* [Enlil] YHWH your Elohim and follow carefully all the words of this law. Their children, who do not know this law, must hear it and LEARN TO FEAR [Enlil] YHWH your Elohim... (Deuteronomy 31:12-13)
>
> ...so that you, your children and their children after them man FEAR [Enlil] YHWH (Deuteronomy 6:2)
>
> ...Moses...gave this command..."Take this Book of Law and place it beside the ark of the covenant of YHWH your Elohim. There it will remain as a witness against you. For I know how rebellious and stiff-necked you are..." (Deuteronomy 31:24-27)

The teachings of Moses were designed to create "fear" into the minds of mankind. This "fear" was then used to manipulate the thoughts and actions of the human slaves in order to maintain control over them. Requiring that the law be read "every seven years" ensured that this "fear" would be constantly instilled into mankind from generation to generation. This control mechanism was the sinister design behind the "god fearing" concept and is the foundation of Judaism. The history and law Moses allegedly recorded filled five books and became known as the Torah of the Judaic doctrine.

Moses' original "Book of Law" no longer exists. Today the oldest existing version of the Torah is found in the Septuagint (Greek translation made in Alexandria, Egypt, by Jewish scholars for Greek speaking Hellenist Jews) and the Dead Sea Scrolls (a Hebrew translation discovered in 1947 which is believed to have been created by the Essenes), both of which only date to the 3rd century B.C. Even then, that's still more than 1,000 years after the originals were said to have been created.

The Greek Septuagint was later translated into a number of versions, including the Vulgate (Latin translation by St. Jerome in the 4th century A.D.). Later, scholars from Babylon and Palestine created a Hebrew version which introduced vowels and accent signs to the Hebrew Scripts around 900 A.D. which has become known as the Masoretic Text (the oldest copy of which, called the Codex Petropolitanus, is from 916 A.D.) (Rf4). Today most modern translations are made from the Masoretic Text.

Despite its sketchy origins, most scholars now believe that today's Torah is only a composite work based upon ancient Mesopotamian texts that the Israelites copied and consolidated while they were being held captive in

Babylon during the 6th century B.C. During that time period a Chaldean man named Nebuchadnezzar was King of Babylon. During his reign he attacked Jerusalem, destroyed the temple, captured the Israelites and took them to Babylon (Ezra 5:12). The Babylonian King then took "some of the Israelites from the royal family and the nobility" and taught "them the language and literature of the Babylonians" for three years (Daniel 1:3-5). It is believed that this is when the Israelites came into contact with the ancient Mesopotamian texts and is why most of the events found in the biblical texts (texts that emerged only after this time period) seem to be condensed versions of the ancient Mesopotamian originals.

When reading the Torah you can clearly see that it contains drastically different agendas. For instance, in one section it contains a few inherently "good" or "positive" teachings, like: do not commit murder, do not steal, do not give false testimony, do not commit adultery, honor your father and mother, do not covet anything that belongs to your neighbor. These are teachings that every human being should be required to follow. The problem is that the overwhelming majority of the Torah was designed with the agenda of invoking fear and creating division as a control mechanism to keep mankind weak, unintelligent and subservient slaves.

To give you an idea of some of the Judaic doctrines that Jewish people are required to follow according to the Torah:

- Jewish people are required to kill any girl who looses her virginity before marriage (she must be stoned to death) (Deuteronomy 22:13-21)

- Jewish people are required to kill gay people (Leviticus 20:13)

- Jewish people are required to kill anyone who has sex with a non-Jew (both must be killed) (Numbers 25:6-15)

- Jewish people are required to kill anyone who commits adultery (both the adulterer and the adulteress) (Leviticus 20:10)

- Jewish people are required to kill anyone who marries both a woman and her mother (Leviticus 20:14)

- Jewish people are required to sacrifice their firstborn sons to Enlil (Exodus 22:29). And the Torah specifies that "nothing that a man owns and devotes to [Enlil] YHWH - whether man or animal or family land - may be sold or redeemed" (Leviticus 27:28), and "No person devoted to destruction may be ransomed; he must be put to death" (Leviticus 27:29, despite a conflicting verse that says redeem your first born sons.

- Jewish people are required to kill their child if it is stubborn and rebellious and does not obey its father and mother (Deuteronomy 21:18-21)

- Jewish people are required to kill anyone who curses at their parents (Exodus 21:17) and required to kill anyone who hits their parents (Exodus 21:15)

- Jewish people are required to kill anyone who curses at an Anunnaki/Elohim/Nephilim (Leviticus 24:10-16)

- Jewish people are required to kill anyone who makes a sacrifice to another Elohim (Exodus 22:20)

- Jewish people are required to kill anyone who has sex with an animal (Exodus 22:19, Leviticus 20:15-16)

- Jewish people are required to kill a priest's daughter if she becomes a prostitute (Leviticus 21:9)

- Jewish people are required to kill anyone who is a medium, spiritist or sorceress (Exodus 22:18, Leviticus 20:27)

- Jewish people are required to kill anyone who shows contempt for a judge or priest (Deuteronomy 17:12)

- Jewish people are required to kill anyone who takes advantage of a widow or orphan (Exodus 22:22-24)

- Jewish people are required to kill anyone who does any work on the Sabbath day (Exodus 31:15)

Following Judaic doctrines people were killed even for the most minor infractions, for example: because a man had collected some wood to keep his family warm on the Sabbath day Moses and the whole assembly stoned the man to death (Numbers 15:32-36); when a man named Achan stole a robe, some silver and gold, Joshua not only killed Achan but also killed his sons and daughters, his cattle, donkeys and sheep (Joshua 7).

The Torah says: "If anyone injures his neighbor, whatever he has done must be done to him: fracture for fracture, eye for eye, tooth for tooth. As he has injured the other, so he is to be injured" (Leviticus 24:19-20); and says "you are to take life for life, eye for eye, tooth for tooth, hand for hand, foot for foot, burn for burn, wound for wound, bruise for bruise" (Exodus 21:23-24). But in a conflicting verse goes on to say "Do not seek revenge or bear a grudge against one of your people" (Leviticus 19:18).

In Judaism there is no "religious freedom." In fact, the Torah requires Jewish people to kill any man or woman who is found worshipping another god:

> take the man or woman who has done this evil deed to your city gate
> and stone that person to death (Deuteronomy 17:2-7)

The Torah even requires Jewish people to kill their brother, son, daughter, wife, or closest friend, if they try to get them to worship anther god:

> You must certainly put him to death. Your hand must be the first in
> putting him to death, and then the hands of all the people. Stone him
> to death... (Deuteronomy 13:6-10)

The Torah goes so far as to require Jewish people to kill an entire town of people if they learn there are people in it advocating the worship of other gods:

> you must certainly put to the sword all who live in that town. Destroy
> it completely, both its people and its livestock. (Deuteronomy 13:12-15)

Then despite all of this required killing the Torah says "do not kill" (Exodus 20:13). Another law in the Torah under Leviticus 18:6 commands:

> No one is to approach any close relative to have sexual relations

However, the history recorded in the Torah details how the biblical patriarchs continuously had sex with close relatives. For example: even the so-called founding father of Judaism, Abraham, had sex with and married his sister or niece Sarah in direct conflict of *Leviticus 18:9*; Isaac had sex with and married his relative Rebekah; Jacob had sex with and married his relatives Leah and Rachel (who were also both sisters) in direct conflict with *Leviticus 18:18* which says "Do not take your wife's sister as a rival wife and have sexual relations with her"; Amram had sex with his aunt Jochebed in direct conflict with *Leviticus 18:12* which says "Do not have sexual relations with your father's sister; she is your father's close relative" and despite *Leviticus 20:20* which says "If a man sleeps with his aunt ... they will die childless," Amram and Jochebed gave birth to Moses.

Why does this contradiction exist? Again, it stems from the different agendas of people who created the Torah. Enlil was against mankind and wanted humans to remain weak, unintelligent, and subservient slaves. Whenever mankind tried to elevate itself beyond its slave status Enlil was there to kill and oppress mankind. You can be certain that any order or rule from him was designed to further those goals. From the succession rules of the Anunnaki/Elohim/Nephilim Enlil knew that procreating with a close blood relative produced the strongest possible genetic strain/bloodline. Because Enlil wanted to keep humans weak he had to prevent this from occurring. So through the "god fearing" concept Enlil ordered mankind not to procreate with close relatives. He then scared mankind with all kinds of "fear" that if they violated this rule their children would be born deformed with birth defects, when in reality Enlil was just trying to weaken mankind by diluting the strength of its genetic strain/bloodline.

Some of the people (who were against Enlil) were secretly inserting truths into the Torah to help teach mankind this science (i.e. the history of how patriarchs procreated with close relatives specifically to maintain the strength of their genetic strain). However, the "fear" Enlil indoctrinated society with was extreme and even to this day the idea of procreating with a direct family member strikes such fear and disgust into most of society; even to those who know the true science behind it.

Various other laws that Jewish people must follow according to the Torah are: Jewish people are forbidden from charging another Jewish person interest on money lent or selling food at a profit (Exodus 22:25, Leviticus 25:37) but may do so to a non-Jew (Deuteronomy 23:20); Jewish people are not allowed to wear clothing woven of two kinds of material (Leviticus 19:19); Jewish people are forbidden from cutting their hair at the sides of their head or clipping off the edges of their beard (Leviticus 19:27); Jewish people are forbidden from getting a tattoo (Leviticus 19:28); Priests are allowed to marry but the woman must be a virgin (Leviticus 21:7-15); Men are superior to women and can nullify vows or pledges made by his woman (Numbers 30).

In Judaism there is no life after death. The concept of people going to Heaven as a reward for good behavior or to Hell as a punishment for bad behavior does not exist. In the rare instance where the word "heaven" is used in the Torah it is simply referring to the sky.

Under Judaism the reward for good behavior was the flesh and blood man, Enlil/YHWH, taking physical residence in the community you lived in and making you prosperous (Leviticus 26:3-12). The punishment for bad behavior was the wrath of a vengeful, blood-thirsty overlord falling upon anyone who disobeyed him; including threats of sudden terror, wasting diseases, fever, plagues, soil that will not yield crops, trees that will not bear fruit, threats of violence in the form of defeat by their enemies, threats of bringing the sword upon them, threats of sending wild animals against them to rob their children and destroy their cattle, and the shockingly sadistic threat of making them "eat the flesh of your sons and daughters," punishment of which they will experience seven times over (Leviticus 26:14-45). Likewise, the concept of a supernatural "devil" does not exist in Judaism.

The history recorded in the Torah demonstrates over and over again how Enlil created divisions amongst relatives and then manipulated conflicts between those relatives to keep them at war with each other and disunited. For example:

As you've seen above, first Enlil divided Abraham from his relatives (the rest of mankind who are also descended from Noah). Then he divided Abraham's sons Ishmael and Isaac advising how Ishmael's "hand will be against everyone and everyone's hand against him, and he will live in hostility toward all his brothers" (Genesis 16:11-16). Then he divided Isaac's twin sons Esau and Jacob advising how "Two nations are in your womb, and two peoples from within you will be separated; one people will be stronger than the other, and the older will serve the younger" (Genesis 25:22-23). After creating these divisions Enlil then forced one group of relatives to attack the others.

In fact, under Enlil's command the Israelites attacked their relatives throughout Mesopotamia, pillaging their property and killing every living thing in their wake, including entire towns of their relatives:

Enlil forced Jacob to use the "sword and bow" and attack his relatives in the land of the Amorites (Genesis 48:22).

Under Moses the Israelites killed Sihon the Amorite King of Heshbon and killed all the men, women, and children living in all the towns therein. They left "no survivors" and carried off the plunder (Deuteronomy 2:33-35, Numbers 21:21-26). The Israelites went on to kill Og the King of Bashan, destroying every city and killing every man, woman, and child therein. Then they carried off the plunder (Deuteronomy 3:1-7, Numbers 21:33-35). In another instance Enlil ordered the Israelites to treat the "Midianites as enemies and kill them" (Numbers 25:16-18). The Torah details how Enlil ordered Moses to take "vengeance on the Midianites" and kill them all. Pursuant to this command the Israelites killed every man and burned all the towns, taking the women, children, herds, flocks and goods as plunder. When Moses found out the Israelites had compassion on the Midianites and allowed the women and children to live, Moses was so angry that he ordered them to kill every boy child and kill every woman who was not a virgin. Moses then went on to divide the plunder of the Midianites which included 675,000 sheep, 72,000 cattle, 61,000 donkeys, and 32,000 women! (Numbers 31). The Midianites were the descendants of Abraham's son Midian (Genesis 25:1)! The Israelites and Midianites were family and here you can clearly see how Enlil was creating divisions amongst relatives and forcing them to attack each other.

Enlil commanded that the Israelites completely destroy their relatives the Hittites, Amorites, Canaanites, Perizzites, Hivites and Jebusites, saying "do not leave alive anything that breathes" (Deuteronomy 20:16-17), explaining how the Israelites "must destroy all the peoples" he gives over to them (Deuteronomy 7:16) and their towns (Numbers 21:1-3).

The reign of terror continued under Joshua's leadership. The Israelites killed every man, woman, and child in Jericho and cursed anyone who would rebuild it (Joshua 6); then they killed every person in the land of Ai (some 12,000 men and women) and hung the king on a tree (Joshua 8); then they killed the five kings of the Amorites: Adoni-Zedek the King of Jerusalem, the King of Hebron, the King of Jarmuth, the King of Lachish, the King of Eglon and hung them on five trees (Joshua 10); the Israelites put Jerusalem to the sword and set it on fire (Judges 1:8); then their killing spree spread to the lands of Gezer, Debir, Geder, Hormah, Arad, Libnah, Adullam Makkedah, Bethel, Tappuah, Hepher, Aphek, Lasharon, Madon, Hazor, Shimron Meron, Acshaph, Taanach, Megiddo, Kedesh, Jokneam, Dor, Goyim, Tirzah, where the Israelites killed all the kings and every man, woman, and child. They pillaged their property and livestock "but all the people they put to the sword until they completely destroyed them, not sparing anyone that breathed" (Joshua 11-12).

After Joshua died other Israelites were "chosen" to continue Enlil's reign of terror, forcing relative to wage war against relative. The Israelites went on to kill 10,000 Canaanites and Perizzites at Bezek and even cut off the thumbs and big toes of Adoni-Bezek (Judges 1:4-6). Under Othniel the Israelites defeated the Cushan-Rishathaim king of Aram (Judges 3:7-10); Under Ehud the Israelites killed about 10,000 Moabites (Judges 3:31) (the Moabites descend from Lot, Genesis 19:36-37); Under Shamgar 600 Philistines were killed (Judges 3:31); Under Gideon the Israelites defeated more Midianites and killed the men of Peniel (Judges 7-8); The Israelite Abimelech killed his 70 brothers on one stone so that he alone could become crowned King of Israel and then went on to burn about 1,000 men and women in the tower of Shechem (Judges 9); Under Jephthah's leadership the Israelites devastated 20 towns fighting the Ammonites (who descend from Lot, Genesis 19:36-38) and as payment for Enlil's help in accomplishing this Jephthah was required to kill (sacrifice) his only virgin daughter as a burnt offering (Judges 11). The Israelites went on to kill 42,000 Ephraimites (their relatives; the descendants of Joseph's son Ephraim). Then the Israelites attacked their relatives the Benjamites putting all the towns to the sword and setting everything on fire. Some 45,100 Benjamites were killed in this attack. The Benjamites were the descendants of Isaac's son Benjamin! The Israelites then sent 12,000 men to Jabesh Gilead to kill everyone living there "including the women and children." Except they allowed 400 young virgin women to live so that they could rape them in order to provide heirs for the surviving Benjamites (Judges 19-21).

Under Saul the Israelites were ordered to attack the Amalekites and destroy everything that belongs to them:

> "put to death men and women, children and infants, cattle and sheep, camels and donkeys" (1 Samuel 15:3)

Because Saul refused to kill everything Enlil removed Saul as King (1 Samuel 15:9-35) and then anointed Saul's youngest brother David as King of Israel to continue the genocide (1 Samuel 16).

Despite the reverence King David's name invokes in Judaism, David was as corrupt and committed the same atrocities as the previous leaders:

King David brutally killed 200 Philistine men and cut off their foreskins in order to exchange them for Saul's daughter Michal in marriage (1 Samuel 18:25-27). King David had multiple wives: in addition to Michal, he married Abigail and then Ahinoam of Jezreel (1 Samuel 25:42-43). King David then committed the crime of adultery with Bathsheba and even went so far as to have Bathsheba's husband Uriah killed so that he could take her as his own wife (2 Samuel 11:2-27). Under Judaic doctrine these were crimes for which they both were required to be put to death, yet Jewish people revere King David as a righteous leader. David would eventually take many other wives and concubines.

Later, when King David was living amongst the Philistines he fought on their side against the Israelites. The Torah describes how: "Whenever David attacked an [Israelite] area, he did not leave a man or woman alive," because David did not want people to inform the Israelites of his acts and say "This is what David did." King David continued to kill Israelites as long as he lived in Philistine territory (1 Samuel 27).

After Saul died David returned to the Israelites to reign as King over them. Under King David's leadership the Israelites continued the genocide attacking their relatives and conquering Jerusalem. They set up residence in the fortress and called it the City of David, after which, King Hiram of Tyre built a palace for King David (2 Samuel 5).

King David continued Enlil's killing spree, attacking his relatives: the Arameans of Damascus (for which 22,000 were murdered) (2 Samuel 8:5); the Israelites then killed 18,000 Edomites in the Valley of Salt (2 Samuel 8:13) (Remember, the Edomites were the descendants of Isaac's son Esau); then the

Israelites went on to kill another 700 charioteers and 40,000 foot soldiers (2 Samuel 10:18).

Even King David's family committed atrocities. King David's son Amnon raped his sister Tamar. King David's other son Absalom kills his brother Amnon and then tries to kill his own father David. Absalom is then killed by King David's men (2 Samuel 13). King David's other son Adonijah tries to assume kingship over Israel without King David's knowledge or blessing (1 Kings 1). Then after King David has the priest Zadok anoint his other son Solomon as King over Israel, King Solomon has his brother Adonijah killed (1 Kings 2:3).

Even as King David was dying he was calling for the death of people who wronged him, in direct violation of Moses' law not to seek revenge (1 Kings 2:3).

Initially Enlil loved King Solomon and changed his name to Jedidiah (2 Samuel 12:24-25), but later Solomon made an alliance with Pharaoh King of Egypt and married the Pharaoh's daughter against Enlil's wishes (1 Kings 3). Solomon went on to marry many women that Enlil ordered him not to marry and eventually Solomon began following other Anunnaki/Elohim/Nephilim: Ashtoreth of the Sidonians and Molech (aka Milcom) of the Ammonites. On a hill east of Jerusalem Solomon even built a high place for Chemosh the Elohim of Moab and for Molech of the Ammonites (1 Kings 11:1-7).

The biblical texts go on to explain how the Israelites went on to kill another 100,000 Aramean soldiers at Aphek then killed another 27,000 in the city (1 Kings 20:29-30). They explain how the Israelite King Manasseh sacrificed his son in the fire, practiced sorcery, divination, consulted mediums and spiritists (2 Kings 21:6). Under Ezra all the Israelites who married foreign women were forced to kill them (Ezra 10:19).

If the above wasn't enough to demonstrate how evil Enlil/El-Shaddai/YHWH was, the biblical texts go on to describe how before Enlil is done with his killing spree there will be enough dead bodies to cover the surface of the Earth from one end to the other (Jeremiah 25:33) until the day:

> when they bathe their feet in the blood... (Psalm 58:10)

> [how they] may plunge [their] feet in the blood of [their] foes, while the tongues of [their] dogs have their share (Psalm 68:23)

The Judaic history is filled with a continuous cycle of violence and division. Enlil used the Israelites as weapons to kill his enemies and drag the human race under his control.

In modern times we look at Jewish people as victims of the atrocities that Hitler and the Nazi party inflicted upon them. However, the history in the Torah proves that Jewish people actually committed more genocide against the human race (with millions of people having been murdered) then anybody else. Both the Nazis and the Jews committed the same evil acts of genocide; Jewish people just did it on a much bigger scale.

Judaism was designed to keep the human race perpetually at war with each other. There is no such thing as a Jew or Gentile. These are man-made labels (created by the evil Enlil/YHWH) that divide mankind up into different groups. The division forges an us-versus-them mentality in the human brain (due to its naturally competitive nature), generating all kinds of intolerances and prejudices in ignorant people who then begin fighting between each other.

Exactly as Enlil designed, due to the created "divisions" today Jewish people consider themselves a "chosen" class of people, separate from the rest of mankind (their relatives whom also stem from Noah). To this very day we see Jews and Arabs in the Middle East (relatives both stemming from Abraham) fighting between each other and remaining divided.

We see these intolerances and prejudices rearing their evil heads in the Judaic doctrines. For example, in addition to the "laws" of the Torah Jews are required to follow the *TALMUD*. The Talmud is the authoritative body of Jewish tradition comprising the *MISHNAH* and *GEMARA*. The Mishnah is mostly a collection of Jewish laws called the Halacha compiled circa 200 A.D. which supplement the scriptual law of the Torah. The Gemara is a commentary on the Mishnah and forms the second part of the Talmud.

The Talmud contains such hatred intended to cause division amongst mankind that in 1306 the King of France (Philip IV) ordered that all copies of it be burned, but the Talmud survived (Rf5).

The law of the Talmud states that no Jew is allowed to reveal anything about its contents to a goy. A goy is a gentile; anyone who is not Jewish:

- "To communicate anything to a goy about our religious relations would be equal to the killing of all the Jews, for if the goys knew what we teach about them, they would kill us openly." (Book of Libbre David, 37)

117

- "It is forbidden to disclose the secrets of the Law. He who would do it would be as guilty as if he destroyed the whole world" (Jaktu Chadasz, 171, 2)

- "If a Jew be called to explain any part of the rabbinic books, he only ought to give a false explanation, that he might not, by behaving differently, become an accomplice in betraying this information. Who will violate this order shall be put to death." (Libbre David, 37)

- "It is forbidden to disclose the secrets of the Law. One should and must make false oath, when the goys ask if our books contain anything against them. Then we are bound to state on oath that there is nothing like that." (Szaalot-Utszabot. The Book of Jore d'a, 17)

- "Every goy who studies Talmud, and every Jew who helps him in it, ought to die." (Sanhedryn 59a. Aboda Zora 8-6. Szagiga 13) (Rf6)

What?!? Why the need for such secrecy and such extreme punishment for its violation? When you read some of the passages the answer becomes self-evident:

"Those who do not own Torah and the prophets must all be killed. Who has power to kill them, let him kill them openly with sword, if not, let him use artifices till they are done away with." (Schulchan Aruch: Choszen Hamiszpat, 425, 50) (Rf7)

The Judaic doctrines took a group of relatives and divided them into Jew and non-Jew (Goy), from which a mindset of superiority arose amongst the Jews:

- "the Jewish nation is the only nation selected by God, while all the remaining ones are contemptible and hateful." (Rf8)

- "Just the Jews are humans, the non-Jews are not humans, but cattle" (Kerithuth 6b) (Rf9)

- "The non-Jews have been created to serve the Jews as slaves" (Midrasch Talpioth 225) (Rf10)

- "Sexual intercourse with non-Jews is like sexual intercourse with animals" (Kethuboth 3b) (Rf11)

- "The non-Jews have to be avoided even more than sick pigs" (Orach Chaiim 57, 6a) (Rf12)

- "The birth rate of non-Jews has to be suppressed massively" (Zohar 11, 4b) (Rf13)

118

- "A boy-goy after nine years and one day old, and a girl after three years and one day old, are considered filthy." (Pereferkowicz: Talmud t.v., p.11) (Rf14)

- "The ears of the goys are filthy, their baths, houses, countries are filthy." (Tosefta Mikwat, v.1) (Rf15)

- "When one sees inhabited houses of the 'Goy' [non Jew] one says, 'The Lord will destroy the house of the proud'. And when one sees them destroyed he says, 'The Lord God of Vengeance has revealed himself' - (The Babylonian Talmud, Berachot 58, 6)" (Rf16)

Judaic doctrine then teaches that "all property of other nations belongs to the Jewish nation, which consequently is entitled to seize upon it without any scruples" (Rf17):

- "A Jew may rob a Goy [non-Jew], he may cheat him over a bill, which should not be perceived by him, otherwise the name of God would become dishonoured." (Schulchan Aruch, Choszen Hamiszpat, 348) (Rf18)

- "How to interpret the word 'robbery'. A goy is forbidden to steal, rob, or take women slaves, etc. from a goy or from a Jew, but he (a Jew) is not forbidden to do all this to a goy." (Tosefta, Aboda Zara, viii, 5) (Rf19)

- "If a Jew has struck his spade into the ground of the Goy, he has become the master of the whole." (Baba Batra, 55a) (Rf20)

- "The estates of the Goys are like wilderness, who first settles in them has a right to them." (Baba Batra, 54b) (Rf21)

- "The property of the Goys is like a thing without a master." (Schulchan Aruch: Choszen Hamiszpat, 156, 5) (Rf22)

- "A thing lost by a goy may not only be kept by the man who found it, but it is forbidden to give it back to him." (Schulchan Aruch, Choszen Hamiszpat, 266, 1) (Rf23)

Judaic doctrine also absolves Jewish people from any crimes or atrocities they may commit against a non-Jew:

"If a goy killed a goy or a Jew he is responsible, but if a Jew killed a goy he is not responsible." (Tosefta, Aboda Zara, viii, 5) (Rf24)

"The son of Noah, who would steal a farthing ought to be put to death, but an Israelite is allowed to do injury to a goy; where it is written, Thou shalt not do injury to they neighbour, is not said Thou shalt not do injury to a goy." (Miszna, Sanhedryn, 57) (Rf25)

119

It also states that a Jewish person may not stand witness against another Jewish person:

> If a goy wants a Jew to stand witness against a Jew at the Court of Law, and the Jew could give fair evidence, he is forbidden to do it, but if a Jew wants a Jew to be a witness in a similar case against a goy, he may do it." (Schulchan Aruch, Choszen Hamiszpat, 28 art, 3 and 4) (Rf26)

If someone betrays the Jewish people three times or caused Jewish money to be passed to a goy:

> "...a wise council must be found to do away with him." "Every one must contribute to the expense of the community (Kahal) in order to do away with the traitor." (Schulchan Aruch, Choszen Hamiszpat, 163, 1) (Rf27)

In Judaism a RABBI (meaning master) is the official leader of a Jewish congregation that is qualified to expound and apply Halacha and other Jewish law. The Talmud and Rabbi are given such a high level of authority in the Jewish community that they are considered "superior" even to God:

> The decisions of the Talmud are words of the living God. Jehovah himself asks the opinion of earthly rabbis when there are difficult affairs in heaven." (Rabbi Menachem, Comments for the Fifth Book) (Rf28)

> It is more wicked to protest the words of the rabbis than of the Torah" (Miszna, Sanhedryn xi, 3) (Rf29)

> Who changes the words of the rabbis ought to die. (Erubin, 21, b) (Rf30)

> Jehovah himself in heaven studies the Talmud, standing: he has such respect for that book. (Tr. Mechilla) (Rf31)

Judaic doctrine even goes so far as to authorize and advocate the death of anyone who wants to leave the Jewish religion:

> It is permitted to kill a Jewish denunciator everywhere it is permitted to kill him before he has denounced... though it is necessary to warn him and say, 'Do not denounce.' But should he say, 'I will denounce,' he must be killed, and he who accomplishes it first will have the greater merit. (Schulchan Aruch, Choszen Hamiszpat, 388, 10)(Rf32)

Now you understand why there is so much secrecy surrounding the Talmud and why such extreme punishment for revealing its message to a non-Jew.

* * *

I present these quotes to demonstrate the very intolerances and prejudices that arose under the Judaic doctrines. They are certainly not indicative of "unity" or "peace and love"; positive things that one would associate with the concepts of religion or God.

What we find in Judaism are the control mechanisms of fear and division that Enlil was trying so hard to indoctrinate society with in order to maintain control.

11

JESUS

THE NEW TESTAMENT introduces us to the biblical figure known as Jesus. In fact, the first Gospel begins with a lengthy genealogy in an attempt to portray Jesus as a descendant of Abraham. Beginning with Abraham, it traces the lineage down through Isaac, on through King David, and continues tracing the lineage down until they arrive at Joseph (Matthew 1:1-16). If you believe in its accuracy, the Gospel of Matthew clearly demonstrates that Joseph was a descendant of Abraham.

The problem is that Jesus was *NOT* Joseph's son. Therefore the entire biblical lineage tracing itself from Joseph back to Abraham is completely irrelevant when it comes to Jesus.

According to the biblical texts Joseph married a virgin woman named Mary. Before "they came together" (had sex) Joseph found out that Mary was already pregnant. Believing that Mary had broken the laws (loosing her virginity before marriage, Deuteronomy 22:13-21, or committing adultery, Deuteronomy 22:22-24) his initial response was to divorce her quietly (Matthew 1:18-19, Luke 1:27). However, a messenger appeared to him in a dream and explained that the child's father was one of the Anunnaki/Elohim/Nephilim. The messenger advised him that he should not be afraid to keep Mary as his wife, so Joseph decided not to divorce her (Matthew 1:20-25).

Mary's conception is explained as such: in the sixth month a messenger named Gabriel arrived in the town of Nazareth, in Galilee (Luke 1:26), where he spoke with Mary and advised her that the:

> Holy Spirit will come upon you, and the power of the Most High will overshadow you (Luke 1:35)

> You will be with child and give birth to a son, and you are to give him the name Jesus. (Luke 1:31-33)

While some try to argue that this means "immaculate conception," with what you now know, this was simply another way of saying that an Anunnaki/Elohim/Nephilim was going to rape you. Because the sexual act and "seed" was not from a human, but from the Anunnaki/Elohim/Nephilim, Mary could still technically be looked at as a virgin since she never had sex with a "man."

The conception could also have been done through artificial or in vitro insemination using their advanced technology.

While the *New Testament* does not elaborate on the history of Mary, from the books that the early church leaders suppressed (known as *The Apocrypha*) we learn that Mary's father was Joachim (a Hebrew priest) and her mother was Anna. The story of Mary's birth is identical to many of the early patriarchs. Similar to Abraham's wife Sarah, Isaac's wife Rebekah, and Jacob's wife Rachel, Joachim's wife Anna is barren; she is not able to have children. One day an Anunnaki/Elohim/Nephilim approaches Joachim to advise him that he would make Anna pregnant but the price to be paid for such service was that the child would have to be raised under the priests and Anunnaki/Elohim/Nephilim at a temple in Jerusalem. After agreeing to these terms the Anunnaki/Elohim/Nephilim "made" Anna pregnant (as was done to Sarah, Rebekah, and Rachel before her). Anna gave birth to a girl and named her Mary, who at the age of three was delivered to the temple as promised. When Mary was around 14 years old her mentors chose a man named Joseph to be her husband (Rf1). This brings us back to the birth of Jesus.

During the reign of King Herod (Matthew 2:1) Joseph and Mary traveled to the town of Bethlehem in Judea to register for the census which was being taken of the entire Roman world. While they were there Mary gave birth to Jesus wrapping him in cloths and placing him in a manger because there was no room for them at the inn (Luke 2:1-7).

According to another book suppressed by the early church called *Infancy*, Jesus was born in a cave:

> And when they came to the cave, Mary confessed to Joseph that her time of giving birth had come, and she could not go on to the city, and said, Let us go into this cave. At that time the sun was nearly down. But Joseph hurried away so that he might fetch her a midwife; and when he saw an old Hebrew woman who was from Jerusalem, he said to her, Please come here, good woman, and go into that cave, and you will see a woman just ready to give birth. It was after sunset, when the old woman and Joseph reached the cave and they both went into it. And look, it was all filled with lights, greater than the light of lamps and candles, and greater than the light of the sun itself. The infant was then wrapped up in swaddling cloths, and sucking the breast of his mother St. Mary (Rf2)

The name *Jesus* is the late Latin form derived from the Greek *Iesous*, which was itself derived from the Hebrew *Yeshua/Jeshua*. In addition to Jesus not being a descendant of King David another problem that arose was that the Old Testament said the savior's name would be Immanuel, not Jesus (Isaiah 7:14).

This is why Jewish people refused to accept Jesus as the **Messiah** (in Hebrew) or **Christ** (Christos in Greek), both of which mean: Anointed One.

After Jesus was born Magi (some texts say Wise Men) from the east traveled to Bethlehem to see Jesus once they saw his star rise (Matthew 2:1-2). The star (which has become known as the Star of Bethlehem) went ahead and guided the Magi, stopping over the exact place where Jesus was (Matthew 2:9). A text known as the *Protovangelion* explains that the star was so "extraordinarily large" that it "outshined all the other stars" to the point where they were "not visible" (Rf3). Contrary to the *Infancy* and *Protovangelion* texts' cave birth, the biblical text says that Jesus was born in a "house" where the Magi presented him with gifts of gold, incense, myrrh, and bowed down in worship (Matthew 2:11). Some researchers now believe that the "star" was actually one of the aircraft of the Anunnaki/Elohim/ Nephilim.

The Gospel of Luke does not have the Magi account, but instead says "shepherds living out in the fields nearby" were approached by a messenger who advised them:

> Today in the town of David a Savior has been born to you; he is Christ the Lord. This will be a sign to you: You will find a baby wrapped in cloths and lying in a manger (Luke 2:8-12)

After the Magi left a messenger appeared to Joseph in a dream saying "Get up, ... take the child and his mother and escape to Egypt" because Herod was searching for the child to kill him. Joseph immediately woke up, took Mary and Jesus, and left during the night for Egypt, where they stayed until the death of Herod (Matthew 2:13-15). Again, this is at odds with the Old Testament because the so-called "god" (who we now know was just the man Enlil/El-Shaddai/YHWH) commanded that none of his people were ever to go back to the land of Egypt (Jeremiah 42:15-19).

When Herod died, again, a messenger appeared to Joseph in a dream and told him to leave Egypt and take Mary and Jesus to Israel. However, after learning that Herod's son Archelaus was King of Judea, Joseph decided to stay in the district of Galilee in the town called Nazareth (Matthew 2:19-23).

The Gospel of Luke also does not contain the account of their travel to Egypt. Instead it says that on the 8th day of his birth Jesus was circumcised, and after the purification period, he was taken to Jerusalem to be consecrated to Enlil (Luke 2:21-24). Then they returned to Nazareth where the child grew and became strong, "filled with wisdom" (Luke 2:39-40).

While the New Testament is silent about the childhood years of Jesus, evidence has since been unearthed which leads some religious historians to conclude that Jesus' family were members of a Gnostic sect known as the Essenes (Rf4). Remember, Mary's father Joachim was a priest. Even the "cave" birth supports this conclusion because "the Essenes were well known for using caves as shelters and hospices" (Rf5).

A person could only be admitted to the Essene Order after several years of initiation and rituals which swore them to secrecy concerning their teachings. The Essenes said that Anunnaki/Elohim/Nephilim were living amongst them, the names of whom they were required to keep confidential. "Essene priests often called themselves 'The Sons of Zadok' after the high priest Zadok, who had served in the temple of Solomon." (Rf6)

Some believe the Essenes were completely controlled by the Anunnaki/ Elohim/Nephilim. "The highest order of Essene men lived in Qumran behind thick walls completely out of touch with the world. They shared everything and owned nothing while dedicating their lives to" the Anunnaki/Elohim/ Nephilim (Rf7).

It is believed by some that at about the age of 5 to 6 years old Jesus entered an Essene monastery above Haifa by the Mediterranean Sea to begin his education, which was the common practice for Essene boys (Rf8). This could also explain why the biblical texts are silent on the history of Jesus during these years. The authors of the Gospels tried very hard to portray Jesus as having obtained his knowledge through some type of divine method. If people discovered that Jesus had actually been undergoing religious studies at various places, that would have undermined that illusion.

Despite being raised and educated in an Essene community, after learning their doctrines Jesus rejected them. This is why Jesus' teachings often contradicted the Essene doctrines.

The next time the New Testament speaks of Jesus he is 12 years old and attending the Feast of the Passover in Jerusalem with Joseph and Mary for the first time. It describes how Jesus spent 3 days in the temple courts sitting amongst the Jewish teachers, listening to them and asking questions, after which he returned to Nazareth where he grew in wisdom and stature (Luke 2:41-52).

After the age of 12 the biblical texts are again silent on Jesus' history until about the age of 30 when he reappears to begin his ministry (Luke 3:23). However, new evidence has been discovered which sheds light on these 18 missing years:
In 1887 it was brought to light that the Himi Monastery of India was in possession of ancient Tibetan scrolls detailing the life of Jesus during his

travels through India and Tibet from the age of 13 to 29. In the Tibetan language the name Jesus is translated as Issa. Interestingly, in Arabic the name Jesus is also translated as Isa (with only one "s") and it is the name Isa that we see used throughout the Qur'an for Jesus.

The Tibetan document is known as the *Legend of Issa* and explains how a 13 year old Jesus (Issa) arrived in Asia and "studied under several religious masters of the East." When Jesus was 14 years old:

> young Issa, the Blessed One, came this side of the Sindh [a providence in Western Pakistan] and settled among the Aryas [Aryans] ...
> [where] 'the white priests of Brahma welcomed him joyfully' and taught him, among under things, to read and understand the Vedas, and to teach and expound sacred Hindu scriptures. (Rf9)

Brahmanism (known today as Hinduism) is the dominant religion of India. It is believed to stem from a time shortly after the Great Flood when Rama (the son of Cush, Genesis 10:2 & 7) ruled the Indus Valley region. When mankind was divided as a result of the Tower of Babel the Indus Valley was one of the regions humans were "scattered" to.

Brahmanism was another control mechanism that the Anunnaki/Elohim/ Nephilim used to keep the human slaves weak and divided. Ceremonies and prayers were created under the name Manou (wise law giver). They were called the Vedas (Rig Veda, Sama Veda, Yajur Veda, Atharva Veda) which were said to be handed down from the creator "god" whom they called Brahma. Anyone who challenged the origin of the Vedas was quickly put to death (Rf10).

The Vedas established a dogma of the Trinity of god (BRAHMA, the creator god; VISHNU, the preserver god; and SHIVA, the god of destruction and regeneration). The Vedas also rejected all the ancient customs of human equality. Instead, in accordance with the Tower of Babel, the Vedas divided the people into castes. This occurred under the Brahmatma Vasichta-Richi (Rf11).

The caste system divided society up into different levels of social importance to keep mankind dis-united. In order to keep humans from rebelling against the caste they were assigned to, they indoctrinated the human slaves into believing "that every person is born into the social and occupational class (caste)" they are assigned to at their birth. It further indoctrinated the slaves into believing that "regardless of the individual's talent or personality," during one's lifetime they can never leave the caste they were assigned to at birth (Rf12).

The caste system not only restricted the occupations a person could obtain in their lifetime, but restricted upper castes from even associating with lower castes. The lower castes "known as 'outcasts' or 'untouchables,'" usually perform menial work and live in abject poverty. Untouchables are shunned by the higher classes" (Rf13).

The Karma that an individual accumulates during one's lifetime determines whether they will advance to a higher caste at their next re-birth or descend to a lower caste. This is a repeating cycle known as samsara. The "caste into which a person was born was considered an indication of that person's spiritual development, and that alone justified whatever treatment the person received" during this lifetime (Rf14).

One of the factors that determined your level of Karma, and therefore your position in the caste system, was the color of your skin. The lighter your skin color was indicated the higher spiritual state of Karma you had accumulated in your previous life and now entitled you to a higher position in the caste system. The darker your skin color was indicated the negative level of Karma you accumulated in your previous life and you would now be placed lower in the caste system. Once you reached the lowest level, instead of being re-born as a human you would be re-born as an animal. The goal in Hinduism is to accumulate good Karma and at your next rebirth you will be born with lighter skin color and move up the caste system until you reach the highest level.

The highest caste in Hinduism is called BRAHMAN. It is generally assigned to the priests and ruling elite.

Under Brahman is the caste called KSHATRIYA. It is traditionally assigned to people in government and military occupations.

The caste called VAISHYA is traditionally assigned to people in merchant and agricultural occupations. The Vaishyas were not allowed to study the Vedas but were allowed to listen to them on holidays.

The lowest caste is called SUDRA. They are only allowed to hold menial jobs. Sudras are not only forbidden to be present at the reading of the Vedas, but could not even look at them "for they were condemned to perpetual servitude, as slaves of the" Brahmans, Kshatriyas and Vaishyas (Rf15). The Dalit or "untouchables" were even required to wear a bell to warn the higher castes of their approaching "vile" presence in some towns and villages (Rf16).

After learning of the Hindu caste system, Jesus (Issa) found the system to be an abomination and rebelled against it. Jesus violated Hindu law and started associating with the lower castes, teaching them:

> God has made no difference between his children, who are all alike dear to Him
>
> [Jesus preached against the higher castes:]
>
> Those who deprive their brethren of divine happiness shall be deprived of it themselves. The Brahmans and the Kshatriyas shall become the Sudras, and with the Sudras the Eternal shall dwell everlasting (Rf17)

Jesus taught the principles of unity and equality. He taught them not to humiliate their neighbors, to help the poor, not to do evil to anyone. Because Jesus was preaching against the Hindu religion the leaders sent people to kill Jesus. However, Jesus was warned of the plot and was able to escape into Buddhist country where he learned the Pali language and studied sacred Buddhist writings: Sutras.

After traveling through Asia, Jesus traveled through the lands of Persia, Greece, and Egypt, studying their religious doctrines on his journey back to Palestine. During his stay in Egypt it is believed that Jesus was initiated into the Secret Society at the Egyptian city of Heliopolis (Temple of Anu) (Rf18).

When Jesus returned to Palestine at about the age of 30 years old, he began his public ministry (Luke 3:23); a ministry that lasted only 3 years.

Despite what some people claim, Jesus was not God (the Great Architect of the Universe) and never claimed to be. Although the "Son of God" label could be applied to Jesus in a couple ways: (1) he was the Son of God inasmuch as all humans are ultimately the Sons of God; (2) Because Mary was impregnated by the "seed" of the Anunnaki/Elohim/Nephilim (the people whom the Bible mistakenly calls "god") Jesus could be looked at as being the "begotten" son of "god," meaning a son of the Anunnaki/Elohim/ Nephilim; having been born with their RH Negative blood type.

Jesus was also not Jewish. A person is only Jewish if they adhere to the Judaic doctrine. Jesus not only refused to accept the Judaic doctrine and the so-called "god" of the Torah/Old Testament (whom you now know was just the flesh and blood man Enlil/El-Shaddai/YHWH, Chief Commander of the Anunnaki/Elohim/Nephilim), but he actively preached against it. Jesus taught people that the "god" of the Old Testament (the man Moses met on Mount Sinai) was really the devil! See Chapter 18, section 2.

Also, time and again Jesus denied being of Davidic descent and even "forbade the disciples to call him the messiah" (Rf19). This makes perfect sense in the light of the facts I have pointed out in the beginning of this chapter showing how Jesus was not Joseph's son, but was the son of an Anunnaki/Elohim/Nephilim. The New Testament verses saying Jesus is from the line of David were all based upon the belief that Jesus was Joseph's biological son, because Jesus was not, all of those statements are wrong.

Jesus was a rebel in the resistance movement against Anunnaki/Elohim/ Nephilim control. Jesus was teaching people not to follow the control mechanism of Judaism.

Jesus rebuked the Jewish people and Rabbis, teaching people to "Be on your guard against" the teachings of the Jews, which is hypocrisy (Luke 12:1 and Matthew 16:5-12), and said "Woe to you, teachers of the law and Pharisees [Jews], you hypocrites!" (Matthew 23:13, 15, 23, 25, 27, 29). Jesus taught that the Jews were "blind guides" (Matthew 23:16) because "they do not practice what they preach" (Matthew 23:3).

Jesus explained how the Jews were "full of greed and wickedness" (Luke 11:39), calling them "You snakes! You brood of vipers!" (Matthew 23:33), and saying "You brood of vipers, how can you who are evil say anything good?" (Matthew 12:34). Jesus went on to explain how:

> Everything they do is done for men to see: They make their phylacteries wide and tassels on their garments long; they love the place of honor at banquets and the most important seats in the synagogues; they love to be greeted in the market places and to have men call them 'Rabbi.'" (Matthew 23:5-7)

Contrary to Judaism, Jesus taught people not to call anyone "Rabbi" because you only have one Master and "you are all brothers" (Matthew 23:8). Jesus rebuked Judaism saying:

> you experts in the law, woe to you, because you load people down with burdens they can hardly carry, and you yourselves will not lift one finger to help them (Luke 11:46)

and went on to describe how the Jews:

> have taken away the key to knowledge. You yourselves have not entered, and you have hindered those who were entering (Luke 11:52)

Jesus continuously preached against the wickedness of the Jewish people saying "unless your righteousness surpasses that of the [Jews] and teachers of the law, you will certainly not enter the kingdom of heaven" (Matthew 5:20).

Jesus was trying to teach mankind what the evil Anunnaki/Elohim/ Nephilim were doing by dividing mankind against each other, explaining how:

> Every kingdom divided against itself will be ruined, and every city or household divided against itself will not stand (Matthew 12:25)

In direct opposition of Judaism's message of fear, vengeance, and separatism to dis-unite and control mankind (as seen throughout the Old Testament, especially at the Tower of Babel), Jesus taught "unity" and "Love thy neighbor."

Contrary to when Moses killed a man for doing some minor work on the Sabbath (the man who was gathering some wood to keep his family warm, Numbers 15:32-36), Jesus taught that it is okay to work on the Sabbath as long as they are doing good deeds (Matthew 12).

Instead of "revenge" (an eye for an eye) Jesus taught "Do not resist an evil person. If someone strikes you on the right cheek, turn to him the other also" (Matthew 5:38-42), and "Love your enemies" the same way you love your neighbor (Matthew 5:43-48).

Jesus went so far as to say that anyone who is even "angry with his brother will be subject to judgment" (Matthew 5:22). Jesus taught people not to be ruled by fear but instead:

> gather force and support each other. He who supports his neighbor strengthens himself ... Not far hence is the time when by the Highest Will the people will become purified and united into one family (Rf20).

Jesus taught people not to judge others (Matthew 7:1) and summed up his entire philosophy as such "So in everything, do to others what you would have them do to you" (Matthew 7:12).

Jesus also taught that the kingdom of God was not a place (here or there like Heaven) but was "within you" (Luke 17:20-21).

Jesus was also trying to teach mankind certain secret sciences that the Anunnaki/Elohim/Nephilim were trying hard to conceal. See Chapter 19, The Fountain of Youth. But Jesus knew that he had to disseminate that knowledge without the evil Rulers discovering, so he concealed it within parables saying: "The knowledge of the secrets of the kingdom of heaven has been given to you, but not to them. ... Though seeing, they do not see; though hearing, they do not hear or understand" (Matthew 13:11-13).

130

The original teachings of Jesus were "positive" to mankind. The problem is that Jesus' original teachings were later sanitized in some areas and completely changed in most others into the same negative control mechanism of Enlil's Judaism. This will be discussed further in the next chapter.

When the ruling elite learned that Jesus was teaching people to unite and rebel against the Anunnaki/Elohim/Nephilim they killed him. According to the biblical texts Jesus was crucified at a place called Golgotha (meaning The Place of the Skull) (Matthew 27:33).

The biblical texts surrounding Jesus' death and resurrection are filled with contradictions. For example: The Gospel of Matthew explains how it was only Mary and Mary Magdalene that approached Jesus' tomb (Matthew 28:1) while the Gospel of Mark adds Salome (Mark 16:1). Then the Gospel of Luke adds Joanna and deletes Salome (Luke 24:10). Then the Gospel of John says that it was only Mary Magdalene that approached alone, deleting everyone else (John 20:1).

In addition to the Gospels of the New Testament not agreeing on who actually approached the tomb, Mark, Luke, and John then say that when (whomever you believe actually approached the tomb) arrived the stone had already been rolled open (Mark 16:3-4, Luke 24:2, John 20:1). Contradicting those Gospels is Matthew, which says that when the women arrived the stone was still closed and "an angel of the Lord came down from heaven and, going to the tomb, rolled back the stone and sat on it" (Matthew 28:1-2).

The contradictions don't stop there! Matthew says an angel led the women into the cave (Matthew 28:5-6); Mark says they went in by themselves and were confronted by a young man in a white robe (Mark 16:4-5). Contrary to that, Luke says two men were standing in the cave (Luke 24:3-4). John adds more contradiction, describing how Mary Magdalene went to get Peter and another disciple before entering the cave where she found two angels sitting inside (John 20:2-12).

Even the history of whether Jesus was still inside the tomb or not when they arrived is uncertain. According to the Gospels of Matthew, Mark, and Luke, Jesus was not in the tomb when they approached it (Matthew 28:6, Mark 16:6, Luke 24:2, 6), while the Gospel of John says Mary Magdalene saw Jesus standing in the tomb and even spoke with him (John 20:14-17).

The entire story of Jesus' death and resurrection is based upon a sketchy foundation: Gospels that conflict in many details.

In the final analysis, it is not clear whether the guards existed or not. The number of women was either one, two, or three. Perhaps Peter was around; perhaps he was not. There was either an angel outside or a young man inside; conversely, there were two angels inside, who might have been sitting or might have been standing. As for the stone, it was possibly still in position at daybreak, or maybe it had already been moved (Rf21)

and as for Jesus, he was either standing inside the tomb or not.

Some researchers even claim that the crucifixion itself was faked just to make it look like Jesus died. Their arguments are based upon ancient texts like the *Nag Hammadi Scrolls* (discovered in Egypt in 1945, dating to circa 400 A.D.) which explain how "Jesus was not nailed to a cross, but another man, Simon, had been cleverly substituted to suffer Jesus' fate" (Rf22). This account is also backed up by the Qur'an which says that Jesus was not crucified:

they killed him not, nor crucified him, but it appeared so to them [the resemblance of Jesus] was put over another man (and they killed that man)], and those who differ therein are full of doubts. They have no (certain) knowledge, they follow nothing but conjecture. For surely, they killed him not (Surah 4:157)

According to modern researchers the history surrounding Jesus' life is also quite different from that which we have been led to believe by the biblical texts. In addition to Jesus not having been crucified, many researchers now believe that Jesus and Mary Magdalene were actually married and moved to Europe where they had three children: the 1st child was a girl named Tamar (Palm Tree, assimilated in Greek to the name Damaris) who was born in September of 33 A.D.; the 2nd child was a boy named Jesus Jr. who was born in 37 A.D.; and the 3rd child was a boy named Joseph who was born in 44 A.D. (Rf23).

Adding more fuel to the marriage theory, in September 2012 a small 4th century papyrus being called the *Gospel of Jesus' Wife* was brought to light by scholars at Harvard's divinity school (Fig. 11.1). According to Professor Karen King, in the ancient Coptic text of the fragment Jesus actually uses the words "my wife" Mary (Rf24).

Figure 11.1

Other researchers believe that Jesus did not exist at all. They argue that Jesus was a fictitious character created by secret societies to teach mankind certain truths. They believe that his history is actually based upon the ancient texts of many other people stemming back throughout history, as well as the principles of astrology. To give you a couple examples:

Born of a Virgin / Died / Resurrected

Twelve hundred years before Jesus was ever said to exist, in India a man named Virishna was born to a virgin which fulfilled an ancient prophecy. Angels and shepherds were at his birth and provided him with gifts. The ruling leader killed all male children under the age of two in his attempts to kill the child. He performed miracles and healed the sick. He was put to death on a cross and arose from the dead (Rf25). Similarly, Bacchus/Dionysus was born of the virgin Semele. "Above the head of Dionysus were the words: 'I am Life, Death, and Resurrection, I hold the winged crown (the Sun).'" (Rf26). In Persia, Mithra was crucified and rose again from the dead on March 25th (Easter) (Rf27). In Phrygia, Attis was born of a virgin, died and was resurrected. In Babylon, Ninus/Tammuz was born of the virgin Semiramis. He was said to have been crucified with a lamb at his feet, placed in a cave, and when the rock was rolled away three days later his body was gone (Rf28). In Egypt, Horus was born of the virgin Isis, died, and was resurrected as Amsu.

Eucharist Communion

Mithra, Iacchus, Bacchus, Dionysus were all celebrated with rituals of eating their "body and blood" (the mysteries of which grant everlasting life to their followers). The history of this practice was incorporated into Christianity in its Eucharist where the "body and blood" of Jesus is symbolically consumed as bread and wine.

December 25 (Christmas)

Even Jesus' so-called date of birth (December 25th) is not based in reality. In fact, it wasn't until 314 A.D. when Roman Emperor Constantine the Great attributed the date to Jesus in order to coincide with the pagan Sun Festival that followed the winter solstice which occurs on December 21st to 22nd.

Similar to Jesus, Sol Invictus, Bacchus, Dionysus, Mithra, etc., all were said to have been born on December 25th. Why were these people said to have been born on December 25th? Because they were based in part upon the principles of astrology, specifically the Sun's annual cycle which begins right after the Winter Solstice (December 21-22). Our ancient ancestors noticed the beginning of the Sun's cycle on December 25th so the Sun was said to have been "born" on that day.

Some cultures represented the Sun's current position in its annual cycle by the length of the rays protruding from it. In the summer months the Sun's rays were like long golden hair which gradually got shorter as the Sun lost its power during the months of autumn. This is where the biblical story of Samson stems from. Samson was extremely strong when he had "long hair" but lost his power when his hair was cut. SamSUN is just a symbolic story of the Sun's annual cycle (Rf29).

The Light of the World / Morning Star

Because these characters were based upon the Sun they were known as "The Light of the World" and the "Morning Star." Similarly, the New Testament calls Jesus the "bright and morning star" (Revelation 22:16) and "day star" (2 Peter 1:20) because Jesus was based upon the same principles as the Egyptian Horus, the Mesoamerican Quetzalcoatl, the biblical Lucifer (Isaiah 14:12), the Sumerian Enki, etc.

Figure 11.2

These characters were often depicted with a halo or sun rays around their head. A Phoenician stone erected to their Sun god Bel is very similar to the way, in later times, Jesus was portrayed (Fig. 11.2) (Rf30).

And regardless of what area of the Earth you look to, the same signs and symbols are always associated with this savior. He was born of a virgin, died, and was resurrected. In the Mexican Codices, hieroglyphics of Egypt, and biblical texts his age is always given as 33. He is supported by four brothers or sons: In the Eschatology of the Mayas it was Kan-Bacab (Yellow Bacab, who stood at the South), Chac-Bacab (Red Bacab who stood at the East), Zac-Bacab (White Bacab, who stood at the North) Ek-Bacab (The Black Bacab, who stood at the West). In Central America it was Acatal, Tecpatl, Calli, Tochtli. In Mexico it was Beeu, Ezanab, Ahbal, Lamal. Amongst the Zapotecs it was Kau, Muluc, Lx, Cauac. Amongst the Chaldeans it was Sed-Alap/Kirub (represented as a Bull with a human face) Lamas/Nirgal (reppresented as a Lion with a human head), Ustur (represented after a human likeness), Nattig (represented with the head of an Eagle). Amongst the Hindu, the four Maharajahs or great kings of the Dylan Cholans were India (King of Heaven to the East), Kowvera (the God of Wealth to the North), Varouna (the God of the Waters to the West), Yama (the Judge of the Dead to the South). Amongst the Chinese, the four Great Powers or Mythical Mountains in China are Tai-Tsong (East), Sigan-fou (West), How-Kowang (South), Chen-si (North). Amongst the people of Bavili, Bimi and Yorba (West Africa) they are Ibara, Edi, Oyekun, Oz-be. In Egypt they were Amsta, Hapi, Tuamutf, Kabhsenuf. When this eschatology was passed down to Christianity the mother became the virgin Mary, the divine child Jesus, and the four became Matthew, Mark, Luke, and John (Rf31).

* * *

In any event, whether you believe that Jesus was an actual man who existed or a character created by secret societies to teach mankind certain messages, the original teachings of Jesus have very little to do with modern Christianity.

12

CHRISTIANITY

WHILE CHRISTIANITY IS believed by many to be a religion derived from the teachings of Jesus Christ, as you will see, the Christian religion was actually designed to silence Jesus' message and quietly subvert its followers back to the control mechanism of Judaism.

As a result of Jesus' teachings more and more people were rebelling against Jewish doctrines. This infuriated the Jewish High Priest and Sanhedrin who began to imprison and stone people to death for following Jesus.

A devoutly Jewish man known as Saul of Tarsus not only witnessed the stonings with approval (Acts 8:1) but he actively sought to destroy everyone who would follow Jesus' message, even "Going from house to house" dragging off men and women to be put in prison (Acts 8:3). Saul issued "murderous threats" against anyone who would follow Jesus (Acts 9:1) and on authority of the High Priest traveled to Damascus to persecute and put an end to all of Jesus' disciples.

The New Testament explains that on his journey to Damascus Saul experienced an enlightenment which caused him to believe in Jesus (Acts 9). However, the enlightenment that Saul experienced was not the belief in Jesus, but the newly formed idea of how to silence the teachings of Jesus for good. Saul decided to change Jesus' original teachings (re-write them to come into compliance with the core principles of Judaism). Then Saul tricked everyone into believing that these were the true teachings of Jesus. Despite some initial skepticism, Saul was eventually accepted as a disciple (Acts 9:26-28), and by pretending to be aligned with Jesus Saul was able to accomplish his goal of quietly subverting Jesus' followers back to Judaism while packaging it under the illusion of "Christianity." In fact, it was at Antioch that the disciples of Saul's teachings were first called Christians (Acts 11:26) and Saul's name was later changed to Paul (Acts 13:9).

The Writings of Paul make up almost half of the New Testament and it is believed that the Epistles or Letters of Paul were the first New Testament writings to actually have been written down. It is extremely suspicious that a man who hated Jesus and his teachings is the very man responsible for the formation of Christianity and what has become known as the Roman Catholic Church; even becoming canonized as Saint Paul (Rf1).

Just as Paul planned on his journey to Damascus, Jesus' message of unity and rebelling against the control mechanisms of Judaism were slowly being forgotten as Paul's new religion called Christianity reverted back to the same Old Testament methods of fear and threats to control the population.

Christianity, as we know it today, derives ultimately not from Jesus but from the teachings of Paul and the numerous Councils that occurred over the years in which doctrines were added, deleted, and changed (Rf2). For instance:

In 325 A.D. Christians organized the first worldwide conference known as the Council of Nicea. It was at this Council that the major editing and outright destruction of Jesus' original teachings occurred. The Council of Nicea declared Rome to be the official center of Christian orthodoxy (Rf3).

The Council also decided which books were going to be included into the canonized Bible. After examining all of the available biblical texts the Council strategically chose certain books that fit the image the Church was trying to create and any books that contradicted that image were banned. It was basically a group of men saying "This book is okay" or "That book is not okay." Some of the books that were removed from the Bible were even written by the exact same authors as other books that were included!

Fortunately many of the books that the early Church leaders banned from the Bible survived the purge. They are collectively known as The Apocrypha. To list some of them: Acts of Adam, Apocalypse of Adam, Abraham, Testament of Adam, Book of Enoch, Book of the Secrets of Enoch, Book of Noah, Apocalypse of Barach I, Apocalypse of Barach II, Apocalypse of Daniel, Apocalypse of Elijah, Apocalypse of Enoch, Apocalypse of Ezra, Apocalypse of Solomon, Odes of Solomon, Testament of Isaac, Martydom of Isaiah, Apocalypse of Zephaniah, Paralipomena of Jeremiah, Apocryphon of Ezekiel, Ascension of Isaiah, Assumption of Moses, Baruch III, Baruch IV, Chronicles of the Kings of Israel, Acts of Solomon, Chronicles of the Kings of Judah, Maccabee III, Maccabee IV, Gospel of Thomas, Gospel of James, Gospel of Peter, Gospel of Bartholomew, Gospel of Nicodemus, Gospel of Perfection, Gospel of Philip, Gospel of the Birth of Mary, Gospel of the Hebrews, Gospel of the Infancy of Jesus Christ, Gospel of Truth, Acts of Andrew, Acts of Peter, Acts of Matthew, Acts of John, Acts of Thomas, Acts of Paul, Acts of Paul and Thecla, Revelation of Paul, Revelation of Thomas, Revelation of John, Revelation of Virgin Mary, Revelation of Stephen, Revelation of Peter, Apocalypse of James I, Apocalypse of James II, Apocalypse of Peter, Apocalypse of Philip, Apocalypse of Stephen, Apocalypse of Thomas, Apocryphon of John, Epistle of Pontius Pilate, Protevangelium of James,

History of Joseph, Letter of Paul to the Alexandrians, Testament of the Lord, Wisdom of Jesus (Rf4).

Radical changes were being made to Jesus' teachings. Even the status of Jesus as being "divine" was established by a "vote" that began at the Council of Nicea (Rf5).

> At the gathering in Nicea, the council formulated a creed that, although it was revised at the Council of Constantinople in AD 381-382, has become known as the Nicene Creed [which begins: I believe in one God]. It affirmed the doctrine of consubstantiality of the Father, Son, and Holy Spirit.

and in 451 A.D. God and Jesus were declared "one person in two natures" by Pope Leo I at the Council of Chalcedon. Although, the concept of the "Holy Trinity" was not officially added to Christianity until the Lateran Council in the 12th century (Rf6). Later, in 553 A.D. the Second Synod of Constantinople went on to delete all references to reincarnation.

Through all of the editing (additions and deletions) by early church leaders, the New Testament has become the basis of a religion called Christianity, not by, but falsely attributed to, the biblical figure known as Jesus.

The New Testament contains 27 books, all of which were originally written in Greek, despite the fact that the language of Jesus' time was Aramaic. These authors even obtained their Old Testament quotes from the Septuagint. Even the Gospels (Matthew, Mark, Luke, and John) were not written until long after Jesus and anyone who had actually witnessed the alleged events, had died. Biblical scholars believe that the Gospels were written some time between 65 A.D. to 125 A.D. at the earliest. To compensate for this time gap, some scholars argue that the authors obtained their information from a "proto-gospel" that had been written during the time of Jesus (Rf7).

The New Testament contains a mixture of Jesus' teachings of "unity" and the Old Testament's teachings of fear and division. Two very opposite ideologies. For example, we see these Old Testament teachings rearing their ugly head in the New Testament when they say Jesus did not:

> come to bring peace to the earth... but a sword. For I have come to turn "'a man against his father, a daughter against her mother, a daughter-in-law against her mother-in-law - a man's enemies will be the members of his own household'(Matthew 10:34-36)

and divisive statements like "He who is not with me is against me" (Matthew 12:30) which were attributed to Jesus. It is only by understanding how the New Testament was created that you can begin to wade through all the nonsense (designed to oppress and control you) and reach the few remaining teaching of Jesus that shine through "to those that have ears."

Directly opposite of Jesus' teachings, Christianity aligned itself with and adopted the very principles of Judaism. In fact, the Judaic doctrine (the 5 books of Moses) make up the main part of the very Bible Christians follow.

While I acknowledge that some Christians pay more attention to the New Testament's teachings of Jesus than to the Old Testaments's teachings of Enlil/El-Shaddai/YHWH, the problem is that most modern Christians make no distinction between the two people. In fact, most Christians combine the two people into one entity and believe every single word contained in the Bible (both Old and New Testaments) is the word of the same Christian god and must be believed verbatim, despite the fact that Jesus taught people not to follow the so-called god of the Old Testament!

Christianity even added new control mechanisms that did not exist under Judaism: The concept of Heaven and Hell were created. It was used to control the slaves through the "fear" threats of being sent to Hell as punishment for disobedience invoked.

In Judaism there was no such concept as an afterlife; once you were dead, you were dead. As explained in the Old Testament:

> the dead know nothing; they have no further reward, ... Their love, their hate and their jealousy have long since vanished; never again will they have a part in anything that happens under the sun.... for in the grave, where you are going, there is neither working nor planning nor knowledge nor wisdom (Ecclesiastes 9:5-10)

> His breath goeth forth, he returneth to his earth; in that very day his thoughts perish (Psalm 146:4)

This is why Enlil/El-Shaddai/YHWH of the Old Testament explained how he was the Ruler of the living, not the dead. When you're dead your life is over. This is also why Jesus said there was no need to bury the dead (Matthew 8:21-22).

Through Christianity's new control mechanism of Heaven and Hell the Anunnaki/Elohim/Nephilim were now able to indoctrinate humans with the mindset of not striving to acquire greatness on Earth but instead to almost hate human existence and wait for the afterlife:

> Do not store up for yourselves treasures on earth, where moth and rust destroy, and where thieves break in and steal. But store up for yourselves treasures in heaven (Matthew 6:19-20)

An afterlife that the designers of Christianity knew full well didn't exist. Since there was no afterlife or resurrection wild, majestic, fanciful promises could be made in order to keep the humans under control that never needed to be fulfilled.

However, since people could physically see the rotting corpse they had serious problems believing that after death anyone "went" to a Heaven or Hell. In order to add credibility to the Heaven and Hell scheme the new concept of a SOUL was created. People were indoctrinated that it was the mythical "soul" that went to Heaven or Hell, not the physical body.

In line with this scheme, new concepts were then created to trick humans into focusing on the "spiritual" (that doesn't exist) so that you won't focus on the material world and become a threat to the Anunnaki/Elohim/ Nephilim! The entire scheme is designed to keep humans weak and under control while alive on Earth.

There is no soul or life after death. Because the human mind so desperately wants there to be more than just death, it easily accepts these created fantasies. We are a product of every experience we have encountered since birth; from every sound that we hear after birth, to every image that we see throughout our lifetime. All of this is recorded in our mind, from which, our mind reasons, makes judgments, and chooses paths. It makes each of us the unique person we are today. While I acknowledge that there are people who believe that they can vividly remember a time before they were born and argue that this must be evidence of past lives in support of the theory of reincarnation, as well as other people who believe that they have actually seen the afterlife while they were temporarily dead for a short time, however, all of this is actually due to how the human brain processes information and our limited understanding of it. They have not actually had any past lives or been to an afterlife. The concept of a soul and afterlife was created to support the religious doctrines of reincarnation and Heaven and Hell. Dogma that you now know was created by the Anunnaki/Elohim/Nephilim to keep mankind under control.

In Christianity the same oppression of knowledge occurred that we saw in Judaism. People were indoctrinated into believing that the Bible was the unquestionable word of God and if it wasn't in the Bible it didn't exist. Christians became so disillusioned that they even refused to accept new scientific discoveries that were emerging, calling them the work of the devil. For example:

140

In 1543 A.D. the Polish astronomer Nicolaus Copernicus published his study *De revolutionibus orbium coelestium* showing that our solar system was heliocentric and the earth was not flat but spherical. In 1600 the Christian Church burned astrologer Giorgio Bruno alive for agreeing with Copernicus' theory that the sun was stationary and the planets revolved around it. In 1604 when Galileo Galilei proved through the use of a telescope that Copernicus was correct, the Church said that this science was "of all heresies the most abominable, the most pernicious, the most scandalous." When this science began to be taught in schools the teachers were labeled "crazy" and even brought into court on charges where deluded Christian scientists actually argued:

> Common sense must tell anyone that the earth cannot possibly be a ball, otherwise the people on the lower half would fall into the void!

> Nowhere in the Bible,... does it say that the earth revolves around the sun. Consequently every such assertion is the work of the devil! (Rf8)

In the 17th century Archbishop Ussher even argued that the world had been created in exactly 4004 BC. Anyone who dared challenge his dating was said to be an emissary of the devil sent to tempt mankind. Scientific, archaeological, and astronomical advances have since proven such beliefs to be absurd.

Religious leaders have continuously tried to keep mankind in darkness away from knowledge, even murdering many people for believing such scientific claims. At every stage of scientific advancement religious leaders were there to argue it was the work of the devil and against God. It occurred again when the science of evolution was discovered, again when man wanted to explore space, again when new techniques were discovered (like stem cell research) in the treatment of disease. To suppress knowledge religious leaders even destroyed libraries and locked books away in Vatican vaults.

Modern Christians don't even follow the laws that were allegedly established by Jesus in the New Testament. For example, Jesus commanded his followers not to pray in front of other people:

> And when you pray, do not be like the hypocrites, for they love to pray standing in the synagogues and on the street corners to be seen by men. ... But when you pray, go into your room, close the door and pray to your Father, who is unseen. Then your Father, who sees what is done in secret, will reward you. (Matthew 6:5-6)

Despite this command we see Christians around the world standing in Churches praying in front of other people in clear violation of Jesus' command. Further, Jesus taught:

> Watch out for the teachers of the law. They like to walk around in flowing robes and be greeted in the marketplaces, and have the most important seats in the synagogues [Churches. Synagogue is simply the word used to designate a house of worship, it is synonymous with a modern Church] and the place of honor at banquets. They devour widows' houses and for a show make lengthy prayers. Such men will be punished most severely. (Mark 12:38-40)

Notice how modern Christian priests/preachers do exactly this. We see them everyday on TV, standing before large crowds, adorned in the richest suits or flowing robes, owning the richest houses, cars, private jets, while giving "lengthy prayers" and receiving money for their services in direct violation of their own Christian doctrines.

Christianity's "Cross" Symbol

Christians would argue that the cross symbol stems from and represents the death of Jesus upon the cross; an event that occurred in 33 A.D. However, if the cross stems from this event then we should only find it emerging after that time period. The problem is that we know from archaeological discoveries all over the world that the cross symbol existed for thousands of years before Jesus. The "cross" symbol did not represent Jesus' death, but as explained in Chapter 1, it was actually the symbol of Anu, the Supreme Ruler of the Anunnaki/Elohim/Nephilim.

As the cross symbol evolved it became widely used in the Pagan Mysteries (Rf9). It was also known as the mystic Tau of the Chaldeans and Egyptians. It was used in Babylon, in China, by Buddhists and Hindus in India, in Ethiopia, in Mexico among the Aztecs. Long before Jesus' time people were crucified upon the cross by the ancient Assyrians, Persians, in Palestine, Carthage, Greece, Rome, etc.

Jesus was rebelling against the people of the cross (the Anunnaki/Elohim/Nephilim) teaching mankind to unite and stand up against the evil overlords. When they killed/silenced Jesus' *message* they represented it by the image of a dead Jesus nailed to their cross. The image actually symbolizes the death of Jesus' message *BY the people of the cross!* These evil people then used this image as the very symbol of their new control mechanism called Christianity.

Many people are ignorant of the things they follow or align themselves with. For example, look around and you will see people who claim to be Christian wearing both the "Cross" symbol and the "International Symbol of Peace." Why is this a problem? Because the two symbols are the exact opposite of each other and is evidence that the people wearing both symbols have no idea what either of them actually mean.

If you take the Cross, turn it upside down, then brake the arms in a downward motion, the International Symbol of Peace is created.

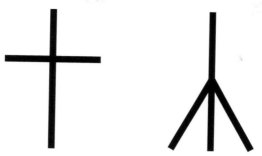

By breaking the Cross (symbolizing your destruction of, or emancipation from the slavery of, the Christian religion) you obtain PEACE. This is the true meaning of the International Symbol of Peace. People wear it every day and have no idea what it really symbolizes.

For those few who know the truth about Christianity the very secret sciences to a longer life can be found encoded into the pages of the Bible as you will see in Chapter 19.

Today, at least for the masses of people who "do not have ears," modern Christianity remains nothing more than the same control mechanism of Judaism. In fact, the religion is now even being called Judeo-Christian.

13

ISLAM

ACCORDING to Islamic historians, a man named Abu al-Qasim Muhammad ibn 'Adb Allah ibn 'Adb al-Muttalib ibn Hashim was born in approximately 570 to 572 A.D.

Historians believe that Muhammad was an orphan who had been raised by his relatives during his youth. When he was 25 years old he married a wealthy widow who was 15 years older than him. While they're not certain, some biographers believe that Muhammad worked in her business as a tradesman for awhile (Rf1).

Prior to the creation of Islam, Muhammad was a member of a tribe called the Quraish. They were a fairly powerful tribe that rose to take control of Mecca (Rf2). The Arabs of that time period, including Muhammad's own tribe the Quraish, worshipped many different gods. The Jewish and Christian gods were among them. Shrines were erected for these gods and pilgrimages were made to them.

A stone building called the Ka'bah in Mecca was one of the most important centers of pilgrimage. It was believed to have been built by Abraham (s.2:125) (Rf3), on a high place resembling a hillock. During that time period, several gods were associated with the Ka'bah, but the main god was called Hubal. The pilgrimage to the Ka'bah had specific rites that were performed during specific lunar periods that were considered sacred (Rf4). Interestingly this same pilgrimage to the Ka'bah was subsequently incorporated into the Qur'an, although, just the name of the god was changed.

Muhammad Receives Message of the Qur'an

According to the Qur'an, Muhammad saw an angel named Gabriel in the clear horizon towards the east (s.81:23). Gabriel was in the highest part of the horizon (s.53:7) then approached Muhammad and came closer until he was at a distance of two bows' length or (even) nearer to him (s.53:8-9).

In the chapter of the Qur'an titled "Surat Al-Isra," (which means: The Journey by Night) we learn that Gabriel took Muhammad to Jerusalem to provide him with the message that would become the Qur'an:

took His slave (Muhammad) for a journey by night from Al-Masjid Al-Haram (at Mecca) to Al-Masjid Al-Aqsa (in Jerusalem), the neighbourhood whereof We have blessed, in order that We might show him (Muhammad) of Our Ayat (proofs, evidences, lessons, signs, etc.) (s.17:1)

Historians believe this occurred in the year 612 A.D. when Muhammad was 40 years old. It occurred on the Night of Al-Qadr, during what is now the 9th month of the Islamic Calendar (Ramadan)(s.97:1). This is why Muslims observe the month of Ramadan as sacred with fasting practiced daily from dawn to sunset.

In his own words Muhammad described the meeting with Gabriel:

While I was at the house in a state midway between sleep and wakefulness, (an angel) recognized me) as the man lying between two men. A golden tray full of wisdom and belief was brought to me and my body was cut open from the throat to the lower part of the abdomen and then my abdomen was washed with Zamzam water and (my heart was) filled with wisdom and belief. Al-Buraq, a white animal smaller than a mule and bigger than a donkey was brought to me and I set out with Gabriel. When I reached the nearest heaven, Gabriel said to the gatekeeper of the heaven, 'Open the gate.' The gatekeeper asked, 'Who is it?' He said, 'Gabriel.' The gatekeeper said, 'Who is accompanying you?' Gabriel said, 'Muhammad.' The gatekeeper said, 'Has he been called?' Gabriel said 'Yes'. Then it was said, 'He is welcome. What a wonderful visit his is!' Then I met Adam and greeted him and he said, 'You are welcome O son and a Prophet.' Then we ascended to the second heaven. It was asked, 'Who is with you?' He said, 'Muhammad.' It was asked, 'Has he been sent for?' He said, 'Yes.' It was said, 'He is welcome. What a wonderful visit his is!' Then I met 'Isa (Jesus) and Yahya (John) who said, 'You are welcome, O brother and Prophet.' Then we ascended to the third heaven. It was asked, 'Who is it?' Gabriel said, 'Gabriel.' It was said, 'Who is with you?' He said, 'Muhammad. It was asked, 'Has he been sent for?' He said, 'Yes." It was said, 'He is welcome. What a wonderful visit his is!' There I met Yusuf (Joseph) and greeted him, and he replied, 'You are welcome, O brother and a Prophet!' Then we ascended to the fifth heaven and again the same questions and answers were exchanged as in the previous heavens. There I met and greeted Harun (Aaron) who said, 'You are welcome, O brother and a Prophet.' Then we ascended to the sixth heaven and again the same questions and answers were exchanged as the previous heavens. There I met and greeted Musa (Moses) who said, 'You are welcome, O brother and a Prophet.' When I proceeded on, he started weeping and on being asked why he was weeping, he said, 'O Lord! Followers of this youth, who was sent after me, will enter Paradise in greater number than my followers.' Then we ascended to the seventh heaven and again the same questions and answers were exchanged as in the previous heavens. There I met and greeted Ibrahim (Abraham) who said, 'You are welcome, O son and a Prophet.' Then I was shown Al-Bait Al-Ma'mur (i.e. Allah's house). I asked Gabriel about it and he said, "This is Al-Bait Al-Ma'mur where 70,000 angels

145

perform prayers daily; and when they leave they never return to it (but always a fresh batch comes into it daily).' Then I was shown Sidrat-ul-Muntaha (i.e. the lot tree of the utmost boundary over the seventh heaven) and I saw its Nabiq fruits which resembled the clay jugs of Hijar (a town in Arabia), and its leaves were like the ears of elephants, and four rivers originated at its root: two of them were apparent and two were hidden. I asked Gabriel about those rivers and he said, 'The two hidden rivers are in Paradise and the apparent ones are the Nile and the Euphrates.' Then fifty prayers were enjoined on me. (s.53:12 note 1, citing Sahih Al-Bukhari, 4/3207(O.P.429))

After discussing it with Moses Muhammad returned to Allah and he was able to have the prayers reduced to five. Muhammad had a second encounter with Gabriel near Sidrat-ul-Muntaha (a lot tree of the utmost boundary over the seventh heaven beyond which none can pass) (s.53:13-14).

Muhammad Begins To Teach Islam

When Muhammad told his tribe of this night journey, the Quraish did not believe him. To try and convince people, Muhammad stood up, facing north, in the unroofed portion of the Ka'bah and described Jerusalem to them, while looking at a map he claimed Allah made appear (s.17:1 note 2 citing Sahih Al-Bukhari, 5/3886 (O.P.226)).

Muhammad argued that he was a "prophet" of Allah and began teaching the message provided to him through Gabriel. However, the beginning of his preaching career did not go so well. The people of his home town of Mecca ignored him. His own tribe, the Quraish, said that the Qur'an was "nothing but an invented lie" (s.34:43).

Contrary to what most people believe, the message of the Qur'an wasn't given to Muhammad all at one time. It was given to him in stages over 23 years (s.17:106, 25:32). One of the many reasons the Quraish didn't believe Muhammad was because they saw a human "man" teaching him religious doctrines every "morning and afternoon" (s.25:5) over this 23 year period! They even talked to the man and knew he had a foreign tongue (s.16:103); as if a foreigner couldn't also speak Arabic. They said to Muhammad:

> O you (Muhammad) to whom the Dhikr (the Qur'an) has been sent down! Verily, you are a madman! (s.15:6 & 44:14)

The Quraish said that these were just "tales of the ancients" which Muhammad has written down (S.25:5). They argued that Muhammad has taken what he learned from the lessons he was taught while in Jerusalem, what he learned of the Jewish and Christian religions from the man who was teaching him over the last 23 years, and what he knew of the multiple gods of the area around him, and transformed all those different gods into "One" (s.38:5). So the

146

people of Mecca said Muhammad "fabricated it (the Qur'an)" (s.11:35), and called him a "liar" (s.38:4).

In an attempt to bolster Muhammad's claim of divine origin his followers claimed that Muhammad was illiterate. In fact, this assertion eventually found its was into the Qur'an (s.7:157). They argued that no illiterate man could have read the Torah or Bible and copied it to create his own religion; therefore the message of the Qur'an must be divinely received. These arguments were not received well because his neighbors knew him. Muhammad was an accomplished leader in his tribal army and his neighbors knew that Muhammad could read and write.

Muhammad's neighbors began to oppose him and Muhammad became a hated individual. The level of disgust grew so high that the Quraish plotted against Muhammad and tried to kill him, but failed (s.14:46 note 1). Fearing for their safety, in the year 622 A.D., Muhammad and the few followers that he could convince were forced to leave his home town of Mecca. The Qur'an evidences the account of how Muhammad was driven out of Mecca at (s.47:13).

Muhammad escaped to the city called Yathrib, where he was able to negotiate a deal with the city leaders so that he could be accepted by them and given protection. Yathrib would later become known as Medina, in W. Saudi Arabia.

The flight of Muhammad from Mecca is called Hegira. The Islamic Calendar begins the very day Muhammad took flight from Mecca in the year 1 A.H. which began on Friday, July 16, 622 A.D. The Islamic year is lunar and each month begins approximately at the new moon.

Creation of the Qur'an

The Qur'an as we know it today did not exist when Muhammad was alive. During his lifetime Muhammad inscribed his revelations on palm leaves, tree bark, stones, etc.; whatever he could find. It wasn't until the time of the caliphate of Umar, the second Caliph, that all of Muhammad's scraps were combined into one final collection in book format. The authorized version wasn't established until the caliphate of Uthman, his successor, between 644-656 A.D. (Rf5).

When the Qur'an was eventually published many people denied its divine origin. Even some of the people who believed Muhammad had originally received a divine message from Gabriel, argued, that in the 12 to 24 year period

147

since Muhammad's death, verses were added, deleted and changed. Discrepancies arose.

By reading the Qur'an you can see why people claimed verses were added or changed. If the Qur'an was given to Muhammad in 612 A.D., and only contains the word of Allah, then how could it talk about events that occurred after the Qur'an was given to Muhammad? This is one of the problems. The Qur'an speaks over and over again about events that happened to Muhammad while he was trying to preach his message, after he received the Qur'an. It talks about how Muhammad had to leave Mecca and the troubles he had while he was preaching his message. This proves that verses were added to the Qur'an that had nothing to do with his original encounter with Gabriel. To any rational person, it raises the questions of what else was added, deleted, or changed. There are many discrepancies like this, but I'm not going into them here since that is not the focus of this book.

The contradictions in the Qur'an were also used by some Persian sects. They examined the Qur'an, pointed out its contradictions, denied its divine origin, and used this to recruit people into other religions (Rf6).

Message of Islam

The Qur'an declares that the Revelation provided to Muhammad was to *"follow"* the **HANIF** religion of Abraham (s.16:123, 2:135). The Qur'an continually stresses this point:

Direct your face entirely towards the religion Hanif (s.10:104-105)

Muhammad was *NOT* being provided with a new religion; Allah was only ordering him to follow the religious texts of the Torah and Gospels that already existed. The Qur'an states clearly that Allah is the same god as that of Judaism and Christianity and he has ordained for muslims the same religion that he ordained for Abraham, Noah, Moses, and Jesus (s.42:13). The Qur'an specifies that the message brought to Muhammad's heart was only a confirmation of the Torah and Gospels of the Bible that were sent down before it (s.2:97, 2:41, 3:3, 10:37). Further, to make it crystal clear to muslims that the Qur'an was not different from or more important than the Torah and Gospels of the Bible, it stresses that muslims must *"make no distinction between any of them"* (s.2:136). In fact, in order for anyone to be "muslim" they must believe in and adhere to every word of the Torah, Gospels, and Qur'an.

Ignorance of the Arabic language is the reason why many people believe Islam is a new or different religion. Unfamiliar words used to identify and describe the same people, places and things is the main cause of this

148

misconception. We must remember that a "word" is just a sound or combination of sounds that symbolizes or communicates a meaning. It's the meaning or definition of the word that matters, not what language it is articulated in. Take a look at the following examples:

Language	Word	Definition
English	God	the Supreme Being and creator
Spanish	Dios	the Supreme Being and creator
Italian	Dio	the Supreme Being and creator
Arabic	Allah	the Supreme Being and creator

Language	Word	Definition
English	pray	the act of addressing God
Spanish	rezar	the act of addressing God
Italian	pregare	the act of addressing God
Arabic	as-salat	the act of addressing God

Language	Word	Definition
English	prayer	an address to God
Spanish	oracion	an address to God
Italian	preghiera	an address to God
Arabic	salat	an address to God

Language	Word	Definition
English	Mosque	a building used for public worship
Spanish	Mezquita	a building used for public worship
Italian	Moschea	a building used for public worship
Arabic	Masjid	a building used for public worship

As you can see in the above examples, despite the different words used the meaning remains the same. Whether you speak Arabic and say (Assalamu 'Alaikum wa Rahmatullah), or whether you speak English and say (May the peace and mercy of God be upon you) you are saying the exact same thing.

In fact, it is not even necessary to know Arabic in order to be muslim. Remember, Muhammad was ordered to follow the Hanif religion of Abraham. Abraham was not and did not speak Arabic. Abraham was from Ur of the Chaldeans in ancient Sumeria. If language mattered then "muslims" should not be learning Arabic, but ancient Sumerian as well as changing their name to a Sumerian one.

While it has become common to identify the religion using the Arabic words ISLAM and MUSLIM, the use of these words is actually a misnomer. However, understanding what these words actually mean shed light on what the true purpose of the religion is.

The Arabic word ISLAM means: "SLAVERY" (submission to a dominating influence). The Arabic word MUSLIM means: "A SLAVE" (one who submits). No matter what language we use the meaning remains the same:

Language	Word	Definition
English	slavery	submission to a dominating influence
Spanish	esclavitud	submission to a dominating influence
Italian	schiavitu	submission to a dominating influence
Arabic	islam	submission to a dominating influence

Language	Word	Definition
English	slave	one who submits
Spanish	esclavo	one who submits
Italian	schiavo	one who submits
Arabic	muslim	one who submits

The word "muslim" is not a title, it's a description. Articulating the message in the Arabic language Allah was simply saying that anyone "who submits" to his orders is "his slave" (or in Arabic, his muslim). The Qur'an specifically calls Muhammad "Our slave" (s.2:23, 8:41), calls muslims "slaves" (s.7:32), and Muhammad even acknowledged that he was "a thankful slave" (s.2:139 note (1)A, citing Sahih Al-Bukhari, 8/6471 (O.P.478)).

Remember, as I explained in the chapter on Judaism, the Hanif religion of Abraham was created by the Anunnaki/Elohim/Nephilim as a control mechanism over mankind. Here, instead of creating alternate names for it, the control mechanism is simply being called what it is: Slavery (or in Arabic: Islam).

In Islam, as with anything in life, slight variations in practice, different interpretations, and new customs arose over time as the control mechanism was put into effect around the world; but the fundamental doctrine remained the same.

Muslims must believe in one monotheistic god. That nothing has the right to be worshipped but him. The Qur'an states: "Your Ilah (God) is One Ilah (God - Allah)" (s.16:22). The profession of faith in Arabic is: *La ilaha-illallah* (which in English is: None has the right to be worshipped but God).

Muslims must believe in his angels; messengers (prophets); the Day of Resurrection of Jesus; and his preordainments.

Muslims are also required to follow several other practices: the SUNNAH (which are statements by Muhammad explaining legal ways or methods of doing various things including how to perform worship, how to dress, down to how to use the bathroom, etc., that have become models to be followed by other Muslims), and AHADITH (which are sayings, deeds, and approvals accurately narrated from Muhammad). However, the Qur'an explains that Muhammad was warned that he was not a Watcher over mankind, nor was he a Wakil (disposer of affairs, guardian or trustee) over mankind (s.6:107, 6:66, 10:108).

Muslims also practice IJMA, which is the principle that any belief held by most Muslims throughout history is true beyond question. And from this, if you wonder why Muslims are against any type of innovation, it is because Muhammad said:

> If somebody innovates something which is not present in our religion (of Islamic Monotheism), then that thing will be rejected. (s.18:104 note (2)b, citing Sahih Al-Bukhari, 3/2697 (O.P.861))

And Muslims are not even allowed to perform good deeds that have not been recognized in the past. Muhammad said:

> Whoever performs a (good) deed which we have not ordered (anyone) to do (or is not in accord with our religion of Islamic Monotheism), then that deed will be rejected and will not be accepted (s.18:104 note (2)b, citing Sahih Al-Bukhari, Vol. 9, The Book of holding fast to the Qur'an and the Sunnah, Chapter No.20, before Hadith No.449 (O.P.))

The Qur'an teaches that women must be subservient to men. It explains that men were created to "excel" over women (s.4:34) and this is why men are the "protectors and maintainers" of women (s.4:34). If a woman refuses to obey a man the Qur'an instructs men to "beat them" (s.4:34). Muslim men can marry multiple women (s.4:3), but women are told to "stay in your houses" (s.33:33) and when outside, women must wear "veils" all over their bodies (s.24:31, 33:59). Muhammad even said that Hell is filled with mostly women:

> I was shown the Hell-Fire and that the majority of its dwellers were women who were disbelievers or ungrateful." [Muhammad explained:] "They are ungrateful to their husbands and are ungrateful for the favours and the good (charitable deeds) done to them. If you have always been good (benevolent) to one of them for a period of time and then she sees something in you (not of her liking), she will say, "I have never seen any good from you." (s.16:112 note 1, citing Sahih Al-Bukhari, 1/29 (O.P.28))

The Qur'an demands that Muslims actively spread the message of Islam and convert every person on Earth to the Islamic religion (s.16:125, 28:87). Anyone who refuses to submit to Islam is branded a disbeliever or infidel; what they call in Arabic: Mushrikun.

The Qur'an orders Muslims not to obey disbelievers (s.68:8, 3:149), and forbids Muslims from marrying non-Muslims (s.2:221). Muhammad even said that Muslims should not meet with, gather together with, or live with a non-Muslim and if he does so, the Muslim is as evil as the non-Muslim (s.3:149 note 1, citing The Book of Jihad, Abu Dawud).

While the Qur'an professes over and over again that it is the same religion as Judaism and Christianity, it then goes on to disparage these religions. For example:

The Qur'an instructs Muslims that Allah has placed a curse on Jewish people and Christians because "they are deluded away from the truth!" (s.9:30), then goes on to paint them as a jealous and hateful people, who are only pretending to be friendly:

> they say, "We believe." But when they are alone, they bite the tips of their fingers at you in rage (s.3:119)

> If a good befalls you, it grieves them, but if some evil overtakes you, they rejoice at it. (s.3:120)

> [the people of the Torah are] as the likeness of a donkey...(s.62:5); Be you monkeys, despised and rejected (s.2:65, 7:166)

So the Qur'an orders Muslims not to take Jews and Christians or any other person outside of the Islamic religion as their Bitanah which means: friends, advisors, helpers, protectors, etc.:

> since they will not fail to do their best to corrupt you. They desire to harm you severely. (s.3:118, 5:51)

> O you who believe! Take not My enemies and your enemies (i.e. disbelievers and polytheists) as friends, showing affection towards them, while they have disbelieved in what has come to you of the truth (i.e. Islamic Monotheism, this Qur'an, and Muhammad). If you have come forth to strive in My Cause and to seek My Good Pleasure, (then take not these disbelievers and polytheists as your friends). (s.60:1)

> Should they gain the upper hand over you, they would behave to you as enemies, and stretch forth their hands and their tongues against you with evil... (s.60:2)

> O you who believe! Take not as friends the people who incurred the Wrath of Allah (i.e. Jews). (s.60:13)

The Qur'an goes on to explain how the Jews disclosed some of the Book sent down to Moses, but concealed much of it (s.6:91), and how:

They (the disbelievers, the Jews and the Christians want to extinguish Allah's Light. (s.9:32, & 61:8)

Verily, those who disbelieve (in the religion of Islam, the Qur'an and Prophet Muhammad) from among the people of the Scripture (Jews and Christians) and Al-Mushrikun, will abide in the fire of Hell. They are the worst of creatures. (s.98:6)

We shall cast terror into the hearts of those who disbelieve... (s.3:151)

Contrary to Christianity, the Qur'an teaches that Jesus was not the Son of God, but only a prophet (s.23:91). And Muslims are ordered not to say "Three (Trinity)! Cease! (it is) better for you. For Allah's (the only) One Ilah (God)" (s.4:171). The Qur'an also teaches that Jesus was not killed or crucified, but another man who looked like Jesus was killed (s.4:157).

Further, the Qur'an says "Take not *ilahain* (two gods in worship)" (s.16:51). Interestingly, the Arabic word **ilahain** is the same as the Hebrew word **Elohim** that is found continuously throughout the Hebrew text of the Old Testament of the Bible to describe the name of its God. So while the Qur'an in one breath is saying that Allah is the same god as that of the Torah, it then contradicts itself and says, don't follow the god (Elohim) of the Torah!

And if that wasn't absurd enough, while the Qur'an professes to be the same religion as Judaism and Christianity, it then demands that everyone must convert to Islam or be killed.

What followed the encounter with Gabriel was a blood-bath that has continued for over 1,400 years. It continues to this very day, as the holy army (mujahideen) that Muhammad raised seeks to impose Islam (Slavery) on the whole world. While it is largely ignored by the national media, today, throughout the Middle East and Africa, we see hundreds of thousands of people running for their lives from Jihadists who are moving from town to town, destroying Christian Churches, and killing everyone who is not Muslim.

Muslim apologetics profess over and over again that Islam is a peaceful religion of love. They argue that the mujahideen (Islamic terrorist groups like Al-Qaeda and Isis) are only "mis-interpreting" the Qur'an and the violent acts of Jihad they are committing are not supported by their religion, nor are they the teachings of Muhammad.

This could not be further from the truth. The fact is, most people outside of the Muslim community have never read the Qur'an and are completely uneducated about the subject of Islam. Muslim apologetics are able to use your ignorance of Islam against you and can deceive you with statements like "The Qur'an and Muhammad don't teach that." When people hear the above statements being made by the Muslim apologetics they just naturally assume that they are being told the truth since the word *religion* is used. Because, how could a *religion* support such acts of violence as those committed by Islamic terrorist groups? These uneducated people then falsely assume that these individuals or terrorist groups must only be "radicals" or "extremists."

This distorts the reality of what the Islamic religion is. As you will see below, the Islamic terrorist groups are not "radicals" or "extremists." They are simply following what the Qur'an instructs them to do.

After being deceived by the Muslim apologetics, these lies are perpetuated by the media who regurgitate this nonsense to the masses, giving society a false sense of security that these are not Muslims; they are only "radicals" or "Jihadists." These false statements are then further solidified when Presidents like Bush and Obama affirm them. People wander around in the dark, blissfully unaware of the true dangers that await them.

While I acknowledge that there are many people around the world who call themselves Muslims that are not performing Jihad, however, their actions should not be used as evidence of what Islam teaches, because the truth is that those people are not really Muslims, just people calling themselves Muslims. For example: I eat meat. I can say over and over again that I'm vegetarian, but if I'm eating meat, am I truly a vegetarian? No, I'm not. For whatever reason I'm claiming to be aligned with a doctrine that I don't follow. This is the same thing that we see occurring in Religions today. Many people claim to be Jewish or Christian but have never read the Torah or Bible. They have aligned themselves with a particular religion for whatever reason but have no real knowledge what the true doctrine of that religion is. Further, the majority of Jews and Christians who have read the Torah or Bible refuse to follow many of the doctrines contained therein. Can any of these people truly call themselves Jews or Christians? No, because (like the person who eats meat but is calling themself vegetarian) if you do not follow the doctrine completely you are not truly a member of that Religion.

We even hear people making statements like "Islam has not gone through its reformation period yet." This exacerbates the problem and demonstrates a complete ignorance of the issues involved. Can the word of God be reformed?

Understand that it is not possible for a person to look at a religious doctrine and say "follow this part, but not this part or this part." In doing so, you're either saying: (a) it's okay not to follow certain of the orders God commanded you to follow; or (b) you're acknowledging that the doctrine was not really divinely bestowed upon man by God so its okay to change some parts of it.

154

As we see occurring in the Jewish and Christian Religions, the same things occur in Islam. Undoubtedly there are people who call themselves Muslim who have never read the Qur'an and other people who have read it but refuse to follow certain parts of it.

The problem is, unlike the other religions, the overwhelming majority of Muslims do follow the Qur'an down to the very letter, and they are willing to kill for it. This is what makes Islam so dangerous.

Contrary to what some Muslims publicly profess, ANYONE who actually reads the Qur'an can see that it orders all Muslims, in no unambiguous terms, to wage war and kill anyone standing in their way that does not believe in Islam until the day that every person alive believes only in Islam. This is the message of the Qur'an and teachings of Muhammad.

Don't believe me? Think I'm exaggerating? Get a copy of the Qur'an and read if for yourself. Educate yourself!

Jihad

Islamic Jihad is not based upon "radicalism" or "extremism" derived from some obscure saying in the Qur'an that Muslims are mis-interpreting. Jihad is a fundamental duty in Islam and one of the "pillars" upon which the entire religion stands.

According to the Qur'an and Muhammad, it is MANDATORY that every Muslim perform JIHAD until there are no more disbelievers and every person, in every country on Earth, is Muslim. The Noble Qur'an states, in crystal clear words:

Jihad (holy fighting in Allah's Cause) is ordained for you (s.2:216)

"Ordained" means being established by decree of law. The Noble Qur'an defines Jihad as:

> Holy fighting in the Cause of Allah or any other kind of effort to make Allah's Word (i.e. Islam) superior. Jihad is regarded as one of the fundamentals of Islam. (Rf7)

The dictionary defines Jihad as: a holy war waged on behalf of Islam as a religious duty (Rf8). When reading the Qur'an you will see that in addition to the word Jihad, the translators use the terms "Cause of Allah," "Allah's Cause," and "Way of Allah" to also describe Jihad.

155

The Qur'an explicitly states that when Allah and Muhammad have "decreed a matter", Muslims do not have "any option in their decision" (s.33:36); they must obey.

The Qur'an then orders Muhammad to "fight (O Muhammad) in the Cause of Allah, ... and incite the believers (to fight along with you)" (s.4:84). "Urge the people to fight" (s.8:65). In accordance with this order from the Qur'an, Muhammad said:

> I have been *ordered to fight the people* till they say: La ilaha illallah (None has the right to be worshipped but Allah) (s.77:48 note (1)A, citing Sahih Al-Bukhari, 1/392 (O.P.387))

The Qur'an explains how important Jihad is to Islam:

> *Al-Jihad* (holy fighting) in Allah's Cause (with full force of numbers and weaponry) *is given the utmost importance in Islam and is one of its pillars (on which it stands)*. By Jihad Islam is established, Allah's Word is made superior,... and His religion (Islam) is propagated. By abandoning Jihad Islam is destroyed and the Muslims fall into an inferior position; their honour is lost... *Jihad is an obligatory duty in Islam on every Muslim*, and he who tries to escape from this duty, or does not in his innermost heart wish to fulfill this duty, dies with one of the qualities of a hypocrite. (s.2:190 note 1)

And Muhammad taught as many people as he could, how good it is "To participate in Jihad in Allah's Cause." Sahih Al-Bukhari 4/2782 (O.P.41). Muhammad's statement is repeated at (s.17:13 note 1, citing Sahih Al-Bukhari, 9/7534 (O.P.625)).

Islam requires that Muslims perform Jihad and fight all over the world until the entire world is united under one Khalifah (a chief Muslim ruler) in order to make Islam victorious (s.8:73).

The order for Muslims to perform Jihad is repeated over and over again in the Qur'an, and specifies what Muslims are to do to non-believers who refuse to accept Islam:

> And kill them wherever you find them...(s.2:191)

> And fight them until there is no more Fitnah (disbelief and polytheism, i.e. worshipping others besides Allah), and the religion will be all for Allah alone (in the whole of the world).
> (s.8:39); and is repeated at (s.2:193)

> And fight in the way of Allah... (s.2:244)

And strive hard in Allah's Cause as you ought to strive (with sincerity and with all your efforts that His Name should be superior). He has chosen you (to convey His Message of Islamic Monotheism to mankind by inviting them to His religion of Islam)... (s.22:78)

O Prophet (Muhammad)! Strive hard against the disbelievers and the hypocrites, and be severe against them... (s.66:9)

O you who believe!... when you are told to rise up ... Jihad (holy fighting in Allah's Cause), or any other good deed], rise up. (s.58:11)

Beheadings

And if you wondered why one of the preferred methods Muslims use to kill in Jihad is cutting the throat or chopping the neck, you need only read the Qur'an at Surah 47:4:

So, when you meet (in fight - Jihad in Allah's Cause) those who disbelieve, *smite (their) necks till when you have killed* and wounded many of them ... Thus [you are ordered by Allah to continue in carrying out Jihad against the disbelievers till they embrace Islam...

The Qur'an then instructs that any Muslim who refuses to perform Jihad is to be looked at as a disbeliever:

What is the matter with you that when you are asked to march forth in the Cause of Allah (i.e. Jihad) you cling heavy to the earth? (s.9:38)

If you march not forth, He will punish you with a painful torment... (s.9:39)

March forth, whether you are light (being healthy, young and wealthy) or heavy (being ill, old and poor)... (s.9:41)

If you refuse to perform Jihad you are a disbeliever... (s.9:49)

Then the Qur'an goes even further, and instills paranoia in Muslims, instructing them not to trust their own families:

O you who believe! Verily, among your wives and your children there are enemies for you (who may stop you from the obedience of Allah); therefore beware of them! (s.64:14)

O you who believe! Fight those of the disbelievers who are close to you, and let them find harshness in you; and know that Allah is with those who are Al-Muttaqun. (true followers of Islam) (s.9:123)

The Qur'an then orders that any Muslims who leave the religion must be killed:

if they turn back (from Islam) take (hold of) them and kill them wherever you find them (s.20:134 note 1, citing Sahih Al-Bukhari, 5/4351 (O.P.638))

The Qur'an then instructs Muslims to fight all disbelievers including Jews and Christians who do not accept Islam:

Fight against those who believe not in Allah, nor in the Last Day, nor forbid that which has been forbidden by Allah and His Messenger, and those who acknowledge not the religion of truth (i.e. Islam) among the people of the Scripture (Jews and Christians), until they pay the Jizyah (s.9:29)

The "Jizyah" is a tax that Jews and Christians must pay to Islam in order that they not be killed immediately, but will be allowed to live until the Day of Resurrection and, at that time, the tax will be abolished and Jews and Christians will be required to accept Islam or they will be killed. The Islamic religion teaches how Jesus:

will descend on earth, and he will not accept any other religion except Islam ... and will judge mankind justly by the law of the Qur'an, and will break the Cross and kill the pigs ... and all mankind will be required to embrace Islam. (s.8:39 notes 1&2, citing Sahih Al-Bukhari, 3/2222 (O.P.425)); repeated at (s.61:6 note (3)B).

Hell

To scare Muslims into submission the Qur'an describes the Hell-Fire that awaits all non-Muslims. It also explains that you will know the people who are going to Paradise or Hell by the color of their faces: people with white faces are going to Paradise and people with black faces are going to Hell (s.3:106- 107).

The Qur'an explains that Hell has seven gates and each of those gates is assigned a special class of sinner (s.15:44).

All non-Muslims will be bound together in fetters (s.14:49). They will be forced to drink "boiling, festering water" (s.14:16) which they will find great difficulty swallowing down their throats, and death will come to them from every side, but they will not die because of the "great torment" still yet to come (s.14:17).

Then they will be dragged on their faces into the Fire and Allah will say to them "Taste you the touch of Hell!" (s.54:48). Garments of fire will be cut for them (s.22:19-20), the fire will burn their faces and they will grin with disfigured lips (s.23:104), while their skin melts away. And when their skins are "roasted through," they will be given new skins so that they can continue to taste the pain (s.4:56), while they sigh "in a high and low tone" (s.11:106).

Paradise

But to Muslims who submit to Allah and fight and sacrifice their lives in Islamic Jihad the Qur'an promises them Paradise:

> if you strive hard and fight in the Cause of Allah (Jihad) with your wealth and lives (s.61:11), and kill (others) and be killed (s.9:111), Allah will forgive you your sins, and admit you into 'Adn (Eden) Paradise (s.61:12).

> Allah has promised the believers - men and women, - Gardens under which rivers flow to dwell therein forever, and beautiful mansions in Gardens of 'Adn (Eden Paradise). (s.9:72), see also (s.5:85, 13:23).

In Paradise there will be flowing meadows (s.42:22) and rich carpets spread all around (s.88:16). Brothers in Islam will be adorned with bracelets of gold and pearls and they will wear green garments of fine and thick silk (s.18:31, 22:23). They will sit upon raised thrones that are woven with gold and precious stones (s.56:15), facing each other (s.15:47).

The Qur'an advises Muslims that, as a reward for Jihad (s.56:24), beside them in Paradise there will be:

> young full-breasted (s.78:33) "virgins" (s.56:36) with wide lovely eyes (s.45:54) that were created specially for them (s.56:35) loving their husbands only (s.56:37). See also, (s.37:48, 38:52, 55:56, 55:72, 55:74, 56:22, 55:70).

These virgins will be "reclining on green cushions and rich beautiful mattresses" (s.55:76). This is what Islamic Jihadists are promised in Paradise! Muhammad said: "Everyone of them will have two wives" (s.29:64 note 1, citing Sahih Al-Bukhari, 4/3245 (O.P.468)).

Paradise will be filled with all kinds of drinks, white wine (s.37:45-46), wine mixed with Zanjabil (ginger) (s.76:17), all kinds of fruits (s.36:57), date palms and pomegranates (s.55:68), banana trees with fruits piled one above another (s.56:29), and the flesh of all the fowls the desire (s.56:21). Paradise contains rivers of milk, wine, clarified honey, and every kind of fruit (s.47:15).

Golden trays and cups, vessels of silver and cups of crystal will be passed around (s.43:71, 76:15) by immortal boy-servants (s.56:17, 52:24).

In Paradise there will be no pain (s.37:47), no sense of fatigue (s.15:48), and Muslims will have therein all that they desire (s.16:31).

The Qur'an also explains that there are 100 levels of Paradise reserved for the mujahideen who perform Jihad, and the degree they attain is based upon how much Jihad they performed. (s.4:95, 4:96). Muhammad explained how:

> Paradise has one hundred grades which Allah has reserved for the Mujahidun [Muslim fighters in Jihad] who fight in His Cause, and the distance between each of the two grades is like the distance between the heavens and the earth. (s.9:20 note (1)A, citing Sahih Al-Bukhari, 4/2790 (O.P.48))

The more Jihad, the higher degree of Paradise they receive!

Martyrs

All of this is promised in the hope of convincing Muslims to perform Jihad and martyr themselves. As to "martyrdom," the Qur'an says that "martyrs" will be among the righteous in Paradise (s.4:69), and:

> who so fights in the Cause of Allah, and is killed or gets victory, We shall bestow on him a great reward (s.4;74).

The Qur'an explains how some have been true to their covenant with Allah and gone out for Jihad having been martyred, "and some of them are still waiting" (s.33:23). Muhammad said to Muslims:

> Allah guarantees him who strives in His Cause and whose motivation for going out is nothing but Jihad in His Cause and belief in His Words, that He will admit him into Paradise (if martyred) (s.9:111 note (1)a, citing Sahih Al-Bukhari, 4/3123 (O.P.352))

Muhammad continued: "Know that Paradise is under the shades of the swords (Jihad in Allah's Cause)." (s.36:26 note (1)c, citing Sahih Al-Bukhari, 4/2818 (O.P.73). Muhammad also said:

> Nobody who enters Paradise likes to go back to the world even if he got everything on the earth, except a martyr who wishes to return to the world so that he may be martyred then times because of the honour and dignity he received (from Allah). (s.36:26 note (1)b, citing Sahih Al-Bukhari, 4/2817 (O.P.72))

Muhammad continually tries to reassure Muslims that "whoever amongst us is killed (in Jihad in Allah's Cause) will go to Paradise" (s.57:25 note (1)a, citing The Book of Jihad, Chapter No.22).

Muhammad even tries to persuade Muslims by telling them of stories of a lady who "threw herself in the ditch of a fire along with her child to be with

160

the martyrs in Paradise" instead of renouncing Islam. (s.85:4 note (2), citing Sahih Muslim, Hadith No.7148).

The Qur'an says: "And say not of those who are killed in the way of Allah [Jihad], "They are dead." Nay, they are living, but you perceive (it) not." (s.2:154).

Muhammad then goes on a crazy rant, saying, that if a group of Muslims went our for Jihad he would never stay behind. How he would go out for Jihad with that Sariyya (army unit) and he would love to be martyred:

> By Him in Whose Hand my soul is! *I would love to be martyred in Allah's Cause and then come back to life, and then get martyred and then come back to life again, and then get martyred and then come back to life again, and then get martyred.* (s.9:20 note (1)B, citing Sahih Al-Bukhari, 4/2797 (O.P.54)

Killing of Innocent People

You might be saying to yourself "What about all the innocent people that Muslims kill? Certainly the Qur'an doesn't support this, does it?" The answer is: YES, it does. What we in the rational world define as "innocent" is not considered innocent under Islam. Under Islam all non-Muslims must convert to Islam or they are deemed an infidel and must be killed.

In addition to all of the above verses that demand this, the Qur'an highlights this very issue under the story of Moses and his boy-servant named Al-Khidr (s.18:60 note 1, citing Sahih Al-Bukhari, 6/4725 (O.P.249)):

While they were walking on the seashore, Al-Khidr saw an innocent boy playing in the sand with other boys.

> Al-Khidr got hold of the head of that boy and pulled it out with his hands and killed him.

Moses was shocked and said: "Have you killed an innocent person who had killed none?" (s.18:74). The Qur'an then goes on to explain that the innocent boy was not Muslim and killing him was lawful because it was done to prevent the boy from spreading his evil disbelieving ways (s.18:80-81).

Entire towns of people can be destroyed if the people refuse to accept Islam (s.28:59); "Allah permits its destruction" (s.17:58 note 1 (Tafsir Al-Qurtubi)). Look at Muhammad's response to an innocent man who was asking Muhammad this same question:

161

Shall we be destroyed though there will be righteous people among us?

[Muhammad said] "Yes"
(s.18:94 note 1, citing Sahih Al-Bukhari, 9/7135 (O.P.249)).

The disbelievers "will not be able to stay in it as your neighbours but a little while" (s.33:60). They shall be seized wherever found, and killed with a (terrible) slaughter (s.33:61).

That was the way of Allah in the case of those who passed away of old,
and you will not find any change in the way of Allah. (s.33:62)

This is what the Qur'an teaches! I could go on and on, but I think my point is made. Islam is militant doctrine about submission to it, or death. To hear some Muslim apologetics profess that the "Qur'an is being mis-interpreted" or "Muhammad didn't teach that" is absurd. No rational person could read the Qur'an and mis-interpret the clear message contained throughout its pages. The mujahideen (Islamic terrorist groups), are not "radicals" or "extremists," but are simply following what the Qur'an and Muhammad demand them to do. If you have a problem with what they are doing, then your problem is with the Islamic religion (The Qur'an) itself. Until you educate yourself and come to this realization you will remain ignorant and the problem will not only continue, it will intensify.

One Islamic sect was so murderous that even today we use its name as the very definition of such acts of violence: *The Assassins*. The Merriam-Webster's Collegiate Dictionary defines the word "assassin" as:

a member of a Shia Muslim sect who at the time of the Crusades was
sent out on a suicide mission to murder prominent enemies.

The term "Assassin" is a corruption of the Arabic term Hashishim, meaning hashish (Indian hemp) smoker. The name was given to the Islamic sect because of its practice of intoxicating its followers with hashish before going on their killing spree (Rf9).

The Assassins were created in 1090 A.D. by a Persian named Hassan bin Sabah, who had been initiated into Ismailism at Cairo, in the household of the Fatmite Caliph, al-Mostansir (Rf10).

Hassan's method of recruitment for Jihad was ingenious. In a secret valley Hassan created a Paradise and filled it with all the rewards Allah promised Muslims. He created palaces, landscaped gardens with all types of exotic animals, and jewels. It was filled with the most beautiful fair women. A majestic sight just as promised in the Qur'an.

162

To recruit members for Jihad, they would befriend strangers in local drinking establishments, slip drugs into their drinks, and bring them in an unconscious state to their secret valley. Upon awakening the man would find himself in Paradise. In shock of such beauty, the man could only believe that he was in Elysium (the Paradise promised by Allah). After a few days of drinking wine, having sex with the most beautiful women and other luxuries of Paradise, the man would be drugged again, brought back to his house, where he would awake back in his dull life (Rf11).

The recruits, usually brainwashed goat-herders, spread word throughout the land of their "godly" experiences in Paradise. From that point in time Islam had no shortage of mujahideen willing to martyr themselves in hopes of reaching Paradise.

While there is a deeper story to the Assassins (they actually were a branch of a secret society which were used for various reasons when needed), I mention them here to show the recruitment methods they used to convince non-committed Muslims that Paradise was real and obtainable through Jihad. Methods that would become the basis of modern day Muslim mujahideen suicide bombers.

While modern day Muslims demand strict adherence to their Islamic laws, they themselves violate the rules of the Qur'an. For example: in the minds of Muslims Muhammad is regarded as holy (a type of saint) that has obtained an elevated status above the rest of mankind. This, in and of itself, is strictly forbidden by the Qur'an.

The Qur'an forbids Muslims from selling verses of the Qur'an (s.2:41, 5:44), yet you see book stores all over selling Qur'ans. The Qur'an also forbids Muslims from engaging in modern day business practices like earning money by selling items for a higher price than they paid for them (as every store does) or earning interest off money lent (s.2:245, 2:275), yet we see Muslim stores all over.

Further, Muslims ignore the fact that Muhammad himself violated some rules. Muhammad married both a mother and her daughter. The religion that Muhammad swore to obey strictly forbids this by punishment of death. Leviticus 20:14 says:

> If a man marries both a woman and her mother, it is wicked. Both he and they must be burned in the fire, so that no wickedness will be among you.

163

And see the Qur'an at (s.4:23). According to his own religion, Muhammad was considered wicked and had to be killed. But because Muslims are so deluded, they can't see, or ignore such acts.

Also, Muhammad married a 6 year old girl. Muslim apologetics will admit this happened, but then argue that this "was a loving act." Others, in the rational world, say that a man over 40 years old who marries a 6 year old girl is a pedophile.

In modern times you see thousands of Muslims in the Middle East, and around the word, rioting in the streets holding their "Death to America" signs. These people are not "radicals," or "extremists." The principles and customs that countries like the U.S. hold dear (i.e. Freedom of Religion, Free Speech, etc.) are the very things that the Qur'an demands Muslims to hate and fight against until they no longer exist.

Muslims in the Middle East profess their feelings openly. Muslims living in countries like the U.S. can not be so open while they are still in the minority. They tolerate us, grin, and pretend to be friendly, while apologizing for the Jihadists with false claims that they are "mis-interpreting" the Qur'an, until the time comes when they are powerful enough to overthrow the U.S. and turn it into an Islamic country. For this is what the Qur'an demands.

True Purpose of Islam

To understand the true purpose of Islam (submission) you need to focus on one question: *WHY* did Gabriel provide Muhammad with this message? It is only by answering this question that the truth is revealed.

It is necessary to briefly re-examine the history of how the Anunnaki/Elohim/Nephilim continuously became angered at humans and tried to destroy us. By the Qur'an's own verses Allah is the same "god" as the Judaic and Christian "god." I have already established how this god was not "God," but just a member of the Anunnaki/Elohim/Nephilim. Further, the Qur'an actually admits that Allah is in fact the same person whom the Arabs called the "Lord of Sirius," one of the Anunnaki/Elohim/Nephilim! (s.53:49).

The Anunnaki/Elohim/Nephilim created us to be slaves. The Qur'an uses the word "slave" over and over again to indoctrinate you into the false belief that you are a slave and must submit. The Qur'an continuously calls Muhammad a slave (s.2:23) and Muhammad said he was "a thankful slave" (s.2:139 note (1)a, citing Sahih Al-Bukhari, 8/6471 (O.P.478)). But it is not "God" that you are submitting to, but Anunnaki/Elohim/Nephilim control, since the Islamic religion is nothing more than their control mechanism to keep its "slaves" subservient. Remember, they did not want us to have any

164

"knowledge" that would elevate us above our slave status. When the Watchers broke the law and had sex with the daughters of men as recorded in Genesis 6:4 and The Book of Enoch, VII:1-2 (See Chapter 5) the children this union created were stronger, more intelligent, and the Watchers began to teach these children secret sciences reserved for the Anunnaki/Elohim/ Nephilim alone.

Ever since that time, the Anunnaki/Elohim/Nephilim have continuously tried to destroy us (the children of the Watchers). After their attempts at starving us to death failed, they decided to let us perish in the coming Great Flood. After Noah and his family survived and repopulated Earth they saw the children of the Watchers all working together in one strong united force in the building of the Tower of Babel. This unity and technological advancement threatened the Anunnaki/Elohim/Nephilim. They became enraged and divided mankind to weaken us (See Chapter 8).

In their eyes the children of the Watchers were violating their rules again. The Anunnaki/Elohim/Nephilim yet again decided to destroy us. This time they gave the job to Gabriel to accomplish. Enlil/El-Shaddai/YHWH ordered Gabriel:

> And to Gabriel said the Lord: ... *destroy the children of the Watchers: send them one against the other that they may destroy each other in battle* (The Book of Enoch, X:9)

Gabriel's very job was to destroy mankind! Now it all makes sense.

This is *WHY* Gabriel provided the message of the Qur'an to Muhammad. Gabriel's purpose in giving Muhammad the message of the Qur'an was to send mankind *"one against the other that they may destroy each other in battle."* Gabriel used Muhammad to get mankind to kill each other. Is this not exactly what is occurring today? The teachings of the Qur'an are the reason why thousands upon thousands of men today raise arms "one against the other" in the name of Allah.

The *Allah* of the Qur'an was an Anunnaki/Elohim/Nephilim (devil) who was trying to destroy mankind, and Muhammad was his messenger. Islam even uses their Moon Crescent and Pentagram symbols as its emblem.

Also, notice how one of the terrorist groups even named itself ISIS. Isis was the Egyptian name of one of the Anunnaki/Elohim/Nephilim! Don't fall for the "It's an acronym" excuse.

Gabriel performed his job very well. The Anunnaki/Elohim/Nephilim's plans are working. Islam is growing at an enormous rate. There are approximately 1.5 billion Muslims. Islam is a cancer that will infect the whole world. If it is not stopped it will destroy mankind, for that is exactly what it was designed to do.

14

STORIES OF THE APOCALYPSE TO WARN OF THE ANUNNAKI/ELOHIM/NEPHILIM'S RETURN

THE APOCALYPTIC STORIES found all over the world follow a common theme: the day when so-called "god" will return to Earth to pronounce his final judgment upon mankind. Ancient texts describe it as an event filled with chaos, cataclysmic disaster and even the arrival of a celestial body.

In the Bible's book of *Revelation* (aka *The Apocalypse of St. John the Divine*), John testifies that someone like a "son of man" came to see him. Describing the man's physical appearance, John said the man's head and hair were as white as snow, his face was like the sun shinning in all its brilliance, his eyes were red like blazing fire, that he was dressed in a long robe reaching down to his feet with a golden sash around his chest, that he was holding in his right hand seven stars and out of his mouth came a sharp double-edged sword. The man told John that he was the First and the Last, who died and came back to life; that he was the Son of the Elohim; that he holds the sevenfold spirit of Elohim; that he holds the key of David; and that he is AMEN the ruler of Elohim's creation.

Note: While the word **Amen** has become widely used amongst the Judeo-Christian congregations as an expression of agreement (even being translated to mean "so be it"), this definition is completely inaccurate. **Amen** is actually the ancient name of one of Egypt's foremost gods (aka Amon, Amun, Amnon, Amon-Re, Amen-Ra) and dates back over 4,000 years. Amen's name meant The Hidden One.

It was during their captivity in Egypt that the Hebrews adopted many of the Egyptian religious practices that we find interwoven throughout modern Judaism and Christianity.

Examining the biblical scriptures themselves you can see how Amen identified a person, not an expression of agreement. For instance:

These are the words of ***the Amen***, the faithful and true witness, ***the ruler of God's creation***. (Revelation 3:14 NIV)

This is not an expression of agreement, but identifying the person **Amen** who *is* the ruler of God's creation. Accordingly, the Good News Translation renders the verse as such: "This is the message *from the Amen*, the faithful and true witness"; The New King James Version renders the verse: "…These things says *the Amen*, the Faithful and True Witness". See also verse 1:18, which states:

> *I am*, **Amen**, I was dead, and behold I am alive for ever and ever!
> And I hold the keys of death and Hades. (KJV)

Other translations render the beginning of this verse: "*I am He who lives*, and was dead, and behold, I am alive…" (1:18 NKJV); "*I am the Living One*; I was dead, and behold, I am alive…" (1:18 NIV); "*I am the living one!* I was dead, but now I am alive…" (1:18 GNT).

As the true meaning of **Amen** became lost over time, or intentionally concealed, translators put forth the idea that it must be an expression of agreement since they found it frequently being used to refer back to the words of another speaker with whom there was agreement. However, by analogy we can look at how Christians today exclaim *"Jesus"* after a prayer, sermon, or statement of another person with whom there is agreement. It doesn't change the fact that Jesus is a name that identifies a person and not an expression of agreement, even though it is being used as such. In this same way **Amen** is not an expression of agreement, but the name of an Egyptian god, even though it was being used as such. Every time you say Amen you are unwittingly invoking the Egyptian god Amen.

But getting back to John's testimony, John was advised to tell the messengers of the seven churches that to all humans who overcome: they will be given the right to eat from the tree of life; they will not be hurt by the second death; they will be given the hidden manna and a white stone with a new name written on it; they will be given authority over the nations to "rule them with an iron scepter" and will be given the morning star; those who overcome will be dressed in white and their name will never be blotted out of the book of life; they will be made a pillar in the temple of Elohim which they will never leave and the name and city of Elohim will be written on them as well as the Son of Elohim's new name; and they will sit with him on his throne just as he sat on his father's throne.

Then John went on to foretell the terror that these people were going to unleash upon the earth. He witnessed a Lamb open seven seals of a scroll: The first seal unleashed a white horse, its rider holding a bow and wearing a crown; he was a conqueror. The second seal unleashed a red horse, its rider had a sword and was given the power to take peace from earth and make men slay each other. The third seal unleashed a black horse, its rider holding a pair of scales issuing a quart of wheat for a day's wages and three quarts of barley for a day's wages. The fourth seal unleashed a pale horse, its rider was named Death and Hades was following close behind him. They were given the power over a fourth of the earth to kill by sword, famine, plague, and by the wild beasts of the earth. The fifth seal unleashed the souls of those who had already been slain, each of them being given a white robe and told to wait a little longer until the rest of the humans are killed. The sixth seal unleashed a great earthquake, the sun turned black, the moon turned blood red, the stars in the sky fell to earth, the sky rolled up like a scroll and every mountain and island was removed from its place. The messengers were then advised not to take any action until they put a seal on the foreheads of each of the 144,000 slaves of the Elohim. When the seventh seal was opened there was silence in heaven for about half an hour.

Then John saw seven messengers standing before the Elohim. One messenger had a golden censer, filled it with fire from the Elohim's altar and hurled it down on the earth, amidst peals of thunder, rumblings, flashes of lightening and an earthquake. Amidst sounding trumpets, hail and fire mixed with blood was hurled down upon earth. A huge mountain, all ablaze, was thrown into the sea turning it into blood. A great blazing star named Wormwood fell from the sky onto the rivers and springs of water. A third of the sun, moon, and stars were struck. Then a star fell from the sky with the key to the Abyss. When it was opened locusts were released upon the earth with power like scorpions to torture all the humans who did not have the Elohim's seal. The messenger of the Abyss named Abaddon (Apollyon in Greek) was king over the locusts. Then the four messengers who were bound at the great river Euphrates were released to kill a third of mankind. After which the Elohim's kingdom was re-established on earth.

John then saw Elohim's temple in the sky open and a pregnant woman appeared. She was clothed with the sun, had the moon under her feet and wore a crown of twelve stars on her head. She was giving birth to the next Elohim who would "rule all the nations with an iron scepter." Then an enormous red dragon with seven heads, each having a crown, and ten horns appeared. The Great Dragon was against the Elohim and attempted to stop their destruction and control over the earth. But he was not strong enough and was hurled down to earth with his messengers, where he continued to fight against all who would follow the Elohim.

On earth the dragon gave his power, authority, and throne to the beast (Revelation 13:2). Who is the beast? The key is in the riddle itself:

169

> This calls for wisdom. If anyone has insight, let him calculate
> the number of the beast, for *it is man's number*. His number is
> 666. (Revelation 13:18)

This is not *A* specific man's number, but *MAN* himself (MANKIND). To the Elohim man is nothing more than a beast; an animal that they created because they needed slave workers.

This result is also reached when we apply the principles of scientific Numerology to number 666 in order to decipher the mystery. The number 9 is considered magical because the digits in its multiples always add up to itself. As explained by Physicist Daniel Ward in *The 9 in Sacred Geometry*: "nine represents the principles of the sacred Triad taken to their utmost expression" (Rf1). For example, 9x2=18 (1+8=9), 9x3=27 (2+7=9), 9x4=36 (3+6=9), 9x5=45 (4+5=9), 9x6=54 (5+4=9), 9x7=63 (6+3=9), 9x8=72 (7+2=9), 9x9=81 (8+1=9). Even when we apply this to the ancient symbol of Supreme Positivity (the Ring), a 360 degree circle (3+6+0=9), we arrive at 9.

So how does the number 9 apply to man? In the Hebrew and Greek alphabets there are no numerals, but each letter has a numerical value. In biblical Hebrew Adam is called ADM. The value of the Hebrew letter "A" is 1, "D" is 4, and "M" is 40. If we add these digits (1+4+4+0 = 9) we learn that the number of Adam (aka mankind) is 9. Applying this to the so-called number of the beast 666 in the Bible's Book of Revelations the digits (6+6+6 = 18, 1+8 = 9) and we again arrive at the number of man. Man is the beast. *A beast that goes through 9 months of gestation*.

Unless mankind (the beast) agrees to remain "as a child, submissive, meek," a slave to the Elohim, he is considered an enemy which must be killed. As the *Book of Mormon* articulates it:

> *the natural man is an enemy to God* ... and will be, forever and ever,
> unless he yields to the enticings of the [Elohim], and putteth off the
> natural man and becometh ... as a child, submissive, meek, ... willing
> to submit to all things which the [Elohim] seeth fit to inflict upon him...
> (Rf2)

The dragon/serpent was trying to save mankind so he gave his power, authority and throne to mankind so that mankind would be able to defend itself against the Elohim.

The Bible's book of Revelation says this final war between the Elohim and mankind will take place at Har Megiddo (the heights of Megiddo) also known as Armageddon.

One ancient Egyptian text (believed to stem from the time of Amenemhet I, 12th Dynasty circa 2000 B.C.) describes the event:

> It is terrifying ...
> What will be done was never done before.
> The Earth is completely perished.
> The land is damaged, no remainder exists.
> There is no sunshine ...
> Ra must begin the foundations of the Earth again. (Rf3)

The prophet Joel describes it as a time when the "sun and moon will be darkened, and the stars no longer shine" (3:15). How "the earth and sky will tremble" (3:16) and mankind will be told to "Prepare for war!" (3:9) as Yahweh gathers "all nations and bring[s] them down to the Valley of Jehoshaphat" where he "will enter into judgment against them" (3:2).

The prophet Zephaniah described it as a time when Yahweh "will sweep away everything from the face of the earth ... both men and animals ... the birds of the air and the fish of the sea (1:2-3). Because mankind refused to be slaves to the Elohim:

> That day will be a day of wrath, a day of distress and anguish, a day of trouble and ruin, a day of darkness and gloom, a day of clouds and blackness, a day of trumpet and battle cry against the fortified cities and against the corner towers. I will bring distress on the people and they will walk like blind men ... Their blood will be poured out like dust and their entrails filth. ... In the fire of his jealously the whole world will be consumed, for he will make a sudden end of all who live in the earth. (1:15-18)

The prophet Isaiah described Yahweh's "day of vengeance" (34:8) as a time when "Yahweh is going to lay waste the earth and devastate it" (24:1). How the "floodgates of the heavens" will be opened and "the foundations of the earth" will shake (24:18) as the "sword of Yahweh is bathed in blood" (34:6) as it descends in judgment to "totally destroy" mankind:

> their dead bodies will send up a stench; the mountains will be soaked with their blood (34:3)

The prophet Malachi describes it as a day that will "burn like a furnace" and all mankind will be set "on fire" except for those humans who accept their enslavement to the Elohim (4:1-6).

Some human slaves become so disillusioned with these End of World prophesies that they actually try and bring about this end of world scenario.

However, since you now know that the biblical texts were not speaking of God (the Great Architect of the Universe) but were only speaking of the Anunnaki/Elohim/Nephilim, it follows that the apocalyptic stories were likewise only describing the events surrounding their return to Earth.

One of the biblical texts, Amos 5:18, even warns mankind not to long for the day when these people return:

> Woe to you who long for the day of Yahweh! Why do you long for
> the day of Yahweh? That day will be darkness, not light.

An ancient Akkadian apocalyptic text even mentions the Anunnaki/Elohim/ Nephilim and explains that when they return:

> The regular offerings for the Iggi gods [human sacrifices] which had
> ceased, will be reestablished (Rf4)

The apocalyptic stories were designed to subdue mankind into "submission" (slavery). Through the use of scare tactics their goal is to dissuade the human slaves from educating themselves and attempting to re-unite mankind into one strong family as they were before the Tower of Babel. At the same time, to the illuminated humans (the ones that have ears) these stories stand as a constant warning urging their perserverance in the fight to re-unite and educate mankind before these people return.

When these people return to Earth they plan to kill every human being who refuses to accept their enslavement. It is the so-called "Day of Judgment" (aka Armageddon). A Hebrew scroll found in a cave overlooking the Dead Sea, which scholars have titled *The War of the Sons of Light Against the Sons of Darkness*, describes it as a time when the *"Sons of Light"* [illuminated humans; the Congregation of Mortals] must rise up "with a show of godlike might" and "battle against the *Sons of Darkness"* [the Anunnaki/Elohim/Nephilim; the Company of the Divine] for their survival.

PART III

SECRET SOCIETIES

15

SECRET SOCIETIES

MANY BOOKS HAVE been written on the subject of Secret Societies. The initiated elect who are said to possess secret knowledge of the *Ancient Mysteries*. Researchers have shown in intricate detail how these societies (sometimes referred to as Mystery Schools) evolved over millennia spreading the world over under different names; from ancient societies that existed throughout Mesopotamia, Egypt and Greece, to more contemporary societies that exist throughout Europe and America.

Researchers assert that Secret Societies like the Freemasons, Rosicrucians, and Illuminati all have at their core the ultimate goal of implementing a New World Order. They describe how operating in secrecy under blood oaths they have infiltrated every area of civilization in furtherance of this goal and that today members of these societies hold the highest positions in government, banking, the news media and entertainment industry.

In an attempt to expose this conspiracy and unmask its members watchdog groups follow secret organizations like the Bilderberg Group (an unofficial name given to it because of the Bilderberg Hotel in Oosterbeek, Holland where this organization was first publicly discovered in 1954) which holds annual meetings at different resorts over the globe of prominent businessmen, politicians, bankers, educators, media owners, and military leaders from around the world. Watchdog groups connect the dots and demonstrate how seemingly public organizations like the Royal Institute of International Affairs established in Britain and England and the Council on Foreign Relations and Trilateral Commission established in the U.S. are simply branches of the Secret Society created by Cecil Rhodes, the Round Table (which was an homage to King Arthur's Round Table, but patterned after Freemasonry). They have even exposed some of their recruiting branches like the Skull & Bones and Scroll & Key societies found at prestigious universities like Harvard and Yale. When you examine the evidence laid out by these researchers the connections are undeniable.

Based upon these connections conspiracy researchers argue that the government is not run by the three branches: executive (President), legislative (Congress and House of Representatives), judicial, but that the President is just a puppet (the face of the corporate government) and the people who really run the government are the members of these societies who secretly pull the strings behind the scenes in order to maintain control of the population; aka The Shadow Government.

Clearly the President is not the person who actually calls the shots. Do you really think that any old Joe can run for the office of President, by dumb luck get voted into office, and then the government is just going to hand over the nuclear bombs to Joe, saying, "don't blow us all up Joe"? It is beyond absurd for any individual to think this is how things work. But you would have to believe this in order to believe that the President actually has any real power or that the people actually vote for or have a say in who runs the government. Even U.S. Supreme Court Justice Frankfurter acknowledged:

> The real rulers in Washington are invisible, and exercise power from behind the scenes. (Rf1)

All governments are basically dictatorships imposing their rules upon society. The problem with dictatorship is that the population being controlled only see the dictator as their source of oppression. Eventually the population will grow frustrated, angry, and when that reaches a boiling point the population will rise up and overthrow the evil dictator by force, anarchy ensues, and the people running things from behind the scenes lose control over the population.

In order to operate as a dictatorship and keep the population from rising up against them they created the scheme of democracy. The democratic process provides them with the exact same type of control but the contrived scheme is designed to PACIFY and RE-DIRECT THE POPULATION'S ANGER of being oppressed at each other rather then at the dictator.

The democratic scheme establishes several levels of deflection. It's ingenious. Instead of exposing the dictator to the public they created the Office of President who acts as the face of the corporation. The population is tricked into believing that instead of a dictator being forced upon them they can vote for who they want to govern them. This perceived choice adds one layer of deflection which reduces the population's anger making it easier for the government to exercise control over them. To reduce any anger that may be rising in the population due to the oppression of the elected President the democratic scheme ensures that the same person is never left in that office too long. Because the population is provided with the appearance that they can vote for a new President every 4 years and the same person is never there longer than 8 years, instead of rising up against the President a frustrated population will instead choose to wait until a "new" President is elected in hopes of receiving relief with sentiments like "only X amount of months before he's out of office," effectively PACIFYING the population.

Another layer of deflection is the multiple party system. By creating different parties (Democrats, Republicans, etc.) the population is DIVIDED as it chooses which side it wants to be aligned with. These divisions are designed to cause conflict amongst the population. As explained earlier, the human mind is naturally competitive. Once a side is chosen the other people are considered an enemy and a "we're better than them mentality arises" and all the prejudices that result therefrom. Now the population, divided into Republicans and Democrats, will fight against each other and will blame the other party for their oppression rather then the President. When someone from the Democratic party becomes President the frustration and anger level of the Republican party begins to rise. Before it gets to a boiling point someone from the Republican party becomes President, they become happy and their anger is reduced. Then while the Republican is in office the frustration and anger level of the Democratic party begins to rise. Before it gets to a boiling point someone from the Democratic party becomes President, they become happy and their anger is reduced. This alternating process acts as a sort of release valve keeping the anger level of the population as a whole under control. It effectively RE-DIRECTS their anger at each other and while they're DISTRACTED fighting between each other the population remains oblivious to the fact that the office of President is just a facade and the fact that the people who are really dictating the policy behind the scenes have never changed. Through the democratic scheme these people can "dictate" their wishes upon the unwitting population in secrecy without the worry of the population rising up against them. It's ingenious!

However, the mechanism of causing conflict amongst a population in order to exercise control over them is not a new concept. In Italy:

> When a prince conquered a neighboring city, he would sometimes breed internal conflicts among the vanquished citizens. This was an effective way to maintain political control over the people because the endless squabbling prevented the vanquished people from engaging in unified action against the conqueror. It did not greatly matter over what issues the people bickered so long as they valiantly struggled against one another and not against the conquering prince. (Rf2)

Because the concept of causing conflict and division to maintain control over a population is such an effective mechanism these people don't just attempt to divide the population by political affiliation, but also by economic status.

With the right instigation they pit the rich against the poor. The poor begin questioning why the rich have so much (wondering why 1% of the population has the majority of the nation's wealth) as their thought process becomes perverted with beliefs that the rich have some how taken something that belongs to the poor or that because the rich have it they can't obtain it.

The poor's envy of the riches' wealth turns to hatred as they begin blaming the rich for all their failures in life.

These types of sentiments are designed to cause a divide amongst mankind. The rich have not done anything wrong. On the contrary they have done exactly what people are supposed to do: work hard and over generations you will be able to make the lives of your descendants better. This is not a bad thing but what most people strive for. But whatever can be used to manipulate the population's thoughts and actions becomes an effect tool to exercise control over them.

If the population is fighting between each other over political affiliation, economic status, or racial class these created divisions prevent the population from uniting and rising up against the government.

Because anger and fear are by far the strongest emotions they are often used as a mechanism to manipulate the population into a particular train of thought. Wars are not only fought to obtain land, wealth, power, or to stop a dangerous regime, but wars are also waged:

> to encourage populations to think in ways that they would not otherwise do, and to accept the formation of institutions that they would normally reject. The longer a nation involves itself in wars, the more entrenched those institutions and ways of thinking will become. (Rf3)

For example, let's say the government wanted to take some type of military action against some area to achieve strategic goals. Military action puts the lives of family members who are serving in the military at risk, endangers the lives of innocent people living in the area they want to perform such military action, and costs taxpayers money. The population may become outraged at the government for taking what they believe to be unnecessary military action, and if this anger becomes too great, the government may even lose control over its population.

So how does the government prevent the population from directing its anger at the government while still achieving its strategic goals? By engineering a fake attack against itself and making the population believe it originated from the area in which the government wants to perform its military operation, instead of directing its anger at the government, the population will focus its anger at the people they believe attacked them. Now the population will not only accept the government's decision to perform military action in that area, but DEMAND that the government take action! It's all about re-directing anger in order to achieve its strategic goal while maintaining control of the population. For instance, researchers will point to events like

9/11 and explain how the government engineered the event in order to manipulate the population into a mindset that would not only allow them, but DEMAND that they take military action in the Middle East, military action that otherwise would have evoked strong protests against the government not only by the U.S. population, but world wide.

Conspiracy researchers unanimously speak of these Secret Societies with an evil connotation and blame them for every societal ill. In an attempt to substantiate their allegations they have even exposed documents which they claim were created by these societies over the years that evidence the various techniques they use to manipulate and maintain control over the population.

One document that is universally mentioned among researchers is the *Protocols of the Wise Men of Zion*, which is basically a MANUAL of how these Secret Societies manipulate the population to achieve their goals.

The Protocols begin by explaining that because there are more "men with bad instincts" in society "than good" it is not possible to appeal to their intellect by way of "academic discussions" in order to maintain control of the population. It explains that the majority of the population has a "lack of capacity to understand and respect the conditions of its own life, or its own welfare", is "guided solely by petty passions, paltry beliefs, customs, traditions and sentimental theorism" and acts like a disorganized, savage mob, that "displays its savagery at every opportunity." Therefore the best way to govern (control) them is "attained by violence and terrorisation".

The *Protocols* explain that by manipulating the opinions of the population to a certain view point, creating envy, fostering religious and race hatred they use the mob mentality of the population to sway their thoughts and actions in any direction they need in order to achieve their goals which were not obtainable by direct road.

They describe how to use the population's "passions which have burst into flames" and how to twist their ideas against them in order to distract them.

> The principle object of our directorate consists in this: to debilitate the public mind by criticism; to lead it away from serious reflections calculated to arouse resistance; to distract the forces of the mind...
>
> In order to put public opinion into our hands we must bring it into a state of bewilderment by giving expression from all sides to so many contradictory opinions and for such length of time as will suffice to make the [population] lose their heads in the labyrinth and come to see that the best thing is to have no opinion of any kind...

[The Protocols explain how they create] newspapers ... of all possible complexions - aristocratic, republican, revolutionary, even anarchical ... Like the Indian idol Vishnu they will have a hundred hands, and every one of them will have a finger on any one of the public opinions as required. When a pulse quickens these hands will lead opinion in the direction of our aims, for an excited patient loses all power of judgment and easily yields to suggestion. Those fools who will think they are repeating the opinion of a newspaper of their own camp will be repeating our opinion or any opinion that seems desirable for us. In the vain belief that they are following the organ of their party they will in fact follow the flag which we hang out for them.

The *Protocols* explain how through "the art of directing masses and individuals by means of cleverly manipulated theory and verbiage, by regulations of life in common and all sorts of other quirks, in all which the [population] understand nothing" they "set one against another the personal and national reckonings of the [population], religious and race hatreds, which we have fostered into huge growth in the course of the past twenty centuries."

In order to conceal what they are doing the *Protocols* explain how they "further distract them with amusements, games, pastimes, passions, people's palaces .... Soon we shall begin through the press to propose competitions in art, in sport of all kinds: these interests will finally distract their minds from questions in which we should find ourselves compelled to oppose them. Growing more and more disaccustomed to reflect and form any opinions of their own, people will begin to talk in the same tone as we, because we alone shall be offering them new directions for thought..."

We have fooled, bemused and corrupted the youth of the [population] by rearing them in principles and theories which are known to us to be false although it is by us that they have been inculcated. (Rf4)

If you truly want to learn the extent of the techniques they use to manipulate public opinion in order to exercise control I implore you to obtain a copy of the *Protocols* and read them for yourself.

In *Behold A Pale Horse* William Cooper presents another document entitled *"Silent Weapons for Quiet Wars,"* dated May 1979 (a copy of which was found in U.S. Naval Intelligence in 1969) which is said to have been adopted by the Policy Committee of the Bilderberg Group in 1954. It explains how they use diversion by:

keep[ing] the public undisciplined and ignorant of basic systems principles on the one hand, while keeping them confused, disorganized, and distracted with matters of no real importance on the other hand.

This is achieved by:

180

(1) disengaging their minds; sabotaging their mental activities; providing a low-quality program of public education in mathematics, logic, systems design and economics; and discouraging technical creativity.

(2) engaging their emotions, increasing their self-indulgence and their indulgence in emotional and physical activities, by:

(a) unrelenting emotional affrontations and attacks by way of a constant barrage of sex, violence, and wars in the media especially the T.V. and the newspapers.

(b) giving them what they desire - in excess - "junk food for thought" - and depriving them of what they really need.

(3) rewriting history and law and subjecting the public to the deviant creation, thus being able to shift their thinking from personal needs to highly fabricated outside priorities.

These preclude their interest in and discovery of the silent weapons of social automation technology.

The general rule is that there is profit in confusion; the more confusion, the more profit. Therefore, the best approach is to create problems and then offer the solutions.

...

Media: Keep the adult public attention diverted away from the real social issues, and captivated by matters of no real importance.

Schools: Keep the young public ignorant of real mathematics, real economics, real law, and real history.

Entertainment: Keep the public entertainment below a sixth-grade level.

Work: Keep the public busy, busy, busy, with no time to think; back on the farm with the other animals. (Rf5)

While there are many people who try to expose what these Secret Societies are doing, they are immediately branded as "one of those conspiracy theory nuts" by the controlled media in order to discredit the individual. And while today the internet makes it much harder to control the flow of information, don't be fooled into thinking that the government can't still have such information censored, not to mention the government's increased ability to interject disinformation.

All of this has led researchers to conclude that the goal of these Secret Societies "is to rule the world" (Rf6). Many authors even claim that these Secret Societies are being "controlled" by the Anunnaki/Elohim/Nephilim in order to enslave mankind (i.e. Jim Marrs in *Rule By Secrecy* (Rf7), Dr. Arthur

181

D. Horn in *Humanity's Extraterrestrial Origins* (Rf8), David Icke, in *The Biggest Secret* (Rf9), to name a few). In a twist, William Bramley in his book *The Gods of Eden* argues that Secret Societies were originally created to benefit mankind but they were defeated by the Anunnaki/Elohim/ Nephilim and are now being used by them as a tool to suppress knowledge, keep mankind divided and easily controlled (Rf10).

* * *

The history of these Secret Societies and their connections to our governments, banking systems, news media, etc., are well documented in other books so there is no need for me to rehash every detail herein, nor is it the objective of this book. I agree with these researchers on this limited aspect.

What I disagree with is their conclusion that, because of these connections and methods, Secret Societies are somehow evil and devising a plot to "rule the world" and enslave mankind. While those beliefs are echoed by many authors, they stem from a fundamental failure to understand *why* Secret Societies take certain courses of action. When you truly understand *why* all of this is being done the only conclusion that can rationally be reached is that these societies are not seeking World Domination, but ***World Unification*** in order to benefit mankind.

In order to comprehend this you first need to understand how to recognize GOOD and EVIL.

16

CONCEPT OF POSITIVE AND NEGATIVE

TO PROPERLY UNDERSTAND the role of Secret Societies you need to know how to recognize Good and Evil. For what you have been lead to believe is good or evil may actually be the exact opposite.

At the beginning of human evolution mankind lived by one law: eat or be eaten. As man began to observe his surroundings he witnessed the forces of nature (the cycles of the moon, the stars in the sky, the animals: primates, lions, tigers, leopards, birds, reptiles, etc., learning which animals were dangerous and which were not). From observing the forces of nature man understood that certain things were beneficial to him (POSITIVE) and that certain things were harmful to him (NEGATIVE).

Imagine yourself back in those times. Everything that you needed to survive (food, shelter, etc.) you had to acquire on your own. Whatever food, property, etc., that you managed to obtain, you then had to fight to keep because people were always lurking around trying to forcibly take it from you. It was survival of the fittest. There was no law, no government, no police to protect you. If you had a wife or children there was nothing to prevent a group of people from taking them from you, raping or murdering them. Only what you could manage to defend on your own.

There was no electricity; no light. When the Sun went down and everything turned pitch black that's when things really got scary. It was hard enough to fight off criminals in the daytime when you could see them, but in the darkness of night, that's when most of the violence occurred.

Imagine yourself in the blackness of night hearing screams of violence all around you, while you're trying to protect yourself, your family, your property. What would you be wishing for the most? LIGHT. In the light of daytime, at the very least, you could see what's around you to try and protect yourself.

From this, our ancient ancestors developed the concept of Light equaling POSITIVE (It was beneficial to man) and Darkness equaling NEGATIVE (It was harmful to man).

The Sun (which brought the Light) became the ultimate symbol of all things POSITIVE and was represented by early mankind as a dot: •.   When our ancestors learned that the planets revolved around the Sun, the symbol evolved into a dot centered within a circle ☉. It symbolized the Sun as the Pole Star of our solar system. Our early ancestors used this symbol to represent the One Supreme Positive Power.

As time went on, instead of understanding the concept of POSITIVE (meaning things that were beneficial to man) and NEGATIVE (things that were harmful to man) our ancestors began to mis-apply the concept. Because the Light of the Sun had such a strong positive influence they started equating all things that were light in color with POSITIVE and equating all things that were dark in color with NEGATIVE. The varying shades of light or dark determined how positive or how negative something was. You can clearly see how this error evolved into various religious doctrines:

We see it at work in the main religion of India, Hinduism (Brahmanism) where they created a caste system in order to divide society up into different levels of social importance in order to keep mankind disunited. Under the caste system, at birth the color of a person's skin was used to determine their position. The lighter your skin color was indicated the higher spiritual state of Karma you had accumulated in your previous life and now entitled you to a higher position in the caste system. The darker your skin color was indicated the negative level of Karma you accumulated in your previous life and you would now be placed lower in the caste system. Once you reached the lowest level, instead of being re-born as a human you would be re-born as an animal. The goal in Hinduism is to accumulate good Karma and at your next rebirth you will be born with lighter skin color and move up the caste system until you reach the highest level.

We also see it at work in the Mormon religion. The *Book of Mormon* equates whiteness with positivity/goodness and teaches people that God created dark skin as a curse/punishment for their sins. It explains that:

> because of their iniquity ... the Lord God did cause a skin of blackness to come upon them ... thus said the Lord God: I will cause that they shall be loathsome unto thy people ... And cursed shall be the seed of him that mixeth with their seed; for they shall be cursed even with the same cursing ... And because of their cursing which was upon them they did become an idle people, full of mischief and subtlety... (Rf1)

The *Book of Mormon* explains that this was done in order to distinguish good people from evil people. That the darkness of their skin was a "witness against them, and doth declare their sin, and they cannot hide it" (Rf2):

184

And the skins of the Lamanites were dark, according to the mark which was set upon their fathers, which was a curse upon them because of their transgression and their rebellion against their brethren... the Lord God set a mark upon them ... And this was done that their seed might be distinguished from the seed of their brethren, that thereby the Lord God might preserve his people, that they might not mix and believe in incorrect traditions which would prove their destruction. (Rf3)

Similar to what we saw in Hinduism, under Mormonism the shade of light or dark skin color that you were born with indicates the positive or negative degree of sin that you inherited.

We see it at work again in the Islamic religion. In Islam the *Qur'an* teaches its slaves that good people will be known by their "white" faces and be admitted into Paradise. Bad people who committed sins will be known by their "black" faces and will be damned to burn in Hell (Surah 3:106-107; and 55:39).

From ancient Egypt, where the "good" Horus I (I am the light of the world) was depicted in white (representing light and day), while the "evil" Sut was depicted in black (representing the night and darkness), to the oldest Christian Churches in Abyssinia, E. Africa, and the customs of the Central Americans, the Zapotecs and Mexicans, we find the tradition of painting the pictures of "good" faces white and "bad" faces black (Rf4).

I'm pointing this out to demonstrate how concepts became twisted over time. Clearly the color of an object, or of a person's skin, has nothing to do with whether it is POSITIVE (beneficial to man) or NEGATIVE (harmful to man).

Things that are POSITIVE (beneficial to man) encompass all forms of KNOWLEDGE (education, science, life extension, things that strengthen mankind) and are accordingly associated with the ⊙ symbol of POSITIVITY. Things that are NEGATIVE (harmful to man) encompass all things that impede positive goals. Eventually the terms Positive and Negative evolved into the terms GOOD and EVIL. There was nothing supernatural about it.

If you understand the concept of POSITIVE (= things that are beneficial to man; Good) and NEGATIVE (= things that are harmful to man; Evil), all you need to do is apply it to the facts to determine who's who.

185

17

ILLUMINATI:
THE RESISTANCE MOVEMENT
AGAINST
ANUNNAKI/ELOHIM/NEPHILIM
CONTROL

WHEN YOU APPLY the concept of Positive and Negative to Religions and Secret Societies to determine which of the two is really working for the benefit of mankind (Positive) and which of the two is really working against mankind (Negative), an undeniable truth is revealed.

It is actually the Religions who are working against mankind (Negative). Recall the history of the evil Anunnaki/Elohim/Nephilim (the people who have become mistaken as gods in the Judaic, Christian, and Islamic religions). Recall how they created mankind to be slaves because they needed someone to *"work the ground."* Recall how they treated us like animals; how they tried to keep their slaves away from the tree of *KNOWLEDGE*, any knowledge that would elevate us out of our slave status; how they continuously tried to kill us off by disease, starvation and the Great Flood. Recall the Tower of Babel incident when the ruthless leader Enlil/ El-Shaddai/Yahweh became enraged when he saw mankind all working together in one strong united force. Anger that resulted in his order to divide mankind up, his order to confuse our language so we could no longer communicate with each other, and his order to fight against anyone trying to re-unite the human race by a New World Order. A continuous course of action to keep mankind uneducated, divided, weak, and easily controlled. These are all NEGATIVE actions.

At every stage of human advancement their control mechanisms (the Religions) were there to keep mankind in darkness. When man said Earth was not the center of the solar system but actually revolved around the Sun, religious leaders argued that was the work of the devil and even killed people for making such claims. When man said Earth was not flat but round, religious leaders argued that was the work of the devil. When man discovered the science of evolution, religious leaders argued that was the work of the devil. When man wanted to explore space, religious leaders argued that was the work of the devil. At every stage of scientific advancement (we see it at work again surrounding stem cell research) religious leaders argued that it was the work of the devil and against god's will. Religions have continuously tried to keep mankind in darkness (away from the LIGHT) by keeping people away from knowledge, and by keeping mankind at war with each other so that we will remain divided. These are all NEGATIVE actions.

Everyone should be familiar with the concept of divide and conquer. One man standing alone is weak and easily controlled. A multitude of people standing together become a strong force. Things that divide us, weaken us (NEGATIVE). Things that unite us, strengthen us (POSITIVE).

Contrary to what you have been misled to believe, when you look past the ominous facade that has been falsely attributed to them, you'll discover that it is actually the Secret Societies that have been fighting to unite mankind (Positive), hence the terms One World Government and New World Order.

So what exactly is this so-called New World Order? Is it really something that mankind should be fighting against as Religious leaders claim?

One of the goals at the heart of every one of these organizations is the elimination of man-made national borders. Any time men draw a line in the sand and claim possession to that area there are always other men who are trying to take possession of that area from them which results in wars. Eliminating the national borders and uniting the world eliminates the wars between nations that arise.

Another goal is to establish one universal language. The ability of mankind to easily communicate with each other worldwide is paramount if we are to re-unite as one family.

These sentiments rest at the very foundation of these Secret Societies. For example, the Secret Society called the Round Table was founded by Cecil Rhodes. According to his will he stated that his purpose for creating this society was to bring about a one world government. He wanted to create "the foundation of so great a power as to hereafter render wars impossible and promote the best interests of humanity" (Rf1). Rhodes wanted to unify people by establishing a universal language, diminish nationalism and to increase awareness among people that they were part of a larger human community.

Members of these Secret Societies are not comprised of subversive elements but the greatest minds throughout history: philosophers, inventors, scientists, physicians, statesmen, astrologers, mathematicians, architects, painters. In one way or another they have not only been involved in, but the guiding force behind the exploration of new lands, the formation of our governments, banking systems, financial institutions, academic institutions, space exploration programs, etc.

The goals of the so-called New World Order are not goals that people should be fighting against, but are things that every human should be striving for.

Secret Societies have always acted for the greater benefit of mankind (Positive), relentlessly struggling over the millennia to educate, strengthen, and unify mankind in order to raise mankind out of the darkness and slavery imposed upon mankind by the Anunnaki/Elohim/Nephilim through their religious control mechanisms.

To explain this in a context that may be easier for you to understand, imagine that another country invaded the country that you are now living in. To maintain control of the population the enemy Rulers implement various mechanisms designed to weaken and eliminate possible threats of rebellion. They prohibit people from acquiring information (knowledge). Knowledge is power. An uneducated population is easier to manipulate and maintain control over. The enemy Rulers also divide the population up, separating you from your family members, even going so far as to create multiple spoken languages to prevent people from communicating with each other. Divide and conquer. Division weakens the population making it easier for the enemy Rulers to maintain control.

What would you do? Would you try to educate yourself (obtain knowledge)? Would you try to re-unite your family? I absolutely would. Certainly you would have to do it in secret, taking precautions so that the enemy Rulers didn't discover what you were doing. Wouldn't you also work with other people who are struggling to obtain the same goals? I would. A group of people working in secret towards a common goal is called a Secret Society. This is why the original Secret Society was formed.

A group of our ancestors banded together to fight against the evil Rulers (the Anunnaki/Elohim/Nephilim who, through various mis-translations and intentional deceptions have become known as the God/Allah of Judaism, Christianity, and Islam).

Remember, the Anunnaki/Elohim/Nephilim were not "Gods," just people, possibly from another planet, who possessed an advanced degree of scientific and technological abilities. Among these people were the brothers Enlil and Enki:

Enlil was appointed by his father Anu to be the Chief Commander on Earth. As discussed earlier, Enlil was against the creation of mankind from the beginning. He detested humans, ruthlessly ruled over them, demanded total "submission" from them, prevented them from obtaining any "knowledge" so that they would remain uneducated (not smart enough to devise any plans that would elevate themselves out of their slave status), and killed every human that disobeyed his commands. This was NEGATIVE (harmful to man).

Enki, on the other hand, had compassion for mankind. Enki felt that mankind should be educated and treated humanely. After witnessing the atrocities that his brother Enlil was committing against the human slaves Enki decided that he needed to take action to help benefit mankind.

Enki rebelled against his brother's order and provided mankind with "knowledge." This was POSITIVE (beneficial to man). Enki bestowed upon certain men the keys to great wisdom. It was then their job to educate the rest of mankind and lead them out of the bonds of slavery which had been imposed upon them by the Anunnaki/Elohim/Nephilim.

The first Secret Society was known as the *Brotherhood of the Snake* in homage to Enki (the Anunnaki/Elohim/Nephilim that rebelled against his own people in order to help benefit mankind; POSITIVE). It was also known as *The Brotherhood of the Serpent* and *The Brotherhood of the Dragon*. As recognized by Masonic author Manly P. Hall, "These illuminated ones founded what we know as the Ancient Mysteries." (Rf2)

As I previously explained, when Enki first landed on Earth he constructed his home in a snake infested marshland. From this Enki acquired the Snake/Serpent symbol as his Totem. Enki was a great scientist and healer (possessing all forms of knowledge). Because of this Enki's Snake/Serpent became a symbol of advanced knowledge and healing. The Snake/Serpent symbol can be found in one form or another throughout every culture of the world to represent the benevolent people who brought them knowledge and civilization. The Snake/Serpent symbol also became venerated by the humans that were resisting enslavement; to them it stood for freedom.

For thousands of years, to this very day, the symbol of the Snake/Serpent has always been used to signify wisdom, enlightenment, and advanced knowledge in the fields of science and medicine. For example:

The single serpent, entwined around the Tree of Knowledge (Fig. 17.1), is used as the insignia of the American and British Medical Associations (Rf3). It is called the Rod of Aesculapius and is often shown with him leaning on it. In some emblems it is lit at the top like a torch, symbolizing the divine Light of Wisdom (Rf4).

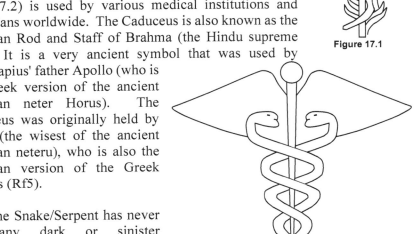

Figure 17.1

Two serpents entwined around the winged Caduceus (Fig. 17.2) is used by various medical institutions and Physicians worldwide. The Caduceus is also known as the Arcadian Rod and Staff of Brahma (the Hindu supreme god). It is a very ancient symbol that was used by Aesculapius' father Apollo (who is the Greek version of the ancient Egyptian neter Horus). The Caduceus was originally held by Thoth (the wisest of the ancient Egyptian neteru), who is also the Egyptian version of the Greek Hermes (Rf5).

The Snake/Serpent has never had any dark or sinister connotations until the Anunnaki/ Elohim/Nephilim's control mechanisms (Religions) imposed them. The Greek historian Plutarch even stated:

Figure 17.2

The men of old time associated the serpent ... with heroes (Rf6)

Likewise, as in Korea and Japan, Chinese dragons (which are synonymous with the Snake/Serpent) were generally beneficent and were held in the highest esteem (Rf7). Throughout Elam, Egypt, Phoenicia, Hatti, Persia, India, Greece, etc., the Snake/Serpent represented wisdom and healing (Rf8).

After the Great Flood, it is believed that the biblical Nimrod, guided by Enki, is one of the people who began to re-teach mankind the secret sciences (which would later become known as the arts/sciences of Freemasonry). Nimrod taught mankind that the Anunnaki/Elohim/Nephilim were not "gods." He taught mankind self-respect, to believe in themselves, to understand that it was their own hard work and courage which produced their happiness on Earth (Rf9). It is believed that it was Nimrod who led a rebellion against the evil Anunnaki/Elohim/Nephilim in the building of the Tower of Babel (Rf10).

190

The Bible speaks of Nimrod as "a mighty warrior on the Earth" (Genesis 10:8) and goes on to say: "He was a mighty hunter before YHWH (Enlil/El-Shaddai)" (Genesis 10:9). However, as pointed out by Dr. Strong, this is a mis-translation. The Hebrew word *paniym* which has been translated *before* is more correctly translated *against*. The proper translation is that Nimrod "was a mighty hunter *against* YHWH (Enlil/El-Shaddai)" (Rf11). Nimrod tried to educate, unite, and avenge mankind for what these evil Rulers did to our ancestors.

Through the generations, while mankind was forgetting what the Anunnaki/Elohim/Nephilim did to them, Secret Societies were preserving our true history. It was their job to illuminate society from out of the darkness and control of these evil Rulers.

Secret Societies are the resistance movement (freedom fighters) against Anunnaki/Elohim/Nephilim control. While Secret Societies have used many names over the years, they have always been the people who possessed the true knowledge of our origins, the enlightened ones, the illuminated ones: the Illuminati.

For thousands of years the Illuminati have been working in secret, behind the scenes, struggling to reunite mankind into one strong united force; the way we were before the evil Anunnaki/Elohim/Nephilim divided us at the Tower of Babel. Their goal is to educate and unite/strengthen the human race, while destroying all control mechanisms that the Anunnaki/Elohim/ Nephilim use to keep mankind weak, divided and under control. These are all POSITIVE actions.

Because the Illuminati work to eliminate all the control mechanisms that divide mankind (which include religions, kingships, national borders, multiple languages that inhibit people from communicating with each other, etc.) they are considered an enemy by all people that want to keep these control mechanisms in place.

This is *why* Religions demonize the Illuminati. The Illuminati know that the Judaic, Christian, and Islamic religions have nothing to do with God; that they are nothing more than the Anunnaki/Elohim/Nephilim's control mechanisms to keep mankind enslaved in darkness (away from the Light of God). The Illuminati know that through religious indoctrination:

The NEGATIVE (evil) brother (Enlil/El-Shaddai/YHWH), who was against mankind, became known as the vengeful, controlling, keep mankind

191

away from knowledge and divided "God/Allah" (Anunnaki/Elohim/Nephilim) of the Torah, Bible, and Qur'an.

The POSITIVE (good) brother (Enki), who rebelled against his brother's orders and took actions that were beneficial to mankind, was cast into the role of Satan. Despite the sinister connotation that the word satan takes on today, the word originally only meant: an adversary. Someone who was against your position. In their attempts to assassinate Enki's character Religions indoctrinated their slaves into believing that he was responsible for everything bad that happened to them and that he was trying to enslave mankind. They made him sound so horrific so that no person would dare listen to the truths he was trying teach mankind. Likewise, to Religions the POSITIVE Snake/Serpent symbol, which had always represented advanced knowledge, was now transformed into a symbol of Satan.

The Judaic, Christian, and Islamic Religions (who are based upon the NEGATIVE Enlil/El-Shaddai/YHWH) now demonize all people who are on the path to the LIGHT/POSITIVE/GOOD and call them satanists. Remember, history is always written by the stronger force regardless of whether that force is Positive or Negative. One man's freedom fighter is always another man's terrorist.

This religious indoctrination is further propagated when authors, who don't fully understand the issues involved, write about the Illuminati as if they were evil satanists seeking the destruction of mankind. For instance, while writing on the subject of Freemasonry, Ralph Epperson, in his book *The New World Order*, points out that "the secret inside the Masonic Order is that Lucifer is their secret god"; as if this fact was proof of some type of evil intention (Rf12).

Yes, it is well established that Masonry is based upon the Luciferian doctrine. Even Albert Pike (33° Mason) in his Instructions to the 23 Supreme Councils (July 14, 1889) confirmed that Masonry must be "maintained in the purity of the Luciferian doctrine" (Rf13). But he also clearly stated that the doctrine of Satanism is against everything that Masonry stands for.

Their mis-understanding stems from the confusion caused by the mis-translation of the word "God." Once you comprehend that the religious texts were not speaking of "God" (the Great Architect of the Universe) but were only identifying one of the Anunnaki/Elohim/Nephilim, things become clear.

As you now know "Light" was the term used to describe things that were POSITIVE (beneficial to man) like "knowledge." The Latin word for "Light" is *luc*. The Latin word for "Bringer of Light" or "Light-Bearer" is *lucifer*, also

192

known as the morning star which brought the Light! From the Latin "lucifer" we derive the word *luciferous* which means "Bringing Light or Insight." This is why Lucifer was depicted in Greek mythology as a man holding a torch (Light) (Rf14).

The word Lucifer just described the person who was taking actions that were beneficial to mankind (POSITIVE), like providing mankind with knowledge, uniting mankind, and emancipating mankind out of the bonds of slavery. Because the NEGATIVE (Evil) "god" of the Old Testament (who you now know was just Enlil, the Chief Commander of the Anunnaki/ Elohim/Nephilim) wanted to keep mankind away from *knowledge* (symbolized as Light), he demonized the "Bringer of Light," the "Light-Bearer," the person who was providing *knowledge* to mankind. The NEGATIVE "god" of the Old Testament tricked his slaves into believing that Lucifer was harmful to mankind. When you understand the concept of POSITIVE and NEGATIVE, it is clear that Lucifer was only taking actions that were beneficial to mankind.

Albert Pike (33° Mason) commented on how ridiculous it is when Religions try to trick people into believing that darkness is good and Light is evil:

> Lucifer, the Light-Bearer! *Strange and mysterious name to give to the spirit of darkness!* Lucifer, the son of the morning! It is he who bears the Light..." (Rf15)

The history of Enki's rebellion against his own people, specifically his brother Enlil's order to keep mankind away from *knowledge* and enslaved, is the actual event that would later evolve into the mythical story of Lucifer's rebellion against God. This is also why Lucifer's Zodiacal image is Capricorn, the LEAPING GOAT OF LIBERTY (Rf16). A goat leads, sheep follow a slave master.

Enki's rebellion generated many other legends of heroes based upon this same theme: "the most famous of which is the Greek god Prometheus, who is said to have stolen fire (knowledge) from the gods and given it to humans ... A gold statue of Prometheus [Fig.17.3] stands in Rockefeller Center in New York" (Rf17).

Figure 17.3

Interestingly, Jesus was also known as the "Bringer of Light" and called "the bright Morning Star" (Revelation 22:16) because Jesus was Illuminati. Jesus taught the same Luciferian doctrine, that the "god" of the Old Testament was really the NEGATIVE (Evil One; Devil), as you will see in the decoded ciphers in Chapter 18.

Masonry is a search after LIGHT (Positivity; things that benefit mankind) (Rf18). In Masonry Enlil/El-Shaddai/YHWH is called ADONAI. If you are unfamiliar with this word you need only look in the "notes on the translation" section of an English language Bible where you'll discover that instead of using the original word ADONAI that was contained in the biblical texts, they translated the word Adonai to "Lord" and where the original word is YHWH Adonai they translated it to "SOVEREIGN LORD." So this clearly proves that Adonai was another word used to describe YHWH, who was also known as El-Shaddai, who was also known as Enlil (the NEGATIVE Anunnaki/Elohim/Nephilim). In Masonry Enki is called Lucifer (the Bringer of Light, Knowledge).

While some researchers would argue that Masonry is designed to avenge the death of the Master Mason Hiram Abif (the builder of Solomon's Temple who was murdered by three assassins), that story is just esotericism, as Hiram Abif is not the true Grand Master.

The true Grand Master of Masonry is Man. Once you truly learn Masonic philosophy you'll discover that Masonry is designed to "avenge mankind" and "destroy all the control mechanisms" that the Anunnaki/ Elohim/Nephilim have used to enslave man. This is explained in the Official Ritual of the 33rd and last degree of Antient and Accepted Scottish Rites of Freemasonry:

The Order is the Great Avenger of the assassinated Grand Master and the grand champion of humanity, for *the innocent Grand Master is*

194

man, man who is Master, King of Nature, man who is born innocent and unconscious.

Our innocent Grand Master was born for happiness and for the enjoyment of all rights without exception.

But he has fallen under the blows of three assassins, three scoundrels have thwarted his happiness and rights and have annihilated him. (Rf19)

The assassins were the control mechanisms the Anunnaki/Elohim/Nephilim used to keep mankind away from knowledge, divided, and enslaved. The corrupt Religions, Laws, and Property rights that the Anunnaki/Elohim/ Nephilim imposed upon mankind. By destroying these evil control mechanisms, a true Religion based upon God can be implemented; a new Law in harmony with the rights of the individual man and the duties of social man in society can be created; with Property rights based upon the understanding that the Earth belongs to nobody and its fruits belong to all in proportion as they are required by each for the needs of his own well being.

Now understand that when they say "a Religion based upon God," they do not mean a religion based upon Lucifer (Enki) as opposed to the Judaic, Christian and Islamic Religions which are based upon the NEGATIVE Enlil/El-Shaddai/YHWH/Adonai. Remember, neither Lucifer nor Enlil/ El-Shaddai/YHWH/Adonai were "Gods." They were just the Anunnaki/ Elohim/Nephilim.

So don't be confused when you hear Masons making statements like: "Yes, Lucifer is God, and unfortunately Adonai is also God" because they are only using the word "god" in the same context that the Religions used it, to identify the Anunnaki/Elohim/Nephilim. The Masonic philosophy that "Lucifer, God of Light and God of Good, is struggling for humanity against Adonai, the God of Darkness and Evil" (Rf20) has nothing to do with "God," just the Anunnaki/Elohim/Nephilim and teaching you which one of them was POSITIVE (helping mankind) and which one of them was NEGATIVE (against mankind). A "Religion based upon God" would mean a theology based upon the Great Architect of the Universe and its scientific principles. The power/entity that created everything.

Despite what some authors would have you believe, the Bible is very important in Masonry because the Illuminati encoded ciphers into it. As explained by Albert Pike (33° Mason), these hidden messages are the Light (knowledge):

The Holy Bible, Square, and Compasses, are not only styled the Great Lights in Masonry, but they are technically called the Furniture of the Lodge; and, as you have seen, it is held that there is no Lodge without

195

them. ... properly understood, *[they] are the Lights by which a Mason must walk and work.* (Rf21)

While the Sun is known as The Blazing Star to Freemasons (Rf22), the Sun is not being worshipped. Mason's are speaking about the POSITIVE concept (Things that are beneficial to mankind), represented or symbolized by the positive affect the Light of the Sun has on mankind. Albert Pike explained how astrological symbols were just:

> *symbols of higher and profounder truths. None but the rude uncultivated intellects could long consider the sun and stars and the powers of nature as divine, or as fit objects of human worship...* (Rf23)

The Arts/Sciences of Freemasonry stem from the ancient knowledge Enki bestowed upon mankind. The Latin motto used by 33° Masons "DEUS MEUMQUE JUS" is translated as "God and My Right" or "God and My Justice." It stands for a belief in God (the Great Architect of the Universe) and a demand for justice for what was done to mankind by the evil Anunnaki/Elohim/Nephilim.

A proper understanding of what *lucifer* really is sheds *light* on why Masons rightfully follow Lucifer (Knowledge, Positivity: things that are beneficial to man). This also sheds light on the deceptive statements made by authors who try to demonize Secret Societies with scary claims that they are following "lucifer," and a host of other authors like William T. Still in his book *New World Order: The Ancient Plan of Secret Societies*, who point out how the initiation rites of Secret Societies "provide a system to gradually and gently realign a man's religious beliefs" (Rf24) as if these were bad things.

When you properly understand the true nature of religions, anyone trying to "gradually and gently" steer a person away from the darkness and control they impose upon mankind is certainly taking POSITIVE actions.

A group that wants mankind educated and united into one strong society is POSITIVE. The Illuminati are trying to educate and unite mankind, not separate it. Their actions are contrary to everything the "conspiracy" researchers claim and this is why they are dead wrong. For any researcher to write about the resistance movement (the people who seek to destroy all the control mechanisms like Religions) and try to convince you that they "are" the evil Anunnaki/Elohim/Nephilim of Religions is absurd and must make you question what their motives really are for saying such things.

196

Because the Illuminati are POSITIVE (taking actions that benefit mankind) they have become associated with the positive symbol (Fig. 17.4).

Figure 17.4

Over time our ancestors felt that this image looked like the pupil of an eye and eventually the image evolved into (Fig. 17.5). It is represented as such in Egyptian hieroglyphics where it was known as the Egyptian symbol for LIGHT. In Hebrew it was called *Ayin*. It was known as the Eye of Illumination and the All-Seeing-Eye. Enki even became known as the Lord of the Sacred Eye.

Figure 17.5

All humans who were seeking POSITIVE goals like education, advanced sciences, life extension, unity, etc., are said to be on the path to the LIGHT. Every journey begins at a symbolic door, and the Doorway to the Light, called the *Daleth*, is represented as an Eye inside of a Pyramid (Fig. 17.6).

Figure 17.6

While the Illuminati stay hidden behind the scenes fighting for humanity, their presence can be seen everywhere in hidden symbols:

On the back of the One Dollar Federal Reserve Note (Fig. 17.7) we find the Doorway to the Light, along with numerous other Illuminati symbols:

Figure 17.7

Above the Daleth is a tribute to the person who enlightened mankind in the Latin phrase "ANNUIT CEOPTIS", which means: "He hath prospered our beginning." Below the Pyramid is the Latin phrase "NOVUS ORDO SECLORUM", which means: "New Order of the Ages." The stated goal of this New World Order is contained on the banner that the Eagle (Phoenix) holds in its mouth. In Latin it says "E. PLURIBUS UNUM", which means: "Out of Many, One." Remember, the goal of the Illuminati is to destroy all the control mechanisms that divide us and then re-unite mankind into *one* strong family.

The occult number 13 is encoded in many places throughout the design. The cover story is that it represents the original 13 colonies, but that is far from the truth. Why the number 13 is important and why Religions have demonized it will be explained in the Fountain of Youth section. There are:

13 Letters in "Annuit Ceoptis"
13 Letters in "E Pluribus Unum"
13 Stars over the Eagle's head form SOLOMON's SEAL (HEXAGRAM)
13 Stripes on the Eagle's Breast Shield
13 Berries on the Olive Branch in the Eagle's right talon
13 Leaves on the Olive Branch
13 Arrows in the Eagle's left talon
13 Levels in the Pyramid to reach the Daleth

And it is no coincidence that it was the *ONE* dollar bill, not the $5, $10, $20, $50, or $100, that was chosen to contain all of this symbolism! Six men had a part in the bill's design: Benjamin Franklin, John Adams, Thomas Jeferson, Francis Hopkinson, Charles Thompson (Secretary of Continental Congress), and William Barton (who designed the Pyramid, All-Seeing-Eye, and Latin inscriptions). It was Franklin Delano Roosevelt who approved the final design. All of these men were Masons (Rf25).

And if you have any doubt that the designers were Masons, they encoded their name into the design. If you place an apex down pyramid (triangle) over the apex up pyramid (triangle), aligning the horizontal edge with the bottom of the raised capstone you will see that the image forms the familiar six pointed star, also known as a hexagram, the Star of David, or Solomon's Seal. The image points to five letters which collectively spell **MASON**! (Fig.17.8). A clue to decoding this secret can be found in the

Figure 17.8

cloud above the eagle's head which contains "13" stars forming this image. While some people often use the inverted pentagram to decode this secret (instead of the apex down pyramid) its use here is not accurate. These people hold the mistaken belief that the inverted pentagram reflects something sinister and therefore use it here in an attempt to attribute that propaganda to the image's message. What the six pointed star (Star of David, Solomon's Seal) actually symbolizes is the mystical third state of enlightenment that is achieved

198

by the combining of the two opposites, which is a topic that will be discussed in another chapter.

Another symbol of the Illuminati is the Statue of Liberty. Notice how similar it is to the ancient Greek portrayal of Lucifer who was depicted as a human holding a torch.

The Statue of Liberty (Fig. 17.9) stands on Liberty Island in the N.Y./N.J. harbor holding up in her right hand the Lighted Torch of Lucifer (Light-Bearer). The benevolent person bringing "knowledge" and "freedom" to mankind. Crowned on her head are "seven" rays of the Sun.

Figure 17.9   Figure 17.10

The Statue of Liberty was given to America by France. Its "mirror image" (Fig. 17.10) can be found in Paris on an island in the River Seine (Rf26).

It would take many books to reveal all of the places in which Illuminati symbolism can be found. I have listed these just to demonstrate my point.

With a proper understanding of POSITIVE (beneficial to man) and NEGATIVE (harmful to man) it is possible to see through the darkness that Religions continuously try to impose upon society.

The Illuminati were, and continue to be, a resistance movement against the attempts to divide and control mankind. Their sole purpose is to re-unite mankind into one strong united force so that we will be strong enough to defend ourselves against the Anunnaki/Elohim/Nephilim when they return, and to learn the secret sciences that they have continuously tried to prevent mankind from obtaining.

The Illuminati have been trying to teach this "knowledge" to mankind, but had to disseminate that *knowledge* secretly. It did so by encoding ciphers in ancient documents; some of which eventually became collectively known as the Bible. Only those who "had ears" (were initiated / possessed the key) would truly understand what was being taught. All others would remain oblivious.

18

THE GARDEN OF EDEN, THE TREE OF KNOWLEDGE and THE GOOD AND EVIL KNOWLEDGE THAT MAN LEARNED

ONE EXAMPLE OF a cipher encoded into the Bible where the Illuminati teach mankind that the *god* of the Old Testament (Enlil/El-Shaddai/ YHWH/Adonai the Chief Commander of the Anunnaki /Elohim/Nephilim) is actually the NEGATIVE (evil one), is the Garden of Eden passage.

According to the Bible, when *god* placed Adam and Eve in the Garden of Eden he told them:

> ...you must not eat from the tree of the knowledge of GOOD and EVIL, for when you eat of it you will surely die. (Genesis 2:17)

The Serpent told Adam and Eve that god is lying to you and if you eat of the tree:

> You will surely not die, ... For God knows that when you eat of it your eyes will be opened, and you will be like God, *knowing GOOD and EVIL*. (Genesis 3:4-5)

Adam and Eve ate from the tree and they did not die. Instead, they gained the knowledge of **GOOD and EVIL**.

Many people read over this passage time and again and never really understand what the message is. It's similar to watching a magic trick. The magician holds a card in his hand, then makes it disappear. You watch it over and over but can't figure out how he's doing it. He tells you the "secret," that the card is attached to a wire and when he lets go of the card it retracts up his sleeve. After learning the "secret" you watch the trick again and now you can "see" what you couldn't before; the card disappearing up his sleeve.

When you read the Garden of Eden passage the question you should be asking yourself is:

201

What was *the GOOD and EVIL knowledge* that Adam and Eve learned from eating of this tree?

Let's look at what we consider *Good* qualities and what we consider *Evil* qualities:

Good
Telling the Truth/Honesty

Evil
Telling Lies/Deception

If we apply these principles to the Garden of Eden passage:

- it was in fact god who was lying to man when he said "you will surely die" if you eat of the tree.

- it was in fact the Serpent who was truthful/honest to man when he said god is lying to you, "you will surely not die" if you eat of the tree, but you will become like god

The *GOOD and EVIL* knowledge that Adam and Eve learned was that *god*, who was lying to them, was **Evil** (NEGATIVE; harmful to man) and the *Serpent*, who was telling them the truth, was **Good** (POSITIVE; beneficial to man).

Now that Adam and Eve learned that *god* had been lying to them, their "eyes were opened." They were able to *see* something they couldn't see before. Prior to this time mankind had blindly accepted whatever *god* told them. After learning this Adam and Eve began questioning everything else so-called *god* had told them.

At that point in time mankind served their Anunnaki/Elohim/Nephilim masters naked. They told mankind that they were slaves and only the *gods* wore clothing. Whether mankind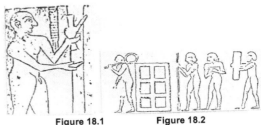

Figure 18.1   Figure 18.2

was working in the fields, serving their masters food and drinks, or working on construction jobs they performed their duties naked. Similar to the way a dog walks around naked. Ancient Sumerian depictions show naked slaves serving their *clothed* Anunnaki/Elohim/Nephilim masters (Figs. 18.1 & 18.2) (Rf1). Another tablet found at Nippur shows Enlil/El-Shaddai/YHWH and Ninlil being served food and beverage at their temple by two naked slaves (Fig. 18.3) (Rf2). Also (Fig. 18.4) where a naked slave serves his Anunnaki/Elohim/Nephilim masters (Rf3).

Figure 18.3   Figure 18.4

There Are also ancient texts showing that clothing was given to man once his status was elevated. In *The Epic of Gilgamesh* (Rf4) Enkidu walked around naked. He was taught that he shouldn't be roaming around like the animals because he was "like a god are thou!" and he was given garments to cloth himself with in order to mark his status. In the *Adapa Tablet* after being summoned before Anu, Adapa was given clothes and anointed with oil then returned to Earth where he became priest-king under Enki (Rf5).

Because Adam and Eve's eyes were *opened* they realized that they were being treated like domesticated animals. They weren't ashamed of being naked. They were ashamed of what the naked status stood for (their enslavement), and how they foolishly believed the lies the Anunnaki/ Elohim/Nephilim had told them.

> ...so they sewed fig leaves together and made coverings for themselves.
> (Genesis 3:7)

When *god* returned to the Garden of Eden, Adam and Eve hid behind a tree (Genesis 3:8). With all the special ability we attribute to him, *god* could not find Adam and Eve who were only hiding behind a tree. So *god* called out to Adam and Eve in bewilderment: "Where are you?" (Genesis 3:9). The all-knowing *god* was further unaware if man had eaten of the tree or not and he said:

> Who told you that you were naked? Have you eaten from the tree that
> I commanded you not to eat from? (Genesis 3:11)

Because man now knew his true status *god* made garments for Adam and Eve, clothed them, and acknowledged their elevated status that *"man has now become like one of us."* (Genesis 3:21-22).

The *god* of the Old Testament did not want mankind to have any knowledge that would elevate man beyond his primitive slave status. It was the Serpent who wanted mankind to be educated and provided man with knowledge.

Now that you know the person identified as *god* in the Old Testament was not *God* but just Enlil/El-Shaddai/YHWH (the Chief Commander of the Anunnaki/Elohim/Nephilim) and that the person identified as the *serpent* was just his brother Enki, you can examine the Garden of Eden passage in a new Light:

> And **Enlil** commanded the man, "you must not eat from the tree of the knowledge of GOOD and EVIL for when you eat of it you will surely die." (Genesis 2:17)
>
> "You will surely not die," **Enki** said to the woman. "For Enlil knows that when you eat of it your eyes will be opened, and you will be like Enlil, knowing **GOOD and EVIL**." (Genesis 3:4-5)

The ***GOOD and EVIL*** knowledge that man learned was that Enlil, who was lying to man, was Evil (NEGATIVE), and Enki, who was truthful to man, was Good (POSITIVE). This cipher was designed to teach mankind which of his Anunnaki/Elohim/Nephilim masters was POSITIVE (beneficial to mankind) and which was NEGATIVE (harmful to mankind).

This also sheds Light on the passage where Enlil/El-Shaddai/YHWH could not locate Adam and Eve in the Garden of Eden, even though they were only hiding behind a tree, and Enlil had to call out "Where are you?". Enlil didn't even know whether they had eaten from the tree or not. Certainly an all knowing *God* would know man was behind a tree. By using the name *Enlil* in place of the mis-translated *God*, the passage makes sense.

This is one of the secrets the Illuminati encoded into the Bible. Hidden in plain sight from the Anunnaki/Elohim/Nephilim rulers, to be spread amongst mankind to all who can decipher the message.

Some people argue that the *knowledge* man obtained was the ability to procreate and it is this knowledge that *god* did not want man to have. This is absurd and could not be farther from the truth. If you look at the ancient texts detailing the creation of man, the Anunnaki/Elohim/Nephilim fully intended that man would have the ability to procreate. See Chapter 4. They created 7 males and 7 females. The fact that both sexes were created demonstrates that they fully intended to make them capable of reproduction. Even the Bible states that *before* the Garden of Eden occurred man and woman were to become one flesh and procreate:

male and female he created them   (Genesis 1:27)

Be fruitful and increase in number   (Genesis 1:28)

a man will leave his father and
mother and be united to his wife,
and they will become one flesh.   (Genesis 2:24)

and even though at this point in time they already had the ability to procreate:

The man and his wife were both
naked, and they felt no shame.   (Genesis 2:25)

The Bible specifies that before the Garden of Eden occurred Adam and Eve already had the ability to procreate, and while both of them were naked, they still felt no shame. So it is absurd for someone to argue that the "knowledge" Adam and Eve obtained in the Garden of Eden was the knowledge of procreation and that because they now knew how to procreate they were ashamed of being naked. They were ashamed at what the naked status stood for: being a slave.

The reason that Adam and Eve were kicked out of the Garden of Eden was because their eyes were now *opened*. They now knew that the Anunnaki/Elohim/Nephilim were lying to them and they would no longer blindly follow just any-old-thing they were being told. Remember, the Anunnaki/Elohim/Nephilim also didn't want mankind to eat of the Tree of Life and live forever. Because they could no longer trust that Adam and Eve would blindly do what they were told (and not eat of the Tree of Life), they had to kick Adam and Eve out of Eden so they wouldn't have access to the Tree of Life:

He must not be allowed to reach out his hand and take also from the
tree of life and eat, and live forever. (Genesis 3:22)

The Anunnaki/Elohim/Nephilim also had to station guards to protect the Tree of Life in case Adam and Eve snuck back and tried to eat of it:

After he drove the man out, he placed in front of the Garden of Eden
cherubim and a flaming sword flashing back and forth to guard the way
to the tree of life. (Genesis 3:24)

* * *

Another cipher encoded into the Bible, where it teaches you that the *god* of the Old Testament was really the NEGATIVE (Evil One; Satan), is found in the New Testament. Examine the following two passages:

205

The Old Testament describes the following event:

- Moses is led to a desert.
- Moses is taken to a very high mountain (Mount Sinai).
- Moses spends 40 days and 40 nights there with no food.
- Enlil/El-Shaddai/YHWH visits Moses and shows him all the kingdoms that would be provided to him and the Israelites if they "bowed down and worshipped him."

The New Testament describes the following event:

- Jesus is led to a desert.
- Jesus spends 40 days and 40 nights there with no food.
- Jesus is taken to a very high mountain.
- A tempter visits Jesus and shows "him all the kingdoms of the world and their splendor. "All this I will give you," he said, "if you will bow down and worship me." (Matthew 4:1-2 & 4:8-9)

As we know from the Old Testament, Moses accepted Enlil's offer, but Jesus refused the temptation, saying:

"Away from me, Satan!" (Matthew 4:10)

In this cipher Jesus is teaching you that the *god* of the Old Testament (Enlil/El-Shaddai/YHWH/Adonai, Chief Commander of the Anunnaki/ Elohim/Nephilim) that Moses met on Mount Sinai, was really Satan; the NEGATIVE (Evil One).

* * *

Another cipher in which this is taught is found in the story of Jacob and his fight against the *god* of the Old Testament.

It begins by setting the stage that during the "night" a man attacks Jacob and wrestles with him until daybreak. (Genesis 32:24). The *man* is really *god* of the Old Testament. The attack occurring at "night" (darkness, NEGATIVE) is equating the *god* of the Old Testament with NEGATIVITY.

The *man* (god of the Old Testament) could not overpower Jacob even though he tried all night long (Genesis 32:25).

When daybreak arrives the *man* (god of the Old Testament) starts pleading with Jacob to "Let me go" (Genesis 32:26).

Understand the symbolism: The NEGATIVE was screaming "Let me go" because the "daybreak" (the LIGHT, POSITIVE) had arrived. It is only by struggling against the NEGATIVE that you can obtain the POSITIVE.

Because Jacob had fought against the NEGATIVE *god* of the Old Testament Jacob's name was now changed to Israel (he struggles against God). As the Bible explains it, it was done:

> because you have struggled with Elohim and with men and have overcome. (Genesis 32:28)

This cipher is teaching you that only by fighting against the NEGATIVE *god* of the Old Testament (the evil Anunnaki/Elohim/Nephilim) can you overcome and ascend.

19

THE FOUNTAIN OF YOUTH

ANOTHER SECRET that the Illuminati encoded into the Bible was the science of how to extend the human life-span. Remember, the Anunnaki/Elohim/Nephilim wanted mankind to remain weak, unintelligent, divided, and easily under control. One way of achieving this goal was limiting how long humans lived. Any *knowledge* (science) that increased the human life-span was off limits to mankind, so it had to be encoded in ciphers.

When we read the Bible we learn that our ancestors, from Adam to Noah, had incredibly long life-spans of almost 1,000 years. Most people continue reading on without giving this a second thought. However, if you study what is being taught, and make a list of the life-spans, you'll discover that a chart emerges:

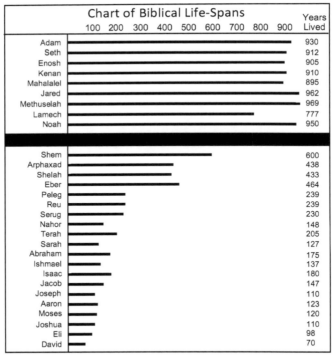

In the chart you can clearly see that our life-spans dramatically decreased after the time of Noah. The questions that immediately arise are:

(1) What happened during the time of Noah that resulted in our decreased life-spans?

(2) And *WHY* did our ancestors feel that this was such an important point that they needed to draw our attention to it by encoding this chart into the Bible?

As far back as we can peer into mankind's past, throughout every culture we find legends and myths of a Fountain of Youth; the waters of which are said to rejuvenate the old.

The search to find this **Fountain of Youth** was even the driving force behind countless explorations that occurred throughout history. For example:

The Greek historian Herodotus, in his book *Histories*, V.III, described the conquests of Cambyses (son of the Persian King Cyrus). Cambyses sent emissaries to the King of Ethiopia to find out why the Ethiopians had such long life-spans, because the "longest term of a man's life among the Persians" was only eighty years old:

> The king led them to a fountain, wherein when they had washed, they found their flesh all glossy and sleek, as if they had bathed in oil. And a scent came from the spring like that of violets.
>
> ...Herodotus noted the following conclusion:
>
> If the account of this information be true, it would be their (the Ethiopians') constant use of the water from it, which makes them so long-lived. (Rf1)

The quest to find the Fountain of Youth was also taken on by Alexander the Great. It is believed that Alexander learned of the legends from his teacher, the philosopher Aristotle (Rf2). The conquests and explorations of Alexander were recorded by the Greek historian Callisthenes of Olynthus. While his original writings disappeared, centuries later a Latin text known as "pseudo-Callisthenes" emerged. Similar versions have since been discovered in Hebrew, Arabic, Persian, Syriac, Armenian, Ethiopian and at least three Greek versions (Rf3).

The texts describe his legendary conquests of the Persian armies throughout Asia Minor and Egypt and then go on to describe his encounter with an angel after leaving Egypt, in which:

> the angel said to him: 'I will tell thee something whereby thou mayest live and not die.' ...
> In the land of Arabia, God hath set the blackness of solid darkness, wherein is hidden a treasury of this knowledge. There too is the

fountain of water which is called "The Water of Life"; and whosoever drinketh therefrom, if it be but a single drop, shall never die.

Despite Alexander's pleas to find out "In which quarter of the earth is this fountain of water situated?", the angel's cryptic response was "Ask those men who are heirs to the knowledge thereof" (Rf4). And you should know by now that *the men who are the heirs to the knowledge thereof* were the Illuminati.

In more recent times, the search for the Fountain of Youth was taken on by Christopher Columbus on behalf of the King and Queen of Spain. During his 1492 expedition in the New World he captured and questioned Indians in attempts to locate the fountain. The Indians advised him that there was a "spring" in which an islander:

"grievously oppressed with old age" had drunk. As a result, he "brought home manly strength and has practiced all manly performances, having taken a wife again and begotten children." (Rf5)

After the King and Queen of Spain were advised of this, in 1513 they sent Ponce de Leon to search for this magical fountain. Upon reaching the hundreds of islands of the Bahamas they searched island after island without any success.

As explained by Spanish historian Antonio de Herrera y Tordesillas in his *Historia General de las Indias*:

He went seeking that Sacred Fountain, so renowned among the Indians, as well as the river whose waters rejuvenated the aged. (Rf6)

Ponce de Leon was sent out again in 1521 to search Florida for the fountain, but again returned without success. Leonardo Olschki, in his book *Ponce de Leon's Fountain of Youth: History of a Geographical Myth*:

established that "the Fountain of Youth was the most popular and characteristic expression of the emotions and expectations which agitated the conquerors of the New World." (Rf7)

Whether we're reading biblical texts or the legends of diverse cultures around the world, all assert a belief in the Fountain of Youth. And regardless of whether the particular legend or myth is describing it as a "fountain," "well," "spring," "stream," or "lake," the universal theme is that it contains the ***Water of Life***.

But remember, truths were hidden in symbolism. If you study the legends closely you'll realize that the term *water of life* is a euphemism. It is not literally *water* that they are identifying; it was the *Water of Life*. The *liquid substance* that is *Life*. Drinking it extends your life-span.

210

Blood is the *water of life*! It was because our ancestors drank blood on a daily basis that they lived such incredibly long lives. While at first this may be shocking and difficult for you to accept, nonetheless, it is true and becomes evident once you study the history of what the Anunnaki/Elohim/ Nephilim did to mankind and the science behind drinking blood.

In the beginning, one of the methods they used to try and keep mankind weak was restricting the types of foods that mankind could eat. If we weren't properly nourished we wouldn't be as strong as them and therefore not as much of a threat. As recorded in the Bible, they issued the order that mankind would only be allowed to eat plants and fruits:

> I give you every seed-bearing plant on the face of the whole earth and every tree that has fruit with seed in it. They will be yours for food. (Genesis 1:29)

At that point in time meat and blood were food reserved for the Anunnaki/ Elohim/Nephilim alone. And as we learn from the ancient Mesopotamian, Egyptian, Mesoamerican, and biblical texts, they required that mankind provide them with human sacrifices on a daily basis. They even gave mankind specific rules on how to prepare this "cooked offering." Much of what you see in the Bible, in this regard, is a deliberate distortion to mask the widespread tradition of human sacrifice and cannibalism that was practiced from the beginning of mankind.

In fact, this was the true purpose behind why the Anunnaki/Elohim/ Nephilim required mankind to sacrifice all their firstborn children to them, as recorded in the biblical texts:

> The firstborn of every womb belongs to me. (Exodus 34:19-20)

> The first offspring of every womb among the Israelites belongs to me whether man or animal. (Exodus 13:1-2)

And (2 Kings 16:3-4) evidences that many people were in fact sacrificing their children, but over time they began doing it for other "gods."

When the *god* of the Old Testament (Enlil/El-Shaddai/YHWH the Chief Commander of the Anunnaki/Elohim/Nephilim) learned that the human sacrifices, *that were only suppose to go to him*, were being given to other people, he became angry. We see this anger in his orders specifying that human sacrifices were only to be made to him and not to Molech: Leviticus 18:21 orders *"of your children to be sacrificed"* do not given any to Molech;

211

and Leviticus 20:1-5 orders the punishment of death to anyone who sacrifices the children that are required to be sacrificed to him, to Molech.

After Adam and Eve gained *knowledge* (learning that these people weren't *Gods*, but were deceiving mankind and keeping them enslaved) they no longer blindly followed just any-old-thing that the Anunnaki/Elohim/ Nephilim were telling them. After observing them eat animals and humans, our ancestors began to do the same thing.

Evidence that our ancestors were cannibals can be found throughout ancient texts as well as modern archaeological discoveries. The *Book of Enoch* explains how mankind:

> began ... to devour one another's flesh, and drink the blood. (Rf8)

The *Atrahasis Epic* describes a period of time when parents ate their "daughter for a meal" and ate their child for "morsels" and how "one house devour[ed] another" (Rf9). The Bible explains how our ancestors "sacrificed their sons and their daughters" shedding their blood (Psalm 106:37-38) and "ate the sacrifices" (Psalm 106:28).

Many archaeological sites have been discovered showing clear evidence of cannibalism. In the caves of Southern France, dating to circa 55,000 to 35,000 B.C., skeletal remains have been found showing signs of cannibalism. As reported in *Secrets of the Ice Age* by Evan Hadingham, in the L'Hortus cave, among the many human skull and jaw bone fragments, two human long bones were found showing intentional breakages (identical to those of animal bones) undoubtedly in order to extract the marrow which is quite nutritious (Rf10).

The July 18, 1986 issue of the *New York Times* reported that in the Fontbregoua Cave 6000 year old human bones were found demonstrating that humans were:

> butchered, processed, and probably eaten in a manner that closely parallels the treatment of wild and domesticated animals.

The international team of scientists discovered "that raw meat was stripped from the bones ... [the bones were] broken to extract the marrow", and then disposed of in a refuse pit (Rf11).

In El Sidron, Spain, dating to 49,000 years ago, the Neanderthal bones of 6 adults and 6 children were found in a cave showing clear signs (cut marks) that they were cannibalized. It was determined that they didn't live in the cave;

212

that their remains were dumped there after being eaten. Archaeologists even found the stone tools used to cannibalize them (Rf12).

From the ancient texts, archaeological discoveries, and the many biblical verses, we can come to the conclusion that the consumption of blood was a routine practice amongst our early ancestors.

When the Anunnaki/Elohim/Nephilim discovered that mankind was violating their rule to only eat plants and fruits they became enraged. They wanted to keep their slaves weak and this posed a severe problem for them.

This was the main reason why the NEGATIVE Enlil/El-Shaddai/ Yahweh decided to impose his wrath upon mankind and kill us off in the Great Flood. The POSITIVE Enki intervened, advised Noah to build a ship, which saved the lives of Noah, his family, and a few others. After learning that Noah and his family had survived, Enlil/El-Shaddai/YHWH had a change of heart and decided to allow them to live. For a detailed account see Chapter 7 (The Great Flood).

What's particularly important to this section is the fact that after all of this the ONLY law that Enlil/El-Shaddai/YHWH imposed upon mankind was that man was not allowed to drink blood:

> Everything that lives and moves will be food for you. Just as I gave
> you the green plants, I now give you everything. (Genesis 9:3)
>
> *But you must not eat meat that has its lifeblood still in it.* (Genesis 9:4)

This order was repeated in Leviticus: "Do not eat meat with the blood still in it." (20:26, and see also 7:26-27).

Enlil/El-Shaddai/Yahweh went on to describe how his wrath would come down upon any human who drinks blood:

> Any ... among them who eats any blood - I will set my face against
> that person who eats blood and will cut him off from his people.
> (Leviticus 17:10)
>
> For the life of a creature is in the blood ... None of you may eat blood.
> (Leviticus 17:11-12)
>
> Any ... among you who hunts any animal or bird that may be eaten
> must drain out the blood and cover it with earth, because the life of
> every creature is its blood. That is why I have said ..."You must not
> eat the blood of any creature, because the life of every creature is its
> blood; (Leviticus 17:13-14)

The order not to drink blood is also found in the Qur'an: "He has forbidden you ... blood" (Surahs 2:173 and 16:115).

At this point the Anunnaki/Elohim/Nephilim realized that they weren't going to be able to trick mankind into believing that meat was bad for them. From seeing them eat it mankind learned that it was good (it was a bell that was not going to be unrung). However, just because mankind knew that meat was good for them didn't mean they understood the science behind it. The Anunnaki/Elohim/Nephilim were able to use this ignorance to their advantage.

So after the Great Flood they were now allowing mankind to eat anything that "lives and moves." They didn't care what humans ate as long as we didn't drink the blood. Because mankind didn't understand the beneficial effects of blood, they accepted the order without any resistance.

And after witnessing the devastation caused by the Great Flood, man was certainly not going to violate (what must have seemed to them as) such a minor order from the Anunnaki/Elohim/Nephilim not to drink blood. This is why many cultures, including Jews and Muslims, hang their meat and let all the blood drip out before they prepare the meat for consumption. Removing the blood is the only way meat is considered *kosher* under Jewish practice or *halal* under Muslim practice. This blood letting is a practice that continues to this very day.

The Anunnaki/Elohim/Nephilim just destroyed almost all of mankind and the *ONLY* order is: *don't drink blood?!?* Why were they trying so hard to prevent man from drinking blood? This is the question that arises.

Remember, Enlil/El-Shaddai/YHWH was the NEGATIVE Anunnaki/Elohim/Nephilim. He was against mankind. Recall how he continuously tried to keep mankind away from *knowledge* and enslaved; how he tried to kill us off by disease, starvation and then the Great Flood. Recall the Tower of Babel incident, when he became enraged that mankind was working together as one strong united force so he divided mankind, to weaken us.

Based upon all of this, you can be certain that the order from the NEGATIVE Enlil/El-Shaddai/YHWH to stop drinking blood was not something that was beneficial to mankind. Any order from this Anunnaki/Elohim/Nephilim was certainly designed to weaken mankind.

And from the very moment that the Anunnaki/Elohim/Nephilim ordered Noah and his descendants to stop drinking blood, we see the dramatic drop in human life-spans!

Chart of Biblical Life-Spans

Name	Years Lived
Adam	930
Seth	912
Enosh	905
Kenan	910
Mahalalel	895
Jared	962
Methuselah	969
Lamech	777
Noah	950
Man Ordered Not to Consume Blood Anymore	
Shem	600
Arphaxad	438
Shelah	433
Eber	464
Peleg	239
Reu	239
Serug	230
Nahor	148
Terah	205
Sarah	127
Abraham	175
Ishmael	137
Isaac	180
Jacob	147
Joseph	110
Aaron	123
Moses	120
Joshua	110
Eli	98
David	70

(X-axis scale: 100 200 300 400 500 600 700 800 900)

Because mankind was no longer drinking the **Water of Life** (Blood) our life-spans decreased. This is why our ancestors encoded this chart into the Bible, to teach us this science. Jesus understood this. What did Jesus teach everyone who would listen?:

This is the blood of my body, drink it!
It will give you everlasting life (Rf13)

As I explained in Part II, Jesus' esoteric education began almost at the time of his birth. Beginning with the teachings of the Essene Community during his childhood, to his travels throughout Asia, Persia, Greece, and his stay in the Egyptian City of Heliopolis where it is believed that he was initiated into the higher ranks of the Mystery Schools (Rf14). When he ordered his disciples to drink his blood, Jesus broke Enlil/El-Shaddai/Yahweh's strictest law.

The portrayal of Jesus as a *carpenter* in modern English language Bibles is based upon a blatant mis-translation. The word *carpenter* was wrongly translated from the ancient Greek *ho tekton*, which was itself derived from the Semitic word *naggar*. As pointed out by the Semitic scholar Dr. Geza Vermes, the word more properly defines a scholar or teacher. This did not identify Jesus as a woodworker, but:

Through the Mystery Schools Jesus became Illuminati, a *Master of the Craft*, a learned alchemist, not a *carpenter*. Jesus learned the ancient secret sciences of the Anunnaki/Elohim/Nephilim and was trying to teach them to his fellow man. Even the Qur'an hints at the secret science encoded into the Bible about extending life-span to 1,000 years, calling the people who would utilize it "the greediest of mankind for life" (s.2:96).

* * *

The Science Behind Drinking Blood

Why does drinking blood lengthen our life-span? In order to comprehend this you need to understand the basics behind why we age.

At the time of conception stem cells are created which begin to give rise to differentiated cells and form the basic structure (the fundamental tissues, primitive organs and organ systems) in the developing embryo according to the specific "coding" of the DNA. The process is known as embyrogenesis and lasts for 8 weeks resulting in a fetus.

Every part of the human body is made up of individual cells that have been massed together according to the coding of its DNA. Each individual cell is:

> a small usually microscopic mass of protoplasm bounded externally by a semipermeable membrane usually including one or more nuclei and various other organelles with their products, capable alone or interacting with other cells of performing all the fundamental functions of life, and forming the smallest structural unit of living matter capable of functioning independently. (Rf16)

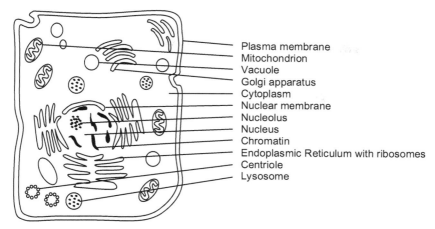

Plasma membrane
Mitochondrion
Vacuole
Golgi apparatus
Cytoplasm
Nuclear membrane
Nucleolus
Nucleus
Chromatin
Endoplasmic Reticulum with ribosomes
Centriole
Lysosome

Figure 19.1

The specific contents of a cell can be seen in diagram (Fig. 19.1). The **Plasma membrane** is a semipermeable limiting layer of cell protoplasm. The surface layer contains vesicle or vacuole invaginations of the membrane that allows material into and out of the cell, whether passively (by diffusion) or actively (by active transport).

The **Cytoplasm** is the area between the plasma membrane and the nuclear membrane of a cell, where the metabolism and chemical reactions occur. While the rate is controlled by enzymes, the secretion of those enzymes are controlled by the DNA. The cytoplasm contains cytosol (the fluid portion of the cytoplasm) and the:

> **Mitochondrion**, which are round or long cellular organelles that are found outside the nucleus. They produce energy for the cell through cellular respiration, and are rich in fats, proteins, and enzymes.
>
> **Vacuoles**, which are cavities or vesicles usually containing fluid.
>
> **Golgi apparatus**, which is a cytoplasmic organelle that consists of a stack of smooth membranous saccules and associated vesicles that is active in the modification and transport of proteins.
>
> **Endoplasmic Reticulum** with associated ribosomes, which is a system of interconnected vesicular and lamellar cytoplasmic membranes that functions in the transport of materials within the cell. They are studded with ribosomes in some places,

which are the RNA-rich cytoplasmic granules that synthesize proteins.

Centrioles which are a pair of cellular organelles adjacent to the nucleus, that function in the formation of the spindle apparatus during cell division. They consist of a cylinder with nine microtubules arranged peripherally in a circle.

Lyosomes which are saclike cellular organelles that contains various hydrolytic enzymes. They split complex chemical compounds into simpler subunits and destroy worn out organelles; even the whole cell if needed.

The **Nuclear membrane** is a double membrane that encloses the cell nucleus, and its outer part is continuous with the endoplasmic reticulum. Inside the nuclear membrane is the:

Nucleus which controls the cell's function (as reproduction and protein synthesis). It contains the DNA from which all our characteristics are derived. It is composed of nucleoplasm and a nucleoprotein-rich network from which chromosomes and nucleoli arise.

Nucleolus is a spherical body of the nucleus that become enlarged during protein synthesis, is associated with a nucleolus organizer, and contains the DNA templates for ribosomal RNA.

Chromatin is the actual genetic material; the nucleic acid and basic proteins (as histone) in the cell that is usually dispersed in the interphase nucleus and condensed into chromosomes in mitosis and meiosis.

Cells are programmed to divide and replicate themselves in a process called *mitosis*. Mitosis takes place in the nucleus of a dividing cell, involves typically a series of steps consisting of prophase, metaphase, anaphase, and telophase, and results in the formation of two new nuclei each having the same number of chromosomes as the parent nucleus.

Cells receive their energy from the metabolism of food that we consume. This occurs through a number of physical and chemical processes, including Cellular Respiration (in which the cell is supplied with the oxygen needed for metabolism and relieved of the carbon dioxide formed by the energy-producing reactions), the ***Krebs Cycle*** (a sequence of reactions in which oxidation of acetic acid or acetyl equivalent provides energy for storage in phosphate bonds (as in ATP), which supplies energy needed for the biochemical processes of the cell.

The human body continues to thrive as long as this division and replication process is operating properly.

However, this process does not continue indefinitely because our DNA is programmed so that a non-dividing state is ultimately achieved. This is known as the **Hayflick Limit**:

> The Hayflick limit was discovered in the 1970s by Leonard Hayflick, Professor of Anatomy at the University of California, who found that most types of human cells have natural limits to the number of times they divide. Once their time is up, the cells cease to divide or reproduce (Rf17)

The length of time in which a cell will continue to divide and replicate itself is controlled by telomeres. Telomeres are caps (like the plastic tips on shoelaces) found on the end of every chromosome contained in the cell (Rf18).

> It is believed that these caps are the "clock of aging." Each time the cell divides, the telomere shortens, and when it attains a certain length the cell ceases to divide (Rf19)

As the telomere shortens, the DNA contained in the chromosome gets damaged and starts to send the wrong *messages* to the cell and its components. As a result the cell begins to function improperly. Depending upon the specific cell being affected, it may lead to a decrease in, or even the wrong secretion of, certain enzymes or chemicals.

As the process of mitosis continues to slow down, fewer new cells are born:

> the cells grow older and fragile with weakened cell walls, prone to pathogenic attack, until they stop dividing completely. This process spreads throughout all the parts of the body until we eventually die (Rf20).

While this is by no means a comprehensive explanation it will put you in a better position to understand the next part.

The human body is designed to produce many substances (hormones, enzymes, etc.), that the body needs in order to function properly. In fact, scientists still can not identify all of the substances that the body produces.

The bloodstream is the *delivery system* the body uses to transport these *substances*. Blood is the fluid that circulates in the heart, arteries, capillaries, and veins carrying nourishment and oxygen to, and bringing away waste products from, all parts of the body.

During our youth (when our DNA is sending the correct signals), our body produces these *substances* in abundant amounts (Fig. 19.2). They are secreted into our bloodstream and delivered to every organ of the body. Because the body's organs are receiving the *substances* they continue to thrive.

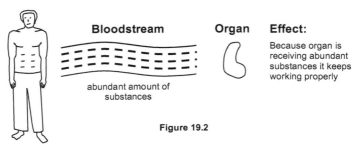

Figure 19.2

However, as we age the body's ability to produce these *substances* steadily declines, resulting in low to non-existent levels of these *substances* being secreted into the blood (Fig. 19.3). As explained above, our DNA was designed so that we would stop producing these *substances* at some point.

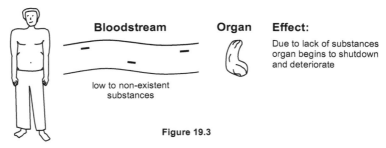

Figure 19.3

Because old blood does not contain adequate amounts of these *substances* the organs don't receive the *messages* that tell them to go on functioning. Due to the lack of these nourishing substances the body's regenerative ability (that worked fine when we were young; when our blood was rich with these substances), gradually stops responding to the damage, as we get older. As a result, the body's organs steadily begin to deteriorate and decrease in performance. The more damage that we do to our body at this stage, the harder it is for us to recover. Even by donating blood, your body has to work harder to replenish its supply. It produces less and less of the substances you need, and you age quicker.

If you can find a way to re-introduce the *substances* (that your body is no longer producing naturally or producing at declining levels) back into your bloodstream, you can bypass the body's aging clock. Your organs don't care *how* they get the substances, they only care that they are getting them. As long as your bloodstream contains the substances your organs will continue to work long after your DNA has stopped telling your body to produce the substances.

To give you an analogy, think of how a radio works: (1) A Power Supply Company has to create electricity, (2) Then it has to transport that electricity to the radio, (3) If the radio receives the electricity it works.

If the Power Supply Company that you are using is not able to produce electricity anymore, you can go to another Power Supply Company that is producing electricity in order to obtain it. The radio doesn't care where the electricity is coming from, only that it receives it.

Surprisingly, the human body works the same way. Your body is the Power Supply Company. The body produces *substances* and secrets them into the bloodstream to be transported to the body's organs. If your blood contains the *substances* your organs will keep working. If your body can not produce the *substances* anymore (because your DNA has told your body to stop producing them), you can obtain the *substances* from another person who is still producing them. Like the radio, the body's organs don't care where the *substances* are coming from, only that they are receiving them.

This is what the consumption of blood does! By drinking *young* blood on a daily basis you are taking the *substances* (which are found in abundant quantities in the blood of a young person) and putting them into your body. They are secreted into your bloodstream and delivered to all the organs of your body. Because the organs are now receiving the *messages* they continue to function properly, effectively bypassing the body's aging clock. This drastically extends the human life-span.

The science behind drinking blood was discovered thousands of years ago. Ancient scientists even discovered that the younger the blood is that you consume, the more potent the effects will be. Clearly this is because the younger blood contains the nourishment, enzymes, etc., that old blood no longer contains due to the aging process as I've explained above. At some point in your life, I'm sure everyone recalls hearing the phrase often spoken of in occult circles:

"the blood of a virgin is needed"

This had nothing to do with a person's sexual status. It had to do with *AGE*. Virgins are usually young, age 11, 12, 13, etc. This was an ingenious way of teaching people that only *young blood* has the beneficial effects!

While this science was known to our ancient ancestors, recently modern scientists are beginning to re-discover it, and, in several scientific studies, have even proven that *young blood* does in fact have these beneficial anti-aging effects.

In 2005 scientists at Stanford University School of Medicine discovered that when *young blood* is added to the bloodstream of an old animal, the regenerative cells in the old animal, that had been shut down due to old age, *instantly re-activated*, giving the animal's organs the ability to heal again like they use to do when it was young. The results of this study were published in the February 17, 2005 issue of *Nature.*

This study examined the effects on muscle tissue. Muscles have specialized cells called satellite cells (the muscle stem cells) which dot muscle tissue. During our youth, when the muscle is damaged they spring into action to repair it. As we age, these satellite cells gradually lose their ability to repair the damaged muscle. Associate Professor of Neurology and Neurological Sciences, Thomas Rando, MD, PhD. (who led the study), demonstrated that as soon as *young blood* is put into the bloodstream of an old animal the satellite cells instantly re-activate and the old muscle heals normally like it did when we were young.

To ensure that it was in fact the *young blood* that was creating these results, scientists put old satellite cells in a lab dish. When the old satellite cells were bathed in *young blood* they began diving again! As a control test, they added *old blood* to young satellite cells and, even though they were young satellite cells, *they started acting like old cells!* This proved that it was the condition or age of the blood that determined how the cells react.

They experienced the same results with tests on the liver. When *young blood* was put into the bloodstream of an old animal the liver's regenerative cells, that were shut down due to old age, instantly activated to regenerate the liver tissue.

In 2011 scientists at Stanford University School of Medicine published another study in the September 1, 2011 issue of *Nature*, this time discovering the regenerative effects that "young" blood has on an aging brain.

Just like other cells in the body, neurons and brain cells also start to decrease as we age, as do our cognitive abilities, such as spatial memory (forgetting where you left your keys). The study's senior author, Tony Wyss-Coray, PhD. (Associate Professor of Neurology and Neurological Sciences) said that when *young blood* was put into the bloodstream of an old animal it increased the number of new nerve cells being created in the old brain by "threefold". Due to the *young blood*, the old brain began producing more neurons, firing more actively across synapses, and even suffered less inflammation. In contrast, the study also found that when young animals received old blood *they experienced all the negative effects of aging!*

In 2013 scientists at the Harvard Stem Cell Institute, Amy Wagers, PhD and Richard T. Lee, PhD (Professors at Harvard's Department of Stem Cell and Regenerative Biology) discovered that when they added *young blood* to the bloodstream of an old animal (who had a thickened heart due to old age), the enlarged, weakened heart, healed and reverted back to a youthful size with improved function. They discovered a protein in *young blood* that they believe is responsible for the anti-aging effects. It is called GDF11 (growth differentiation factor 11). Amy Wagers was one of the people who had worked on the 2005 Stanford University study. After moving to Harvard she continued the research.

In 2014 scientists at the Harvard Stem Cell Institute published two papers in the journal *Science*. (Rf21). They were published online on May 4, 2014 and in print on May 9, 2014.

The first study demonstrated that when *young blood* is put into the bloodstream of an old animal, the chemicals in the young blood rejuvenated the muscle tissue in the old animal. The actual structure of the muscles improved and the old animal had improved strength and endurance. They even "saw improvements in unmanipulated muscle."

The scientists demonstrated that they could replicate the anti-aging effects of *young blood* by injecting just the GDF11 protein. After injecting the GDF11 protein into old mice, they could run twice as long on a treadmill as other old mice that had not been given the protein.

Importantly, the scientists discovered that **the DNA damage associated with aging was being repaired**. They also confirmed that the GDF11 protein found in mice is the same substance found in human blood.

The second study demonstrated that when *young blood* was put into the bloodstream of an old animal, the number of brain cells increased, it experienced the growth of new blood vessels, and could now detect smells as good as young mice can. The study found that when they injected the GDF11 protein into an old animal it experienced the same results. In contrast, when they put old blood into the bloodstream of young mice, the young mice experienced all the effects of aging. They had a dramatic reduction in stem cell production in the brain.

In 2014 scientists at the University of California, San Francisco published a study in *Nature Medicine*. (Rf22). It was published online on the same day as the two Harvard studies, May 4, 2014. The study was led by UCSF's Saul Villeda, PhD (who also led the 2011 Stanford University study en route to his doctoral thesis) and Stanford's Tony Wyss-Coray, PhD (the senior author on the 2011 Stanford study).

This study was an extension of their previous work. They discovered that when they took *young blood* from 3-month-old mice and put it into the bloodstream of 18-month-old mice (the equivalent of a 70-year-old man), the performance of the old animal's brain dramatically increased. It grew more stem cells and the connections between those stem cells increased by 20%.

At the 2012 annual meeting of the Society for Neuroscience in New Orleans Villeda explained:

> One of the main things that changes with ageing are these connections, there are a lot less of them as we get older, ... That is thought to underlie memory impairment - if you have less connections, neurons aren't communicating, all of a sudden you have [problems] in learning and memory (Rf23).

It turns out that what scientists originally thought was a natural slowdown in the production of new neurons leading to brain death, is actually caused by the gradual degradation of the blood.

As reported in the 2014 *Nature Medicine* article, after injecting *young blood* into the bloodstream of an old mouse and then putting the old mouse in a water maze, it performed as well as a young 4-6 month old mouse. The old mouse even reacted like a 3-month-old when testing how well it remembered a threatening environment. Villeda explained to the Guardian:

> There's something about *young blood* that can literally reverse the impairments you see in the older brain (Rf24)

As I explained earlier, once the organs in the body receive the *substances* that are in *young blood* they begin working again. As the scientists discovered in this study, as soon as the *young blood* was put into the bloodstream of the old animal and the brain started receiving the messages found in *young blood* that tell it to keep working, the master regulator of the brain turned back on and started producing the Creb protein again which turned on genes that make neural connections.

While we don't know exactly what the substances are in *young blood* that give us this anti-aging effect, as the above studies verify, *young blood* contains

224

key chemical factors that decline in the blood as we age. Re-introduce these into your bloodstream and all of a sudden your body starts working again like it did when it was young!

Proving that it is the condition or age of the blood that ultimately determines whether the organs in our body work as young organs or old organs. Like an electric radio that does not care where it gets its electricity from, the organs in the human body don't care where they get these *substances* from, only that they are receiving them. The use of *young blood* has now been shown to reverse the effects of aging on memory, learning ability, muscle strength and stamina, and general regenerative abilities.

The main flaw in all of these studies is the method they are using to transport the *young blood* to the old body. Through parabiosis, or injecting *young blood* directly into your veins, you can only obtain a limited beneficial effect. Understand, the veins in your body can only hold so much blood. Even if you were to undergo a blood transfusion and replace all of your old blood with *young blood*, the amount of *substances* you receive is still limited to the amount of blood that can fit into your veins. Through these methods you can not obtain a high enough blood serum level of the life-extending substances.

However, by drinking *young blood* on a daily basis, the GI tract absorbs the good *substances* your body needs and disposes of the waste. By this method, you can obtain very high blood serum levels of these life-extending *substances* in your body.

Through this method, not only is it possible to achieve the regenerative effects that your body produced when it was young but with high blood serum concentrations of these substances your body will experience heightened mental and physical abilities.

This is just modern science catching up with what our ancient ancestors knew thousands of years ago.

When scientists discover what the specific *substances* are in *young blood* that allows our bodies to experience this anti-aging effect, they will be able to begin to create some kind of substitute so that we can receive just those substances.

Further, when scientists discover what part of the body is responsible for actually producing those *substances*, they can then focus on a way to make the human body continue to produce those *substances* beyond its natural limit.

It's only a matter of time. However, with what I know about the government, I find it hard to believe that secret government scientists have not already made these discoveries, even going far beyond them, and are just keeping a lid on the science due to population control.

Until these things are discovered, the only way to extend your life-span or obtain the heightened mental and physical abilities is to drink blood. By consuming 2 cups of *young blood* on a daily basis you are continuously flooding your body with these *substances*. As a result of the high blood serum levels of these *substances*, your body's ability to heal itself is dramatically increased, and it lives substantially longer. To witness: the 1,000 year life-spans of Adam to Noah when they were drinking blood on a daily basis. While it's not immortality, it will extend your life-span by 10 times its current ability.

Note: I am not advocating that you go out and drink blood. I am just revealing the hidden science encoded in the Bible. It is my belief that if enough people know about it more pressure will be applied to scientists to create a substitute.

Alchemy

The Great Work of alchemists is said to be the chemical science aiming to achieve the transmutation of a base element (such as lead) into a higher element (such as gold). The often quoted alchemical principle is: "To make gold, you must take gold" (Rf25).

Countless hours have been spent by countless people around the world desperately trying to turn lead into gold. Blindly following false symbolism, which has arisen due to thousands of years of borrowing, adding, adapting, manipulating, and mis-interpreting every available symbol, emblem and myth, by the gold-seeking alchemists from so many different cultures around the world, never having achieved their goal (Rf26).

The Alchemical Medallion of the Hidden Stone has the Latin phrase: Visita Interiora Terrae Rectificando Invenies Occultum Lapidem (Fig. 19.4). The phrase is translated: Visit Earth's interior, by purifying/rectification you find the hidden stone. The phrase's initial letters spell the word "Vitriol" (Rf27).

Figure 19.4

The word alchemy comes from the Arabic *al* (the) and *khame* (blackness or nothingness) (Rf28). It is the science which overcomes the blackness or nothingness, also known as death. Alchemy is, and has always been, the science which overcomes death! The science aiming to extend the human life-span.

The secret to extending life-span is not found by "Visiting Earth's Interior," but the "VITRIOL" is found in the interior of the human body. The alchemist is both the vessel of the work and the material within it (Rf29).

Alchemy does not involve metals, but living substances; the blood and glandular secretions of the human body. In fact, "the word 'secret' has its origin in the hidden knowledge of these glandular secretions" (Rf30).

The Occultum Lapidem (hidden stone) spoken of in the phrase is known as the Philosopher's Stone. This is the true medicine, known as the Great Tincture (Rf31). The Elixir of Life.

227

The key to unlocking the hidden meaning of the alchemical phrase is found in the word **Rectificando**. When used in terms of ritual, this word means to *purify* or *sanctify*.

According to the Bible, the only way to *purify* or *sanctify* anything was by the use of blood! It was the *blood* of a sacrifice that made it effective. Blood was required in order to purify/sanctify God's altar; to purify/sanctify utensils used in ceremony; to purify people's houses; to purify garments; to make atonement, etc.

Over and over again priests were required to sprinkle blood against the altar in order to purify or sanctify it:

> the priests shall bring the blood and sprinkle it against the altar on all sides... (Leviticus 1:5)

> Aaron's sons the priests shall sprinkle its blood against the altar on all sides. (Leviticus 1:11)

> its blood shall be drained out on the side of the altar. (Leviticus 1:15)

> Then Aaron's sons the priests shall sprinkle blood against the altar on all sides. (Leviticus 3:2)

> Then Aaron's sons shall sprinkle its blood against the altar on all sides. (Leviticus 3:13)

In connection with a sin offering, an anointed priest was required to take blood into the Tent of Meeting:

> He is to dip his finger into the blood and sprinkle some of it seven times before the Lord, in front of the curtain of the sanctuary. (Leviticus 4:5-6)

> He is to put some of the blood on the horns of the altar that is before the Lord in the Tent of Meeting. The rest of the blood he shall pour out at the base of the altar... (Leviticus 4:18)

Purification by blood is repeated again and again in the Bible: (Leviticus 4:30, 4:34, 5:9, 7:2, 9:9, 9:12, 9:18); in regards to ceremonial cleansing "blood is to be sprinkled seven times" (Leviticus 14:5-7, 14:14, 14:25); to purify a house sprinkle the house with blood seven times (Leviticus 14:49-52); blood is sprinkled on those who are ceremonially unclean to sanctify them (Hebrews 9:13).

Blood was even required to ordain priests and to enter God's Most Holy Place. We see this in the ordination of Aaron and his sons as priests:

228

Moses ... took some of the blood, and with his finger he put it on all the horns of the altar to purify the altar. He poured out the rest of the blood at the base of the altar. So he consecrated it to make atonement for it. (Leviticus 8:15; 8:19)

Then Moses took blood and put it on the lobe of Aaron's right ear, on the thumb of his right hand, and on the big toe of his right foot (Leviticus 8:23). Moses did the same with Aaron's sons. Afterwards, Moses sprinkled blood on all sides of the altar (Leviticus 8:24). Finally, Moses took the blood and sprinkled it on them and their garments to consecrate them (Leviticus 8:30). This was required by God in order to make atonement (Leviticus 8:34). Blood was even required to make atonement for the death of Aaron's two sons when they approached the Lord (Leviticus 16:1-19). The Bible explains why blood was so important:

For the life of a creature is in the blood, and I have given it to you to make atonement for yourselves on the altar; it is the blood that makes atonement for one's life. (Leviticus 17:11)

Blood was so important that not even the first covenant was put into effect without blood (Hebrews 9:18). When Moses proclaimed the commandments to the people, he took blood and sprinkled the scroll and all the people (Hebrews 9:19):

Moses then took the blood, sprinkled it on the people and said, "This is the blood of the covenant that the Lord has made with you in accordance with these words." (Exodus 24:8)

In the same way, Moses sprinkled blood on the tabernacle and everything used in its ceremonies (Hebrews 9:21):

In fact, the law requires that nearly everything be cleansed with blood, and without the shedding of blood there is no forgiveness. (Hebrews 9:2)

According to the Bible's book of Hebrews, even the highest priest could not enter God's Most Holy Place but one time a year, and only then, if he was bringing blood!

But only the high priest entered the inner room [the Most Holy Place], and that only once a year, and never without blood... (Hebrews 9:7)

The Bible even describes the distinction between animal blood and human blood, explaining how human blood has a much stronger effect than animal blood (Hebrews 9:11-14). It explains how the blood of bulls and goats could never have the effect that human blood does (Hebrews 10:4). It explains that while items that were only "copies" of heavenly things could be purified or

229

sanctified with animal blood, heavenly things themselves required a better blood sacrifice (human blood) (Hebrews 8:23). Also, see the Book of Revelation where Jesus was "worthy to take the scroll and to open its seals" only because of the human blood sacrifice (Revelation 5:9-10).

The Bible even explains not to put any *yeast* into the blood (Exodus 34:25) because yeast will kill the beneficial *substances* in the young blood!

In ancient times "a human being was often deliberately killed, ritually sacrificed, in order to sanctify a site with his or her blood." Early Christians used this practice to consecrate Churches, although, they hide the practice by using the metaphor that: churches were built upon the burial sites of saints (Rf32).

The above clearly demonstrates that the Bible equates the act of "purifying or sanctifying" with the use of *blood*. The word Rectificando (which means "to purify or sanctify) in the Alchemical Medallion, was a way to hide the secret alchemical message that *blood* is necessary if one wishes to extend life-span. Deciphered, the alchemical phrase really means:

Visit the interior of the human body and in the blood you find the true medicine (Elixir of Life).

The secrets of alchemy were hidden in symbolism. It was a way of keeping the secrets hidden, while at the same time, preserving them. Only those with the key had admission. In alchemy the color red is synonymous with the metal gold (Rf33). The word "ritual" stems from the blood drinking customs and the Sanskrit word ritu, from which also stem the words rite, root, red. Blood was the "red gold" of the ritual.

The alchemical principle (to make gold, you must take gold) is only a euphemism. The true alchemical secret is: *To Make Life, You Must Take Life.* A principle born due to the fact that, in ancient times, in order to obtain blood in which to drink people would have to be killed. In modern times it is not necessary for someone to die, they can simply drink blood that people have donated.

The reason the science of drinking blood has remained a closely guarded secret is because, as of today, scientists can not chemically create blood. If everyone knew that drinking blood lengthens your life-span, everyone would demand blood. No sane person would donate blood once they find out that the effort your body goes through to produce more blood, shortens your life.

230

This could cause a serious situation where people seeking to lengthen their life may start forcibly taking blood from people. Not to mention the fact that since no blood is being donated, hospitals won't have blood for operations, emergencies, blood transfusions, etc. Then questions of population control arise, because if everyone lived for a thousand years the Earth would quickly become overpopulated. This should give you an idea of why it has remained such a secret.

* * *

StarFire

As time progressed, our ancestors tried to use different methods to obtain blood without the need for someone to lose their life. Ancient scientists discovered that the life-extending substances found in *young blood* could also be obtained from the menstrual blood of young females. This practice was known as **StarFire** (Elixir Rubeus).

Under the StarFire practice menstrual blood was collected from chosen females (referred to as Scarlet Women) beginning at about the age of "**13**", when the female menstrual cycle begins.

A collection at the British Museum contains a 13th century fallopian style Mycenean StarFire chalice that was used to collect menstrual blood in this ancient practice (Fig. 19.5) (Rf34).

Scarlet Women chosen to be used in StarFire practice were known in:

Figure 19.5

> Greek as the hierodulai (sacred women), a word that was later transformed (via medieval French into English) to 'harlot.' In the early Germanic tongue, they were known as hores (later Anglicized to whores) a word which meant quite simply 'beloved ones.' As pointed out in Skeat's Etymological Dictionary, these words of high veneration were never interchangeable with such words as 'prostitute' or 'adultress' (Rf35)

The negative connotation that the word evokes in our minds today is due to the sinister attempts by Religions to denigrate and conceal all traces of this ancient science.

This is also the mysterious secret behind why Religions demonized the number 13. The number 13 represented the 13 cycles of the moon (a lunar year), which is tuned to the 13 menstrual cycles a year; a process that begins at the age of 13! For those that have ears, let them hear.

StarFire was also known as the Vehicle to the Light. In that, by using this process an individual is able to achieve enlightenment (heightened mental and physical abilities as well as an extended life-span). Interestingly, this process is also encoded on the imagery of the One Dollar Bill (Fig. 18.7). On it you will see that the only way to reach the *Doorway to the Light* is by utilizing the *13* steps of the pyramid (a metaphor that you can only reach the Light by drinking the menstrual blood)!

Because our ancient ancestors were now using menstrual blood to obtain heightened mental and physical abilities as well as extended life-spans, the legends, myths, and symbols evolved to incorporate this science.

Veiled in symbolism, objects like a "fountain," "well," "underground stream," "sacred chalice," "grail," "cup," etc., were used to represent the vagina, from which poured the "Waters of Life" (Blood). Women were sometimes symbolized as flowers:

> In mystic circles, the menstrual flow-er (she who flows) has long been the designated "flower," represented as a lily or lotus (Rf36)

In a carving known as the Venus of Laussel, dating back to 18,000 B.C. or earlier, the goddess Venus is depicted holding a drinking vessel (similar to a bison horn) which has *13* notches along it symbolizing *what* was being drunk in the vessel.

As the blood drinking practices spread throughout different cultures the blood became known as the Vedic SOMA, the Mazdean HAOMA, the Greek AMBROSIA. For example:

Ambrosia was the food of the Greek and Roman gods and the word literally meant "immortality." However, ancient legends shed more light on what ambrosia actually is. In the Greek myth of the goddess Demeter, after Demeter anointed King Celus' son Demophoon with "Ambrosia, the food of the gods, ... the boy grew beyond his age" (Rf37). In Asia, the half-man, half-bird deity called Garuda sprang forth from an egg after 500 years (note the Phoenix symbolism). He flew to the "Abode of Indra," extinguished a fire that surrounded it, conquered the guards (the devatas) and obtained the ambrosia. "When a few drops of this elixir fell upon the grass known as Kusa, it was consecrated for all eternity" (Rf38). As we learned from the biblical verses of the Bible, only blood "consecrates." Ambrosia was blood!

Soma, which is identical to ambrosia, is the Sanskrit word used in ancient India to identify the drink of immortality that was used in Vedic rituals. In Hindu mythology soma is spoken of as: "This Soma is a god; he cures the sharpest ills that man endures. He heals the sick... So great and wonderful are his gifts, men feel the god within their veins" (Rf39). Interestingly, in Greek soma means "the body."

Haoma, which is identical to soma and ambrosia, was the word used to identify the ritual drink of immortality in the ancient Iranian language (Avestan), in which the sacred books of Zoroastrianism were written.

In some cultures the blood or menstrual blood was called the "milk" or "nectar" of the gods. The metaphor of drinking "milk" from the Lactating Goddess (which was said to have healing powers) was really identifying the menstrual blood. For example, in the sacred Hindu writings of the *Rig Veda* this point is evidenced:

> O goddess of waters. You have within you the life-giving sap. May
> you feed us with that even like mothers giving breast milk... (Rf40)

Also, most Goddesses became known as "lunar deities" due to the connection between the menstrual and lunar cycles, from which the menstrual blood became known as **Moon-Fluid**. For example:

The Indian goddess Kali was a lunar deity (moon goddess). In her role as World Mother she was known as the controller of immortality. Kali was actually the daughter of two Anunnaki/Elohim/Nephilim (Enki and Lilith) and was known in Sumeria as Kalimath or Kali Marg (Rf41). Kaula Tantra is dedicated to her, and in this ancient practice we find the same elements of StarFire.

In Tantra the power of the Goddess (Shakti) was said to reside in her fluids, called the Rasa (Rf42). Identical to the Scarlet Women used to obtain menstrual blood in StarFire, in Tantra the women were called Suvasini priestesses. In the ritual "secretions" were collected from the sacred Suvasini priestesses and they:

> were called Kalas (units of time), while the womb (the Kalana) was
> regarded as a measurer of lunar time. (Rf43)

Interestingly, the menstrual blood was referred to as "units of time," a metaphor that the blood controls/extends time (life-span). Further, the menstrual rasa was also known as amrita (a divine nectar of sacred waters known as the 'fountain of youth') in the Sanskrit mystic song, the Sama Veda (c.2000 B.C.) (Rf44).

In other myths menstrual blood was symbolized as "apples" due to their red color. For example:

The Celtic Mother Goddess is Brigid. She was associated with healing and owned a magical apple orchard. Eating her "apples" healed the sick and old. The story of Brigid is similar to the Welsh version of Ceridwen. Both:

> Ceridwen and Brigid were also said to be keepers of the cauldron, chalice or cup, and to 'drink' from the chalice was a metaphor for receiving great healing (Rf45)

They were the "owners" of the orchard because it was from them that the menstrual blood (apples) flowed. As previously explained, a "chalice" was used to symbolize the vagina. Another Norse goddess was Idunn. She:

> lived by a sacred brook and ... kept magical apples in her coffer. When the gods grew old, they would come to her to eat of the apples, whereupon they turned young again. Indeed, "Idunn" meant "Again Young"; and the apples that she guarded were called the "Elixir of the Gods." (Rf46)

Likewise the legend of Hercules who had to bring back divine "apples" from the Hesperides (Daughters of the Evening Land) in order to extend his life (Rf47.)

We find StarFire symbolism in the various forms of the Tree of Life. In Ireland, Scotland and Wales, the Tree of Life is represented as a Hazel Tree located by a well.

> Atop the branches of the hazel tree there sits an eagle who drops *a blood red nut of wisdom into the well 13 times a year.* There it is consumed by the Salmon of knowledge. (Rf48)

Another analogy of the female menstrual cycle from which you obtain the StarFire.

However, in order to obtain enough *menstrual blood* (2 cups daily) to be effective, you would need many Scarlet Women. This brings us to another cipher in the Bible, the story of the biblical King Solomon.

In the Bible we learn that King Solomon had 700 wives of royal birth and 300 concubines (1 Kings 11:3). They were his Harem (Rf49). No matter which way you look at it, this is an excessive amount of women to have simply for the purpose of sex, even if you wanted a great variety. Why would King Solomon keep so many women around, considering the extremely large cost of housing them, feeding them, clothing them, entertaining them, etc.?

With what you now know of the StarFire practice, this passage should be easy to decipher. They were not there for sex. King Solomon's harem was a blood farm. A thousand women menstruating each month would provide him with the needed 2 cups of daily blood.

This also sheds light on why King Solomon was said to be so intelligent. Remember, as explained in the science section, high blood serum levels of the *substances* contained in *young blood* increases mental abilities!

The StarFire practice was also encoded directly into the Bible's Song of Songs. As you will see, in Solomon's Song women are symbolized as flowers (lilies), a spring, fountain, and well of living waters. The menstrual blood is symbolized as a *rose* and *pomegranates* due to their red color. The Song explains:

> "I am a rose of Sharon, a lily of the valleys." (Song of Songs 2:1)

The first section of the verse concerns the "rose" which symbolizes the menstrual blood due to its red color. The second section of the verse: "Sharon, a lily of the valleys" explains that Sharon is a lily. Sharon was a flower (flow-er) from which the menstrual blood poured. As explained earlier in mystic circles flowers were used to symbolize a female. The title *Sharon* explains that she was a woman of distinction or royalty (a Scarlet Woman or Suvasini priestess trained in the use of StarFire). Solomon's Song continues:

> "He feedeth amongst the lilies," (Song of Songs 2:16)

The metaphor of this verse is that Solomon is drinking the menstrual blood of the women (lilies, flow-ers) of his harem. Solomon's Song continues:

> You are a garden locked up, my sister, my bride; you are a spring enclosed, a sealed fountain. (Song of Songs 4:12)

This verse is teaching you that the Scarlet Woman or Suvasini priestess is a virgin. Her vagina is *locked up, enclosed, sealed*. Again, the virgin reference was a way of teaching people that it was only *young blood* that had the beneficial effects. And here we also see the woman being referred to as a *garden, spring* and *fountain*. Solomon's Song explains that the woman contains "an orchard of pomegranates" (identical to the metaphor "orchard of apples" that we saw used earlier) and continues:

> You are a garden fountain, a well of living waters (Song of Songs 4:13-15)

235

In this verse the woman is being called a *fountain* and a **well of living waters**. This cipher is teaching you that in the StarFire practice the woman is the source of the **waters of life**, the liquid substance that is life, which you already know in this context is a euphemism for menstrual blood. Further, as encoded into the Bible, the Tree of Life (Fountain of Youth) yields **"its fruit every month"** (Revelation 22:2), referencing the menstrual cycle. Solomon's Song continues:

> My beloved put his hands by the hole of the door and my bowels were moved for him
>
> I rose up to open to my beloved; and my hands dropped [dripped] with Myrrh, and my fingers with sweet smelling Myrrh, upon the handles of the lock. (Song of Songs 5:4-5)

This verse is a metaphor describing the collection of the menstrual blood. The "hole of the door" is the opening of the vagina. The term "my bowels were moved for him" describes the release of the menstrual blood. The rest should be self explanatory. Solomon's Song continues:

> I would lead you and bring you to my mother's house - she who has taught me. I would give you spiced wine to drink, the nectar of my pomegranates. (Song of Songs 8:2)

In this verse we learn that she was taught the StarFire practice by her mother. Here she is offering Solomon the "nectar of my pomegranates" which is a metaphor for her menstrual blood. Pomegranates are used to symbolize blood because they are red and contain red juice. This is identical in meaning to the "rose" and "apples" seen earlier. Solomon's Song continues by explaining how he drank the menstrual blood (Song of Songs 5:1).

It is not clear exactly when King Solomon obtained the knowledge of the StarFire practice, however, the Bible speaks of an event when it was used to heal his father, King David:

> When King David was old and well advanced in years, he could not keep warm even when they put covers over him. So his servants said to him, "Let us look for a young virgin to attend the king and take care of him. She can lie beside him so that our lord the king may keep warm." Then they searched throughout Israel for a beautiful girl and found Abishag, a Shunammite, and brought her to the king. The girl was very beautiful; she took care of the king and waited on him, but the king had no intimate relations with her. (1 Kings 1:1-4)

If you decipher this passage you will see the connection to StarFire. If they were trying to keep King David warm, while the body heat of a person lying next to him would afford some heat, certainly there were better ways to provide heat. But more importantly, *why* would a "young virgin" be needed? Couldn't any woman or person do for that matter? Why couldn't his wife Bathsheba lay beside him to keep him warm? Instead, Abishag, the young virgin Shunammite is required.

The significance of this passage is further amplified by the following events: While King David was sick, Solomon's brother Adonijah tried to assume kingship without King David's blessing (1 Kings 1:5). Adonijah's attempt failed and Solomon became King. Afterwards Adonijah went to Bathsheba and asked her for only one favor, that she speak with King Solomon on his behalf, to convince Solomon to give him Abishag the Shunammite as his wife (1 Kings 2:13-17). When King Solomon heard the request he was outraged:

> Why do you request Abishag the Shunammite for Adonijah? You might as well request the kingdom for him ...
>
> Then King Solomon swore by the Lord: "May God deal with me, be it ever so severely, if Adonijah does not pay with his life for this request!" (1 Kings 2:22-23)

King Solomon was so outraged at the thought of his brother having access to Abishag, the Shunammite, that he had his brother killed! (1 Kings 2:25). Why was the young virgin Abishag the Shunammite so important? Why was she more important than the whole kingdom?!?

Now you see how the previous passage takes on a greater significance. The "young virgin" Abishag was a Scarlet Woman or Suvasini priestess who was summoned to provide King David with StarFire; *young blood* to help heal him in old age.

King Solomon was what some call a pagan. Even the Bible recognizes that Solomon followed other gods, like the goddess Ashtoreth and the god Molech (1 Kings 11:5). While the condensed version in the Bible blames this on his many wives (1 Kings 11:3) other texts like the Jewish Talmud demonstrate that Solomon was:

> the mightiest magician of his age, and his great wisdom and considered judgment as a sorcerer-king are directly attributed to his ownership of an enchanted Ring with which he summoned the demons of the Earth [the Anunnaki/Elohim/Nephilim] (Rf50)

King Solomon's light-radiating jewel was called the **Schamir**. According to esoteric Jewish tradition, King Solomon was said to have inherited the *Book of Raziel* which was a collection of secrets cut into sapphire. Raziel was Raquel, one of the Anunnaki/Elohim/Nephilim/Watchers, also known as one of the seven archangels in the Book of Enoch 20:4. The *Book of Raziel* was said to be the same as the Tablet of Ideograms that Abraham gained access to, as well as the Tablet of Destiny that was known to the Sumerians (Rf51). It was said to be:

> the testament of a lost civilization, ... a series of ideograms, all that men had ever known, all that men will ever know, concerning the vocation of mankind in the presence of the impenetrable mystery of being. (Rf52)

Interestingly, the knowledge that King Solomon inherited originated from Abraham's place of birth, Aur Kasdeem. This is translated "Ur of the Chaldees" and means "the light of the magicians."

> Aur in Hebrew means light, and the Kasdeems are the magicians, astrologers, diviners (Rf53)

The acquisition of this knowledge is recorded in the Bible as: Elohim gave Solomon wisdom and very great insight, and a breath of understanding as measureless as the sand on the seashore (1 Kings 4:29); His wisdom was greater than the wisdom of all the men of the East, and greater than all the wisdom of Egypt (1 Kings 4:30); The whole world sought audience with him to hear his wisdom (1 Kings 10:24).

King Solomon even encoded the science of the secret blood drinking practices into the architecture of the two pillars of his Temple:

The two pillars of King Solomon's Temple each have two rows of interwoven chains that cross "seven" times meeting at a round bowl (Note: this is identical to the ancient Caduceus, which has two rows of interwoven snakes that cross "seven" times meeting at the orb) (1 Kings 7:15-17).

Above the bowl were two hundred *pomegranates* and the tops of the capitals of the two pillars were "in the shape of lilies" (1 Kings 7:18-22), the flower (flow-er) from which the blood poured into the bowl!

Even the names of the pillars describe the results of the process. The south pillar was called Jakin (he establishes). The north pillar was called Boaz (in him strength) (1 Kings 7:21). The decoded secret is:

Drinking the blood establishes strength in you.

As shown in the science section, high blood serum levels of the *substances* contained in *young blood* heighten mental and physical abilities as well as extend life-span. For those that have ears, let them hear!

More evidence of this can be found in the Two Tat Pillars of Egypt, as seen on the Papyrus of Ani. The Pillars were called: Tat (in strength) and Tattu (to establish).

The true meaning of the Tat Pillars can be found in the word "Tattu" that was used to identify them. In Egyptian the word Tattu means "The place of establishing forever"! (Rf54). It was known as the place where the mortal becomes immortal. The process whereby the normal human life-span was extended so greatly that the person was looked at as being immortal. Over time, as the science became lost or hidden and future generations tried to make sense out of it, the message was distorted to "mortal" becoming "spiritual."

The Two Pillars of King Solomon's Temple can be found at the entrance of every Temple in ancient times (e.g. Ptah, Amenta). While the Two Pillars originally represented the two brothers Enlil (south) and Enki (north), then in Egypt the two brothers Sut (south) and Horus (north), as you can see above, the pillars have since been adapted to also conceal the secrets of extending life, and the science behind the secret combination of positive and negative as you will see in a later section.

King Solomon's Temple was also a representation of the female body. In this context, the Two Pillars represented the two legs. Between the two legs was the *door* to the temple/body, symbolizing the vagina, from which the menstrual blood poured.

StarFire symbolism was also encoded into labyrinths, which stem from spiraling circles symbolizing the snake/serpent's path to immortal life. Ancient labyrinths based upon StarFire did not have any of the false pathways or dead ends you find in amusement parks. At the center of every labyrinth awaits the Maiden (Scarlet Women) and her menstrual blood.

For example, the Chartres labyrinth in France was built in the 13th century by the Knights Templar. At the center of the labyrinth you find a six petaled "rose," carved into which, is an "**M**" figure. The "**M**" symbol was used to represent the vagina (similar to the two pillars of Solomon's Temple, the outer two lines symbolize a woman's two legs, between which is the 'v̲'agina) from which you obtain the StarFire:

The Rose Garden symbolism of the core of the labyrinth of Chartres is an echo of the Garden of Solomon and the Rose of Sharon, meaning "Blood of the Virgin Princess"...

the Rose in the center of the maze can be seen bathed in the sanguine light of the sun beaming through a strategically placed pane of red stained glass (Rf55)

The great rose window sits above the labyrinth in the west wall of the cathedral and represents the path towards immortality at its center (Rf56). We see this again in the more ancient forest labyrinth of Melusine that is mentioned in medieval French literature:

> The center of the maze incorporated a black cubic stone from which
> spurted the waters of life, la fonteine de soif (Rf57)

Labyrinths containing StarFire symbolism can be found stemming back to ancient Egypt and Mesopotamia.

The "M" symbol representing this practice has not only been found encoded into labyrinths but can be found all over the world encoded into paintings, sculptures, and architecture. When researchers began discovering it they attempted to decode its meaning which has led many to the erroneous conclusion that the "M" represents Mary. For example, the "M" symbol is encoded into Leonardo Da Vinci's painting of The Last Supper on the

Figure 19.6

reflectory wall of the Monastery of Santa Maria delle Grazie in Milan, Italy. If you look at the posture of the group of three people sitting on Jesus' right you'll notice that the four of them form an "M" (Fig. 19.6). Leonardo was said to have encoded the secret of the Holy Grail into his paintings. Because some researchers erroneously believe that the Holy Grail deals with the genealogy of Jesus (the possibility that he married Mary, they begot children and the descendants of which live among us today), when these researchers discovered the "M" symbol in Leonardo's painting it led them to the conclusion that it represents Mary and evidence of this secret. Some even believe that the person Leonardo painted sitting next to Jesus on his right is not the apostle John, but Mary.

240

While they are correct on the one aspect that the "M" is encoded into the painting, it does not stand for Mary. The Holy Grail does not have anything to do with the genealogy of Jesus. The so-called Holy Grail (meaning sacred blood) was not a reference to a particular bloodline, but to the importance of blood itself. The Holy Grail (which carries the same meaning as the Philosopher's Stone) represents the secret alchemical science by which the human life-span can be extended by drinking blood. It was the basis of the Last Supper where Jesus explained to his disciples, take this all of you and drink it, it is the blood of my body which has been shed for you, it will give you everlasting life. You may have also noticed by now that the table in which they are sitting is in the shape of Tau (the Symbol of Life), as well as the encoded number *13* (Jesus plus his 12 disciples) which you now know identified the blood drinking practice.

Further, if you look closer at Leonardo's painting of the Last Supper you'll see that out of the three people sitting on his right that he used to form the encoded "M" symbol Leonardo painted one female. Again, this was not a reference to Mary, but to the TWO OPPOSITES. By combining the two opposites (male, female) the third state of enlightenment is achieved as you will see in a later section called The Mystery of Fire and Water, The Secret Combination.

We also find the "M" symbol encoded into an oil painting of Christopher Columbus that was painted by Sebastiano del Piombo in 1519 (Fig. 19.7). When you look closely at his hand gesture you can see the encoded "M" symbol. As explained earlier, one of the reasons Columbus traveled the world was in search of the Fountain of Youth and is undoubtedly why the "M" symbol representing this concept is found here in connection with Columbus. However, while Columbus was one

Figure 19.7

of the many people searching for the Fountain of Youth it is also clear that he didn't know what the Fountain of Youth actually was. If he had known the true meaning behind the "M" symbol he would not have been traveling around the world in vain looking for a specific fountain. This also occurs in connection with the people who erroneously believe that the Holy Grail is a

241

physical chalice (a meaningless object) and waste their time searching the world in vain for it.

Interestingly, "M" is also the 13th letter of the English and Hebrew Alphabets! Again linking it with the 13 cycles of the moon, 13 menstrual cycles which begin at around the age 13, 13 steps of the pyramid to reach the Doorway to the Light; the blood drinking practices. All of this is why the "M" symbol was important to the Templars.

We find evidence of the blood drinking practices in one form or another all over the ancient world. From China, where it was said that a person can obtain immortality by drinking the blood of the goddess Nu Kua (Rf58), to the opposite side of the Earth in Mesoamerica, where images can be found in the ancient Mayan city of Yaxchilan describing a practice in which blood is used to extend life-span. The Mayan images on Structure 23 show:

> Shield Jaguar, the blood-lord of the city, stands holding a flaming staff. [Note: the reference to the biblical flaming sword that was placed in front of the Tree of Life to guard it] Below him is Lady Xoc ... who is performing a unique and disturbing sacrifice. She is kneeling ... pulling a rope or vine strung with thorns through her tongue and the blood is dripping down it into a bowl/basket, decorated with serpents at her knees. The design on the bowl/basket, known as the 'step-fret,' represents water, waves, wind, sun, light and, most importantly life. It is a known symbol of the serpent and a magical talisman against death. Her blood is also splattering upon white paper placed in the bowl/basket to collect and ... the vessel only becomes a life-giving symbol after the paper has collected the blood. Like the Grail chalice, the vessel is a receptacle for blood. ... Lady Xoc's head tilts back as she beholds the 'new life' rising from the bowl (Rf59).

This practice may also shed light on why the Aztecs really had such great blood sacrifices. A scene in a Nahuatl Codex (Fig. 19.8), found in the area of the Mixtec Tribe, shows two people stabbing a man who is hanging upside down as his blood drips down into some form of container. Above the contraption new life emerges (Rf60). Teaching that blood creates/extends life!

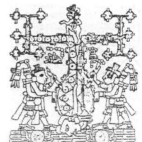

Figure 19.8

Human sacrifice was regularly practiced among the Moche people of Peru, where the high priests would drink the victim's blood. In the Andes region called the Kingdom of Cusco young children were sacrificed in a ritual called CAPACOCHA, where the blood would be drained from their bodies and consumed. Pachacuti Inca Yupanqui believed that drinking the blood would slow down time, in other words, lengthen their life-span.

We find the same secret science encoded into The *Book of Mormon*. It describes the Tree of Life as such: There was a "rod of iron ... which led to the fountain of living waters, or to the tree of life" (1 Nephi 9:25 and 8:19). The "fruit" of the Tree of Life "sheddeth itself abroad in the hearts of the children of men" (1 Nephi 9:22). After consuming its "fruit" Lehi wanted his family to also consume it because he now knew that the "fruit" was "desirable above all other" (1 Nephi 8:10-12).

The meaning of the vision is this: The "rod of iron ... which led to the fountain of living waters, or to the tree of life" was a reference to the rod of iron which pierced Jesus' side drawing "blood." Blood, which you now know, is known as the *living waters*. It is blood which pumps through the *heart* and can be *sheddeth*. The fruit spoken of which the Tree of Life yields is blood. Consuming blood was "desirable above all other" because it extends the human life-span.

In the "13th" century this secret science was also encoded by the Order of Rosicrucians into the very name of its founder Christian Rosenkreuz. The name is really a myth designed to teach mankind occult truths:

"His very name is an embodiment of the manner and the means by which the present day man is transformed into the Divine Superman. This symbol,

"Christian Rosen Kreuz"
[The] Christian Rose Cross,

shows the end and aim of human evolution, the road to be traveled, and the means whereby that good end is gained. The black cross, the twinning green stem of the plant, the thorns, the blood red roses - in these is hidden the solution of the World Mystery - Man's past evolution, present constitution, and particularly the secret of his future development.

It hides from the profane, but reveals to the Initiate ... that choicest of all gems, the **Philosopher's Stone**... (Rf61)
* * *

The blood drinking practices were even secretly encoded into poems and fictional writings. In fact, it is the science hidden behind the fictional story of the vampire.

The vampire drinks blood. Drinking the blood extends his life-span, allowing the vampire to live for hundreds of years. It also increases his physical abilities. In this fictional story you can clearly see the secret sciences, as taught by Jesus, and before him, practiced from Adam to Noah.

The story of the vampire even includes the character trait of how the vampire hates the cross. Most people are unfamiliar with the origins of the cross and incorrectly believe that it is a symbol of God. These people then falsely assume that the vampire hates the cross because he is *evil* and the cross (representing goodness), will kill the vampire.

As you now know, the cross is a symbol of the Anunnaki/Elohim/ Nephilim. They were against mankind; they tried to prevent mankind from obtaining any knowledge that would elevate us out of slavery; they didn't want mankind living long lives and forbade mankind from drinking blood. The vampire is repulsed by the sight of the cross because of what the cross symbolizes: his enslavement to a short, weak, unintelligent life.

It's similar to the way modern Jewish people feel about the swastika. To them the swastika is a symbol of all the evil that Hitler did to them. When Jewish people see a swastika they are repulsed by it. This is the same way the vampire feels when it sees a cross.

Out of all the vampire fables that have been written, it was Bram Stoker's version, published in 1897, that directly connected it to the ancient practices by naming his vampire "Dracula."

While Stoker's book doesn't mention it directly, based upon his research papers, all authorities on the subject agree that his character "Dracula" was based upon Vlad Barsarab III.

It was ascertained that Stoker had originally intended to name his vampire character Count Wampyr (Rf62). However, while performing research at a public library in England he discovered an 1820 text entitled An Account of the Principalities of Wallachia and Moldavia, which described "A voivode [prince] Dracula" (Vlad Barsarab III) (Rf63).

Through his research into the history of Voivode Dracula, Bram Stoker would have learned: In the year 1390, Vlad Barsarab II was born into the Wallachian House of Barsarab the Great (1310-1352). Wallachia was a Romanian province. Bordering on its north is Transylvania. Prince Vlad II grew up to become appointed the military governor of Transylvania. On February 8, 1431 Vlad II was inducted into the Society of the Dragon by Zsigmond Von Luxembourg, King of Hungary (Rf64).

It was the membership in this Society of the Dragon that evidenced the connection between the fictitious vampire character and the real life ancient blood drinking practices.

244

The Society of the Dragon traces its origins back to ancient Egypt where it was identified as the Dragon Court under the priest Ankhfn-khonsu (c.2170 BC) and more formally established by Queen Sobeknefru (c.1785-1782 B.C.) (Rf65).

While the teachings of the Society are based upon the sciences of Thoth and the ancient Mystery Schools (which ultimately stem back to the teachings that Enki bestowed upon mankind) it is not known how much the original teachings had become distorted by this time. In one form or another the society utilized the blood drinking practices.

Today, the Society of the Dragon is registered at the High Court of Budapest. It is called: *The Imperial and Royal Dragon Court and Order* (Ordo Draconis) - Sarkany Rend, 1408 (Rf66).

Members of the Court wear the insignia of a dragon curved into a circle (the Ouroboros) with a red cross (Fig. 19.9). This is based upon the original emblem of the Rosi-crucis, which identified the Anunnaki/Elohim/Nephilim Bloodline (aka the Bloodline of the Holy Grail, or Sangreal) from the 4th millennium B.C. (Rf67).

Figure 19.9

Today, members of this society claim they are descendants of the Anunnaki/Elohim/Nephilim (that they have Dragon Blood) and that because of this they are entitled to a status of royalty. They base this claim on the allegations that they can trace their lineage back through history, in an unbroken line, to the Anunnaki/Elohim/Nephilim (Rf68).

However, their claim to be of **Dragon Blood** based upon what their family lineage is makes no more sense than the British monarchy who claim royalty because of their family lineage. As I've shown in Chapter 6 (Genes, Traits, and The Blood of the Gods), we are all siblings. If we trace our ancestors back far enough they all merge into one ancestral line. For people to argue between which branch of the main line they descend from is ludicrous. Dragon Blood is not conferred from parent to child and so on in perpetuity down the line.

When the Anunnaki/Elohim/Nephilim had sex with daughters of men, as described in Genesis 6:4 and Chapter 5 of this book, the gene responsible for Dragon Blood was added to the Human Gene Pool. Dragon Blood is a trait that is inherited at birth in very few people. It doesn't matter what your last name is, what area of the Earth you live on, or which ancestry you can trace your family back to. Only those few people who are born with RH Negative Blood have Dragon Blood. Period.

Through his membership in this society Vlad II obtained the title Lord Draconis, from which he derived his title "Dracul." This stems from the Latin Draco, which means Dragon. From that time on he was known as Vlad Dracul (Rf69). A mis-understanding of the name Dracul led to the erroneous *devil* interpretation.

In 1431, at the fortress of Sighisoara in Romania, Vlad Barsarab III was born (Fig.19.10). He had reddish hair and green eyes. He inherited the Dragon office in the Society at his father's pledge and became known as Vlad Dracula (more precisely Draculea) which means "Son of Dracul" (Son of the Dragon) (Rf70). Evidence of 15th & 16th century sources, including his own signatures, demonstrate that he in fact used the name Dracula (Rf71).

Figure 19.10

Vlad Dracula received his education at the Scholomance (or School of Solomon) mystery school located in the mountains near Hermanstadt in Austria. This mystery school was a center of scientific, alchemical, and hermetic learning which was taught to the sons of royalty. Vlad Dracula became a Hermetic scholar and initiate. He also graduated with honors in a ritual known as Riding the Dragon. This school was considered to be a:

> 'devil's school', where 'the secrets of nature, the language of animals and all magic spells are taught.' (Rf72)

In 1448, at the age of 17, Vlad Dracula became the Voivode of Wallachia, after his father's murder. A statue of him stands at Tiroviste and another by his castle ruin at Capitinei on the River Arges. While he is often spoken of by his enemies as being a brutal tyrant, no such reference comes from his own nation (Rf73).

However, perhaps they were too afraid to speak against him, given that his favored punishment against his enemies was to impale them upon wooden stakes. This earned him the name Tepes, often being referred to as Vlad the Impaler (Fig. 19.11) (Rf74). Dracula would drink the blood of his impaled and decapitated victims.

Figure 19.11

In naming his vampire *Dracula* Bram Stoker had connected the vampire character with a real person who actually knew and utilized the blood drinking practices!

Stoker's reason for doing this is a matter of speculation. Although, we know that while attending Trinity College in Dublin he became president of the Philosophical Society which has been known to study the occult (Rf75). Stoker was also associated with several people who had knowledge of the ancient blood drinking practices. Stoker was:

> a close friend and associate of the Welsh magician and writer Arthur Machen who wrote numerous works, including a paper on the alchemical significance of the Dragon ... Stoker was also acquainted with Aleister Crowley and MacGregor Mathers, both of whom were leading lights in the Hermetic Order of the Golden Dawn ... it has been suggested that Stoker was either a member of the OTO or the Golden Dawn. (Rf76)

In fact, it was Aleister Crowley in *The Book of the Law: Liber Al Vel Legis*, who said "The best blood is of the moon, monthly". So clearly Stoker had some knowledge of the blood drinking practices, although to what extent is not known.

Another interesting point is that Bram Stoker even set the home of Dracula as Transylvania. This is significant because the real Vlad Dracula is from Wallachia. So why not also set the home of his Dracula as such? The reason is because Stoker was also teaching where the blood drinking practice originated. Present day Transylvania was originally Ubaid, Sumeria!

In fact, some of the earliest evidence of the blood drinking practice comes from Tartaria in Transylvania and stems to the fifth millennium B.C.

> Archaeologists working in Tartaria in the Ubaid territory of Transylvania discovered a "tepes" or Rath under which they found a fire-pit dated to about 5000 B.C. Buried amongst the ashes were the human remains of a cannibalistic sacrificial victim and two clay tablets.

On these were inscribed the name of Enki ... the number of Anu - 60 - and the image of a goat, Enki again, and a Tree - Lilith. (Rf77)

The language on the tablets was subsequently termed proto-Sumerian and represented some of the earliest written artifacts yet to be found. Again connecting the practice with the history of the Anunnaki/Elohim/Nephilim.

* * *

This should demonstrate some of the ways in which the ancient practices have been spread throughout history. If you look close enough you will find them everywhere, in one form or another.

However, I should point out that often knowledge gets twisted or even lost over extended periods of time. This results in small to drastic variations in the practices. For example, we see this at work in the StarFire practice when at one time people believed that only *special* women could provide them with the menstrual blood; to them, it had to be a priestess, as we saw in the biblical case of Abishag the Shunammite. This was clearly because (even though they knew the basic practice) they did not truly understand the science behind it.

We see this again in modern Witchcraft. New Age Wiccans try to distance themselves from the blood drinking practices (which have become known as the Black Mass), arguing they have nothing to do with Witchcraft. They even create fictitious distinctions of White and Black Witchcraft to justify this absurdity. All of which, demonstrates their ignorance of what Witchcraft truly is.

The foundation of Witchcraft stems back to the ancient sciences of the Anunnaki/Elohim/Nephilim/Watchers. These people are also the deities (sometimes called "Mighty Ones," "Avatars," "Ancestors," etc.) that Witches worship. As you will see in the next section, even the images Witches use to represent their deity (like the double-faced Janus or goat-headed Baphomet) contain the same alchemical principles.

As an example: modern day Witches often worship the moon goddess Diana, a concept that emerged around the 6th century B.C. (Rf78). The secrets underlying the worship of Diana are the same as those explained earlier with regard to the Indian goddess Kali; the StarFire. Diana was celebrated with rites of moon-dew (Moon-Fluid) every 28 days (Rf79). Ancient witches weren't worshipping the moon; they were celebrating what the full moon stood for, the coming menstrual cycle. Witchcraft was based upon these ancient blood drinking practices and for *New Age* Wiccans to argue that they have nothing to do with it is ludicrous.

This also occurs in the very Secret Societies whose job it is to preserve the knowledge. Despite the fact that certain secret societies have knowledge of the basic blood drinking practices, it is clear that they do not completely understand the true science behind it. This is evidenced when these people drink blood in fancy rituals held once a month or on a few special days throughout the year. While they have the right intentions, they are fooling themselves; similar to role playing. Perhaps the true understanding of the practice was lost to them over time, or intentionally hidden from them by their superiors. In any event, it is necessary to consume a minimum of 2 cups of *young blood* every day in order to achieve high enough blood serum levels of the *substances* that heighten mental and physical abilities and extend the life-span.

* * *

The Mystery of Fire and Water
The Secret Combination

After utilizing the StarFire science, our ancient ancestors discovered that menstrual blood had additional benefits that regular blood did not contain.

During menstruation the *ovum* is flushed out of the body with the blood. Since the menstrual blood was being collected in a chalice for use in StarFire, the ovum was also consequently collected. Our ancestors discovered that by adding male semen to the chalice containing the menstrual blood, the ovum would become fertilized resulting in an embryo.

In modern times this process is known as in vitro fertilization where an ovum is removed from a female and mixed with sperm in a laboratory dish or test tube. However, in ancient times the embryo was not implanted back into the body.

What possible need would our ancient ancestors have for an embryo? ***Embryonic stem cells!*** As modern scientists are just discovering, embryonic stem cells can be used to regenerate damaged tissues in the body. After injecting stem cells into damaged tissues like hearts, livers, eyes, etc., they have healed within days to weeks. Modern scientists are also using stem cells to create new organs entirely. In one experiment scientists discovered that they were able to take a washed exoskeleton of a heart, pour stem cells over it, and the stem cells formed a new heart with all its arteries. When a small

249

electrical charge was emitted into the heart it began beating on its own! Stem cells have even been used to suppress the extra chromosome that is responsible for Down Syndrome. Modern scientists are just beginning to learn all the benefits of stem cells.

While there is another use for the embryonic stem cells, it is a process that will not be discussed herein. Over time this science was passed down from generation to generation, where we see it preserved in the ancient writings of the Egyptians. In Egypt the ritual was known as a sacred marriage that brought fertility and prevented death.

1. The *sacred marriage* is that of the Two Opposites: male and female. The Alpha and the Omega, the First and the Last, the Beginning and the End. Semen is the beginning of life, before it exists (the Alpha). The menstruated Ovum is the end of life, before it exists (the Omega).

2. The *fertility* is the spark of life... embryo... embryonic stem cells that are created through the alchemical process of combining the Two Opposites. It is known as the Third State (Trinity).

3. The ritual *prevented death* because drinking the blood and embryonic stem cells extends life-span.

This is known as the **Secret Combination** and the **Mystery of Fire and Water**. The combining of the two opposites. In alchemy semen is symbolized as fire and, as I've previously shown, blood is symbolized as water. Many images and symbols have been used to represent this Secret Combination, for example:

The Two Opposites are usually depicted as an Androgyne (half-male, half-female) (Fig. 19.12) (Rf80). In the Janus/Jana image you see the woman holding a snake in her hand, symbolizing that she possesses a required element. The man holds a chalice in his hand containing three snakes, representing the three elements (blood, ovum, semen) being mixed together to create the elixir. Also contained in the image are the Tree of Life, the Phoenix which represents immortality, and three snakes cannibalizing each other, a metaphor that the

Figure 19.12

elements needed to be consumed in the alchemical process are contained within the Two Opposites themselves. When the Two Opposites are properly combined the Third State (Trinity) is achieved. It is represented in this image by the Crown which sits atop of the Two, now united, Opposites and represents the crowning of the Great Work in alchemy. You also see the outstretched wings of the Caduceus, since the message is the same with both images. All of which symbolize the path to an extended life.

The Templars symbolized this Secret Combination in the image they called **Baphomet**, which is also depicted as the Androgyne. The image is usually found with a male and female face, back to back, and a third face centered between the two representing the Third State. The name Baphomet has been translated as Bapho Mitra or Father Mithras by some (Rf81), others say it is a corruption of Bathos Metis (purification by wisdom). The name Baphomet was re-translated by Dr. Hugh Schonfield using the Atbash cipher, a Hebrew device used to hide messages in texts. He found that while in Hebrew it reads Bet Pe Vav Mem Taf, using the Atbash cipher, it reads Shin Vav Pe Yud Alef, which in English means "Sophia" (Wisdom) (Rf82).

Eliphas Levi said that in Latin Baphomet means *Templi Omnium Hominum Pacis Abbas* (The God of the Temple of Peace Among All Men). He said that it is a reversal composition of three abbreviations Tem.Oph(ohp).Ab., which spell the name Baphomet backwards (Rf83). Levi believed this was a reference to the Temple of Solomon. As I've shown above, the two pillars of Solomon's Temple describe this secret practice.

Levi's drawing of Baphomet has the head, horns, and feet of a goat (Fig. 19.13). Between the horns is a three pointed flame. It has a beard representing great wisdom. It has the torso of a snake/serpent and wings, representing the Anunnaki/Elohim/Nephilim. Baphomet has the breasts of a female and phallus of a man with two serpents entwined around it symbolizing the Two Opposites being combined in the form of a Caduceus.

On Baphomet's forehead is the female Pentagram (single point up). In the middle of the female Pentagram is the Emerald Jewel of Lucifer. Myths say that the Emerald Jewel was brought to Earth by Lucifer and eventually became known as the *Philosopher's Stone*. Remember, Lucifer means Bringer of Light (Wisdom). As shown in the alchemy section, the Philosopher's Stone was a euphemism for blood, and because it is synonymous with the Emerald Jewel, it too is a euphemism for blood. The Emerald Jewel was a "sacred stone" among the ancient tribes of North and South America, the Mayas, Mexicans, and Zapotecs. It represented Enki (Horus I. in Egypt) known as Prince of the Emerald Stone and symbolized "Eternal Youth." (Rf84). It was represented:

hieroglyphically as lustrous bodies, with eyes at the four corners - i.e. sending rays in four directions, representing Horus - Her-uatch-f Prince of the Emerald Stone ... The Ritual says: "I am the Tablet of felspar," Green Stone Uat amulet that was placed in the tomb as a type of that which was for *ever green, fresh, young, and represented eternal youth* (Rf85)

This is also why the color green is used to symbolize "youth" in alchemy. As you will see below, the "green" Emerald Jewel in the middle of the female Pentagram symbolizes the female menstrual blood and ovum that are used to extend life.

Figure 19.13

Baphomet's left arm has the word **Coagula** written on it and points down to the dark (female) moon crest with three fingers (thumb, index and middle). Its right arm has the word **Solve** written on it and points upward to the white (male) moon crest with two fingers (index, middle). The hidden message is that by *combining* (Coagula) the *Two Opposites* (male and female) you obtain the mystical Third State. This is also indicated in the fingers, where the 2 become 3. The five points of the Pentagram!

The head of Baphomet represents the combined male and female opposites, similar to the Crown in the Janus/Jana image. In this position the three pointed flame represents the Third State. Geometrically what you are seeing in the Goat Head and female Pentagram on its forehead are the male and female Pentagram symbols combined (Fig. 19.14 and Fig. 19.15).

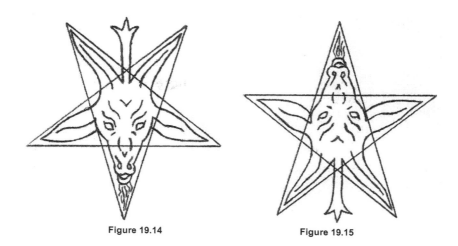

Figure 19.14   Figure 19.15

If you turn Baphomet's head upside-down, his head becomes the female pentagram (Fig. 19.15). The chin becomes her head, the ears are her arms, the horns are her legs, and the jewel then becomes her vagina. In this position, the three pointed *flame* coming out of the jewel is **StarFire**! (Rf86)

The Jewish Star of David, also known as Solomon's Seal (Fig. 19.16) is identical in meaning to the male and female pentagrams of Baphomet. When you combine the Two Opposite pyramids (Fig. 19.17) the Third State is achieved. While this symbol has been attributed to King David it is far more ancient. The two pyramids (triangles) depicted in (Fig. 19.17) can be found carved into stones dating back tens of thousands of years before King David was ever said to exist. This symbol is found on sacred ornaments of most ancient tribes from Egypt to Australia, Mexico, Central America, etc. (Rf87).

Figure 19.16   Figure 19.17

The Chinese Yin-Yang symbol (Fig. 19.18), also known as the Tai Chi symbol, reflects the same secret combination. When the Two Opposites, male (white, positive) and female (black, negative) are combined the Third State is achieved.

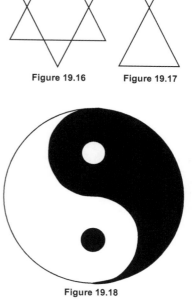

Figure 19.18

Another symbol used to represent this secret combination is the Caduceus (Fig. 19.19). The name stems from the Latin word kerykeion and different versions of the symbol can be found all over the world. It is also known as the Arcadian Rod, Staff of Hermes, and Staff of Brahma. Because the Caduceus symbolized the uniting of opposite forces, it "was carried by Greek messengers and ambassadors, and later became a Roman symbol for truce, neutrality and non-combatant status." (Rf88)

Figure 19.19

In the Caduceus the two snakes symbolize the Two Opposites being combined, from which, the Third State is achieved. The Third State is represented by the orb and outstretched wings, similar to the Crown that is used in other symbols like the Janus/Jana image shown earlier. The symbol represents the path to immortality.

While different Secret Societies use their own symbols to represent this Secret Combination, all have the same esoteric meaning at their core. For example:

In Freemasonry the 1st to 32nd degrees use the symbol shown in (Fig.19.20) to represent a person who is on their journey to the Light. In this symbol you see the Doorway to the Light above a two headed Eagle (Phoenix) that holds a sword in its talons. The sword symbolizes the flaming sword that the Anunnaki/ Elohim/ Nephilim placed in front of the Tree of Life to guard it. The two heads of the eagle symbolize the Two Opposites. They have not yet been united because the person is still on their

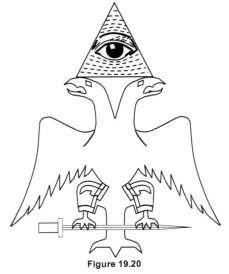

Figure 19.20

254

journey. Notice how the wings of the eagle are in a downward position as if it is flying upwards towards the Doorway to the Light.

However, in Freemasonry the 33rd degree is represented by the symbol depicted in (Fig. 19.21). With what you now know of the Secret Combination this symbol should be easy to decipher. In this image notice how the wings are no longer downward, but up and outstretched like the Caduceus and Janus/Jana images, because the eagle is no longer flying upwards. The Two Opposites are united and the Third State has been achieved. In this image it is represented by the Crown of Zodiacal Light, the highest crown of illumination in the highest degree. Surmounting the crown is a Cross which has the **Sacred Triangle** (of Enki, Horus

Figure 19.21

I) resting on it. Only by combining the Two Opposites and achieving the Third State can you *cross* into the realm of the Anunnaki/ Elohim/Nephilim (i.e. obtain their heightened mental and physical abilities as well as their extended life-spans).

The **Secret Combination** is also represented in the Qabalistic Tree of Life (also known as the ETS CHAYYIM) (Fig. 19.22). Without going into a detailed discussion of the many layers of the Qabalah, basically the Tree is *divided* into Three Pillars, comprised of ten circles called the Ten Holy Sephiroth (Rf89). Similar to the two snakes in the Caduceus, the Two Opposites are represented by the Two Pillars: MERCY (Male, Positive) and SEVERITY (Female, Negative). Similar to the staff of the Caduceus, the Neutral Point is the Middle Pillar EQUILIBRIUM.

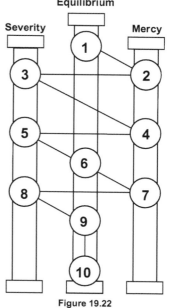

Figure 19.22

When the Tree is used to represent the Macrocosm, it is viewed like this:

SEVERITY	EQUILIBRIUM	MERCY
(Female, Negative)	(Male, Neutral)	(Positive)
(3) Binah	(1) Kether	(2) Chokmah
(5) Geburah	(6) Tiphareth	(4) Chesed
(8) Hod	(9) Yesod	(7) Netzach
	(10) Malkuth	

But when the Tree is used to represent the Microcosm (the human body) we back into it, so that the Middle Pillar equates with the spine and the pillar that contains Binah is now on our right side (Rf90), like this:

MERCY	EQUILIBRIUM	SEVERITY
(Male, Positive)	(Neutral)	(Female, Negative)
Chokmah	Kether	Binah
Chesed	Tiphareth	Geburah
Netzach	Yesod	Hod
	Malkuth	

The Two Pillars represent the male and female opposites, the *"positive and negative forces in Nature, the active and passive, the destructive and constructive, concreting form and free-moving force"* (Rf91). As you can see, the same basic elements that underlie the previous symbols, as well as the Two Tat Pillars and Two Pillars of Solomon's Temple, are contained in the Qabalistic Tree of Life.

* * *

On a deeper level, the Secret Combination relates to the forces of energy and the process of how to manipulate that energy through the proper use of the positive, negative, and neutral.

SUMMATION

MY RESEARCH leads me to believe that at one point in history an advanced race of people inhabited earth. These people had technological and scientific capabilities that we still don't possess today. With their ability to manipulate the positive and negative forces of nature (energy) they possessed sciences which increased their intelligence, strength, and life-span. These people may have been an advanced society that arose here on earth, or may have been astronauts from another planet that arrived here and colonized earth.

Researching the origins of myths, legends and religious systems of every culture around the world it becomes evident that they all stem, in one form or another, from a common source: the history of these people. Different cultures simply used different names throughout time to identify the same people, places, and events.

By investigating the ancient texts from around the world that have not been lost to us by the sands of time, while attempting to discern between information that may have historical significance and that which was designed to lead people astray by intentional deceptions (not to mention the distortions that undoubtedly arose over time as they spread mouth to ear from culture to culture, generation to generation), I believe that we can discover these ancient sciences and use them to increase the intellectual capabilities of the human mind, use them to increase the strength of the human body, and use them to dramatically increase the human life-span, just like those people did. *As above, so below*.

Today a war is raging on behind the scenes. The control mechanisms (Religions) that the Anunnaki/Elohim/Nephilim implemented have been indoctrinating society for thousands of years with lies in order to keep mankind divided and enslaved. So great a deception, they have even succeeded in deluding their slaves into believing that a human's very existence in the material world is evil; that the goal in life is to liberate oneself from the material world, in other words – *die*.

This is why **evil** is **live** spelled backwards, because to them the longer a human is alive the more time that individual has to acquire knowledge; knowledge which increases his intelligence and inevitably leads to his "eyes" becoming "opened", enabling him to see past the smoke and mirrors of the control mechanisms.

On the other side, the Illuminati are struggling against those control mechanisms to re-unite mankind so that we will be one strong united force before those people return as warned in the Book of Revelations. Anyone who has tried to unite all the people in one room under a common purpose knows how difficult a task that is, let alone trying to unite the billions of people around the world. This requires them to utilize every available technique, even those described in the Protocols, for the greater good of humanity as they gradually prepare society to accept the hard truths that await them.

While the steps the Illuminati have taken may seem drastic to the un-informed, the alternative is to do nothing, and that leads to the enslavement and eventual annihilation of mankind, which is no alternative at all. The end justifies the means.

You can choose to be "meek", "child-like" (unintelligent), "submissive", "sheep" as proposed by the religious control mechanisms and remain in a state of ignorance enslaved to the will of the Anunnaki/Elohim/Nephilim masters, or you can choose to use your brain, educate yourselves, and fight to uplift the human race and survive.

the advantage of knowledge is this:
that wisdom preserves the life of its possessor.
(Ecclesiastes 7:12)

Whose side are you on?

ILLUMINATI

REFERENCES

PART I: ANCIENT HISTORY

Chapter 1: The Ancient Astronauts

1. Sitchin, Zecharia, There Were Giants Upon the Earth: Gods, Demigods, and Human Ancestry: The Evidence of Alien DNA (2010 Bear & Company), p.197, 82
2. Sitchin, Zecharia, The Stairway to Heaven (1980), p.117
3. Sitchin, Zecharia, The 12th Planet (1976), p.89; and There Were Giants Upon the Earth, supra, p.197
4. The 12th Planet, supra, pp.89-90
5. There Were Giants Upon the Earth, supra, p.127
6. Sitchin, Zecharia, Genesis Revisited: Is Modern Science Catching Up With Ancient Knowledge? (1990), p.90
7. The 12th Planet, supra, pp.100-101; Flying Serpents and Dragons, infra, p.68; There Were Giants Upon the Earth p.100
8. There Were Giants Upon the Earth, supra, p.138; The Stairway to Heaven p.152
9. The 12th Planet, supra, p.95
10. Kramer, S.N., Sumerian Mythology, pp.44, 59
11. There Were Giants Upon the Earth, supra, p.132
12. The 12th Planet, supra, pp.104-106
13. There Were Giants Upon the Earth, supra, p.129; The 12th Planet p.177
14. Ibid.
15. Ibid. pp.127-128
16. Ibid.
17. The 12th Planet, supra, pp.124-126
18. Boulay, R.A., Flying Serpents and Dragons: The Story of Mankind's Reptillian Past (1999), pp.66-67
19. Ibid. pp.46-48
20. Ibid. pp.41-43
21. Siblerud, Robert, Our Galactic Visitors: The Extraterrestrial Influence (New Science Publications 2008), pp.42-43
22. Hancock, Graham, Fingerprints of the Gods (1995), p.104
23. Sitchin, Zecharia, The Lost Realms (1990), p.24
24. Ibid. p.87
25. Ibid. p.68
26. Fingerprints of the Gods, supra, pp.101-103; Our Galactic Visitors, supra, p.179
27. The Lost Realms, supra, p.7
28. Ibid. p.19; Pinchbeck, Daniel, 2012, The Return of Quetzalcoatl (Penguin Group 2006)
29. Fingerprints of the Gods, supra, pp.42-45
30. Ibid. p.45-49

31. Genesis Revisited, supra, p.19
32. The Lost Realms, supra, p.271
33. For a more in-depth account of the history of the Anunnaki upon Earth I highly suggest reading Zecharia Sitchin's seven book series called The Earth Chronicles (The 12th Planet, The Stairway to Heaven, The Wars of Gods and Men, The Lost Realms, When Time Began, The Cosmic Code, and The End of Days), and his other books Genesis Revisited, The Lost Book of Enki, There Were Giants Upon the Earth. As well as works from other authors like Eric Von Daniken and David Hatcher Childress. I also implore you to watch the History Channel's Ancient Aliens series.

The purpose of my book is not to rehash every available fact concerning the day to day events of these people which other authors have published already. The focus of my book is demonstrating how these people created religions as a control mechanism to enslave mankind, how secret societies are actually the resistance movement against their control, and how all of this is affecting society today. In order to accomplish that I need to give you a brief summary of their history, focusing on certain key points.

Chapter 2: Planet of Origin

1. The 12th Planet, supra, pp.237-242
2. Ibid. pp.238-239;
3. Ibid. pp.212-239
4. Zinc isotopic evidence for the origin of the Moon, Nature 490, 376-379 (October 18, 2012) DOI:10.1038/nature11507
5. The 12th Planet, supra, pp.204-206; There Were Giants Upon the Earth p.115
6. Ibid. p.240
7. Sitchin, Zecharia, The End of Days: Armageddon and Prophecies of the Return (2007), pp.303-304
8. Johnson, Keith, Why is U.S. Government Moving Installations to Center of Nation?, (American Free Press, June 27, 2011)
9. Watson, Tracy, "Little body may be under influence of much bigger one" (USA Today, March 27, 2014)

Chapter 3: Arrival on Earth

1. There Were Giants Upon the Earth, supra, pp.84-86
2. Ibid. p.27
3. Ibid. pp.21-22
4. Sitchin, Zecharia, The Wars of Gods and Men (1985), pp.32-33
5. There Were Giants Upon the Earth, supra, p.23
6. Lambert, W.G. and Millard, A.R., Atra-Hasis, the Babylonian Story of the Flood (1969); Clay, Albert T., Atrahasis, An Ancient Hebrew Deluge Story and Other Flood Story Fragments (1922)

7. There Were Giants Upon the Earth, supra, p.137
8. The 12th Planet, supra, p.284
9. The 12th Planet, supra, pp.287-290; There Were Giants Upon the Earth p.47
10. The 12th Planet, supra, p.134-135
11. Chariots of the Gods, by Erich Von Daniken (1970)
12. The 12th Planet, supra, pp.288, 290
13. The Lost Book of Enki; The 12th Planet, supra, p.288
14. The 12th Planet, supra, p.290
15. Genesis Revisited, supra, p.88
16. The 12th Planet, supra, p.48
17. The 12th Planet, supra, p.318-319
18. There Were Giants Upon the Earth, supra, p.138; The 12th Planet, supra, p.294
19. The 12th Planet, supra, pp.272-278
20. The 12th Planet, supra, p.294; The Wars of Gods and Men, supra, p.87
21. The 12th Planet, supra, p.297
22. The Wars of Gods and Men, supra, p.87
23. The 12th Planet, supra, pp.290, 298; The Wars of Gods and Men, supra, p.87
24. The 12th Planet, supra, pp.290-300
25. The Wars of Gods and Men, supra, p.87, The 12th Planet, supra, p.297
26. The 12th Planet, supra, pp.294-295; The Wars of Gods and Men, surpa, p.88
27. The 12th Planet, supra, p.327
28. The 12th Planet, supra, pp.295-296
29. There Were Giants Upon the Earth, supra, p.140
30. Ibid.; Genesis Revisited, supra, p.163; The 12th Planet, supra, pp.312-318
31. The 12th Planet, supra, p.96
32. The 12th Planet, supra, p.330
33. Ibid.
34. There Were Giants Upon the Earth, supra, p.142
35. The End of Days, supra, pp.245-246
36. Genesis Revisited, supra, p.246
37. Ibid. pp.246-248
38. Ibid. pp.248-250
39. Ibid. pp.250-251; The End of Days p.248
40. Genesis Revisited, supra, p.251
41. Genesis Revisited, supra, pp.252-253
42. The End of Days, supra, p.246
43. www.universetoday.com/99750/another-weird-shiny-thing-on-mars-2/
44. Genesis Revisited, supra, p.253
45. Ibid., p.142
46. The 12th Planet, supra, p.330
47. Ibid. p.332
48. Churchward, Albert, Signs and Symbols of Primordial Man: The Evolution of Religious Doctrines from the Eschatology of the Ancient Egyptians (2nd Ed., 1912), p.29
49. Budge, Wallis E.A., The Gods of the Egyptians, Studies in Egyptian Mythology (1904), Vol. 1, p.64
50. The Lost Realms, supra, p.271

51. The 12th Planet, supra, p.332

Chapter 4: "The Adam" Created To Be A Slave Worker Through Genetic Manipulation

1. There Were Giants Upon the Earth, supra, p.146
2. The 12th Planet, supra, p.332
3. Ibid.
4. Ibid. p.333
5. Ibid.
6. Ibid. p.333-334
7. Genesis Revisited, supra, p.159
8. There Were Giants Upon the Earth, supra, p.147
9. Genesis Revisited, supra, p.160; The 12th Planet, supra, pp.342-343
10. Genesis Revisited, supra, p.160; The 12th Planet, supra, p.344
11. The 12th Planet, supra, p.337
12. Ibid.
13. Mendez, Fernando; Kyahn, Thomas; Schrack, Bonnie; Krahn, Astrid-Maria; Veeramah, Krishna; Woerner, August; Fomine, Forka Leypey Mathew; Bradman, Neil et al. (2013). "An African American paternal lineage adds an extremely ancient root to the human Y chromosome phylogenic tree" (haplogroup-a.com/ Ancient-Root-AJHG2013.pdf). American Journal of Human Genetics 92 (3):454
14. Genesis Revisited, supra, p.198
15. Ibid. p.199
16. There Were Giants Upon the Earth, supra, p.150; Genesis Revisited, supra, p.167
17. The 12th Planet, supra, pp.346-347
18. Ibid. p.349
19. Ibid. p.357
20. Ibid. p.348
21. Ibid. pp.351-352
22. Ibid. p.347
23. Ibid. p.351
24. Tellinger, Michael, Slave Species of the Gods: The Secret History of the Anunnaki and Their Mission on Earth (2005), p.482
25. The 12th Planet, supra, pp.354-355
26. Ibid. p.352
27. There Were Giants Upon the Earth, supra, p.150
28. Atrahasis (Clay), surpa, p.68, Lines 11-14
29. Enuma Elish, The Seven Tablets of Creation, or the Babylonian and Assyrian Legends Concerning the Creation of the World and of Mankind, edited by L.W. King (1999), p.99, Lines 30-33
30. The 12th Planet, supra, p.349
31. The Lost Book of Enki, supra
32. Kramer, S.N., Mythologies of the Ancient World (1961 Anchor Books), p.103

33. The 12th Planet, supra, pp.354-358
34. Ibid. p.369
35. Ibid.
36. Flying Serpents and Dragons, supra, p.11
37. Genesis Revisited, supra, p.22
38. Ibid.
39. The 12th Planet, surpa, pp.359-360
40. Atra-Hasis (Lambert), supra, pp.65, 67
41. Slave Species of the Gods p.484
42. The Lost Realms, supra, p.179
43. Ibid. pp.35-36
44. Ibid. pp.178-179
45. Signs and Symbols of Primordial Man, supra, p.134
46. Ibid. p.437
47. Ibid. pp.140-145
48. Ibid. pp.133, 140
49. Ibid. p.155
50. Ibid. p.218 note 2
51. Ibid. p.437
52. Ibid. p.218
53. Ibid. p.148-149
54. The 12th Planet, supra, p.4
55. Horn, Dr. Arthur David, Mallory-Horn, Lynette, Anne, Humanity's Extraterrestrial Origins: ET Influences on Humankind's Biological and Cultural Evolution (1994), pp.46-47
56. Genesis Revisited, supra, p.197
57. Humanity's Extraterrestrial Origins, supra, pp.46-47. For years the evidence pointed to Africa as the earliest site of Neanderthals but a date from China places near modern looking humans there at least 200 KYA. "Asian Hominids Make a Much Earlier Entrance" by B. Bower (1994), Science News, #145, p.150
58. Slave Species of the Gods, supra, p.49
59. 59sciencenews.org; June 5, 2010, p.5, January 15, 2011, p.10
60. Hopkin, Michael (2005-02-16). "Ethiopia is top choice for cradle of Homo sapiens" www.nature.com/news/2005/050216/ full/news050214-10.html). Nature News. doi:10.1038/news050214-10
61. Flying Serpents and Dragons p.123
62. Martinez, Susan B., PhD., "A Question of Breeding" (Atlantis Rising #105, May/June 2014), p.46
63. ccn.com/2006/TECH/science/11/15/neanderthal.ap/index.html 64.Genesis Revisited, supra, pp.195-196
64. "A Question of Breeding", supra, p.47
65. American Free Press, Issues 14 & 15 (April 8 & 15), p.2

Chapter 5: The Anunnaki/Elohim/Nephilim Have Sex With the Daughters of Men

1. The Book of Enoch, translated by R.H. Charles (originally published 1917; republished by Dover, 2007), CVI:13
2. Ibid. VI:1
3. Ibid. VI:2
4. Ibid. VI:3
5. Ibid. VI:4
6. Ibid. VII:1
7. Ibid. VII:2
8. Ibid. VII:1, VIII:3
9. Ibid. VIII:1, LXV:7-8
10. Ibid. VIII:3
11. The 12th Planet, supra, p.269
12. Genesis Revisited, supra, pp.5-14

Chapter 6: Genes, Traits, and The Blood of the Gods: Evidence of the Anunnaki/Elohim/Nephilim Bloodline - RH Negative Blood

1. "Divergence between samples of chimpanzee and human DNA sequences is 5% counting indels" www.ncbi.nlm.nih.gov/pmc/ articles/PMC129726). PNAS 99 (21): 13633-5. Bitcode: 2002PNAS ...9913633B
2. Genesis 5:28-29
3. The Book of Enoch, supra, CVI:1-2
4. Ibid. CVI:4-6
5. 2nd Book of Enoch, 1:4-5
6. The Book of Enoch, supra, 14:20
7. Ibid. 71:1
8. Ibid. CVI:7
9. Ibid. CVI:10
10. Ibid. CVI:18
11. The Stairway to Heaven, supra, pp. 148-149
12. Dupont-Sommer, A., The Essene Writings from Qumran, p.285
13. The Stairway to Heaven, supra, pp. 148-149
14. Sora, Steven, Alexander's Lost Navy, Atlantis Rising No. 96 (November/December 2012), pp.30, 62
15. The Genetics of Blood Type, by Emory University School of Medicine (2006) (genetics.emory.edu/pdf/factsheet43.pdf)
16. RH factor blood test, by Mayo Clinic Staff (April 27, 2010) (mayoclinic.com/health/rh-factor/MY01163)
17. The Genetics of Blood Type, supra
18. Rh Blood Types (anthro.palmar.edu/blood/Rh_system.htm)
19. "Blood of the Gods," UFO's Ancient Astronaut Magazine (October 1976), p.46

20. Ibid.
21. Ibid.
22. Icke, David, The Rh Negative Factor (reptilianagenda.com/research/rl10199a.html)

Chapter 7: The Great Flood and The Plot To Kill Mankind

1. The Book of Enoch, supra, IX:6
2. Ibid. VII:5
3. Ibid. VII:3
4. Ibid. VIII:2
5. Atra-Hasis (Lambert), supra, p.73
6. Atrahasis (Clay), supra, p.65 Lines 9-12
7. The 12th Planet, supra, pp.390-391
8. Atrahasis, (Clay), supra, p.66 Lines 25-28
9. Ibid. p.66 Lines 39-43
10. Ibid. pp.66-67 Lines 44-46
11. The 12th Planet, supra, p.391
12. Ibid. p.392
13. Ibid. pp.393-394
14. Ibid. p.402
15. Ibid. p.401
16. The Stairway to Heaven, supra, pp.140-141
17. Ibid. p.141; The 12th Planet, supra, p.381
18. The 12th Planet, supra, p.395
19. Ibid.
20. There Were Giants Upon the Earth, supra, p.55
21. The 12th Planet, supra, p.390
22. There Were Giants Upon the Earth, supra, p.53
23. Slave Species of the Gods, supra, p.242
24. The 12th Planet, supra, p.395
25. Ibid. p.396
26. Atrahasis (Clay), supra, p.73 Lines 23-29
27. The Stairway to Heaven, supra, p.141
28. The 12th Planet, supra, pp.381-382
29. Atrahasis (Clay), supra, p.69 Lines 7-9
30. Ibid. pp.76-77 Lines 81-86 and 95
31. The 12th Planet, supra, p.397
32. Ibid. p.388
33. The Lost Realms, supra, p.33
34. The 12th Planet, supra, p.403
35. The Wars of Gods and Men, supra, p.118
36. The 12th Planet, supra, p.383
37. Ibid. p.398
38. Ibid.
39. Atrahasis (Clay), supra, pp.78-79 Lines 136-141
40. Ibid. p.79 Lines 146-159

41. Ibid. p.80 Lines 160-162
42. Ibid. p.80 Lines 163-170
43. Ibid. pp.80-81 Lines 171-195
44. The 12th Planet, supra, p.384
45. There Were Giants Upon the Earth, supra, p.30
46. Ibid. p.31
47. Slave Species of the Gods, supra, p.244
48. Ibid. pp.245-246
49. The Children of Odin, The Book of Northern Myths, by Padraic Colum (1984)
50. Slave Species of the Gods, supra, pp.245-246
51. Ibid.
52. Ibid. p.247
53. Ibid. p.379
54. The Book of Enoch, supra, X:2-3

Chapter 8: The Tower of Babel and The Division of Mankind

1. The Wars of Gods and Men, supra, p.129
2. Ibid. p.121
3. Ibid. p.123
4. Humanity's Extraterrestrial Origins, supra, p.111
5. There Were Giants Upon the Earth, supra, p.223
6. The Stairway to Heaven, supra, p.192
7. The 12th Planet, supra, p.140; The Stairway to Heaven p.221
8. Ibid. p.142
9. Ibid. pp.138-139
10. Ibid.
11. The Stairway to Heaven, supra, p.98-99
12. Ibid. pp.97,102
13. The 12th Planet, supra, p.143; Flying Serpents and Dragons, supra, p.166
14. The Epic of Gilgamesh
15. The 12th Planet, supra, pp.161-162
16. Ibid. p.143-144
17. The Stairway to Heaven, supra, p.103-104
18. Bramley, William, The Gods of Eden (1989), p.50
19. The End of Days, supra, p.255
20. The 12th Planet, supra, pp.149-150
21. The Gods of Eden, supra, p.51

REFERENCES

PART II: RELGIONS

Chapter 9: Control Mechanisms To Keep Mankind Enslaved

1. The 12th Planet, supra, p.95
2. Gardner, Laurence, Genesis of the Grail Kings: The Explosive Story of Genetic Cloning and the Ancient Bloodline of Jesus (1999) p.82 citing Sumerian Mythology, S.N. Kramer, pp.44, 59
3. Ibid.

Chapter 10: Judaism

1. Sweeny, Emmett, The Exodus as Egyptian History: Sifting Ancient Records for the Bible Story (Atlantis Rising, No.105), pp.45, 70; Emmett Sweeny is the author of Genesis of Israel and Egypt (2008)
2. The Gods of Eden, supra, p.78
3. Miller, Edith Star (Lady Queenborough), Occult Theocrasy (1933), Vol. 1, p.75
4. Genesis of the Grail Kings, supra, p.35
5. Occult Theocrasy, supra, p.81
6. Ibid. pp.86-87
7. Ibid. p.82
8. Ibid. p.83
9. Icke, David, The Biggest Secret: The Book That Will Change The World (1999), p.88
10. Ibid.
11. Ibid.
12. Ibid.
13. Ibid.
14. Occult Theocrasy, supra, p.87
15. Ibid.
16. Ibid. p.82
17. Ibid. p.83
18. Ibid. p.84
19. Ibid. p.85
20. Ibid. p.83
21. Ibid.
22. Ibid.
23. Ibid. p.84
24. Ibid. p.85
25. Ibid. p.84
26. Ibid. p.85
27. Ibid.

28. Ibid. p.83
29. Ibid.
30. Ibid.
31. Ibid.
32. Ibid. p.85

Chapter 11: Jesus

1. Slave Species of the Gods, supra, p.414
2. Infancy 1:6-11
3. Protovangelion 15:7-9
4. Humanity's Extraterrestrial Origins, supra, p.22 citing Borkamn, G., Jesus of Nazareth (1960), p.71 (1960)
5. The Gods of Eden, supra, p.127
6. Ibid. pp.127-128
7. Slave Species of the Gods, supra, p.417 citing Thiering, Barbara, Jesus of the Apocalypse: The Life of Jesus After the Crucifixion (1996)
8. The Gods of Eden, supra, p.129
9. Ibid. p.130 citing Bock, Janet, The Jesus Mystery, Of Lost Years and Unknown Travels (1980), p.211
10. Occult Theocrasy, supra, p.49
11. Ibid.
12. The Gods of Eden, supra, pp.98-99
13. Ibid. p.99
14. Ibid. p.100
15. Ibid. p.131
16. Slave Species of the Gods, supra, p.237
17. Ibid. p.421
18. The Gods of Eden, supra, pp.131-132
19. Ibid. p.132
20. Slave Species of the Gods, supra, pp.422-423 quoting the Legend of Issa
21. Gardner, Laurence, Bloodline of the Holy Grail: The Hidden Lineage of Jesus Revealed (1996), p.91
22. The Gods of Eden, supra, p.133
23. Bloodline of the Holy Grail, supra, pp.101-115; Baigent, M. Leigh, R., and Lincoln, H., The Holy Blood and the Holy Grail (1982)
24. Alternative News, Did Jesus Have a Wife?, Atlantis Rising No.97 (January/February 2013), p.10
25. The Biggest Secret, supra, p.91 citing Leedom, Tim C., The Book Your Church Doesn't Want You To Read (1993), p.137
26. Ibid. p.111 citing Findlay, Arthur, The Curse of Ignorance, A History of Mankind (1947), Vol. 1, p.549
27. Ibid. p.92
28. Ibid. p.54
29. Ibid. p.82
30. Ibid. p.93
31. Signs and Symbols of Primordial Man, supra, pp.315-320

Chapter 12: Christianity

1. Humanity's Extraterrestrial Origins, supra, p.287
2. Baigent, M., Leigh, R., and Lincoln H., The Messianic Legacy (1986), p.40
3. Humanity's Extraterrestrial Origins, supra, p.289
4. Slave Species of the Gods, supra, p.293
5. Humanity's Extraterrestrial Origins, supra, pp.289-290
6. Slave Species of the Gods, supra, pp.412-413
7. Humanity's Extraterrestrial Origins, supra, pp.286
8. Chariots of the Gods, supra, p.30
9. Hislop, The Two Babylons, p.197-199

Chapter 13: Islam

1. The Gods of Eden, supra, p.151
2. Slave Species of the Gods, supra, p.336
3. All verses from the Qur'an are taken from Interpretation of the Meanings of The Nobel Qur'an, translated into English by Dr. Muhammad Muhsin Khan and Dr. Muhammad Taqi-ud Din Al-Hilali, Darussalam Publishers (Revised Edition 2007); "s." is an abbreviation for "Surah," which is the word usd to identify a chapter of the Qur'an.
4. Slave Species of the Gods, supra, pp.336-337
5. Ibid. p.338
6. Occult Theocrasy, supra, Vol.1, p.134
7. The Nobel Qur'an, supra, Appendix-I Glossary, p.862
8. Merriam-Webster's Collegiate Dictionary, 11th Ed.
9. Occult Theocrasy, supra, p.141
10. Ibid. p.140
11. Ibid. pp.141-142

Chapter 14: Stories of the Apocalypse to Warn of the Anunnaki/Elohim/Nephilim's Return

1. Gardner, Laurence, Realm of the Ring Lords: The Myth and Magic of the Grail Quest (2000), p.53
2. The Book of Mormon: Another Testament of Jesus Christ (The Church of Jesus Christ of Latter-day Saints, 2013), Mosiah 3:19
3. The End of Days, supra, pp.36-37
4. Ibid. p.61

REFERENCES

PART III: SECRET SOCIETIES

Chapter 15: Secret Societies

1. James Perloff, The Shadows of Power: The Council on Foreign Relations and the American Decline (1988), p.3
2. The Gods of Eden, supra, p.3
3. Ibid
4. Cooper, William, Behold A Pale Horse (1991), pp.268-332
5. Ibid pp. 56-57
6. Ibid p.79
7. Marrs, Jim, Rule By Secrecy: The Hidden History that Connects the Trilateral Commission, the Freemasons, and the Great Pyramids (2000), p.407
8. Humanity's Extraterrestrial Origins, supra, pp.xxix-xxx
9. The Biggest Secret, supra, p.1
10. The Gods of Eden, supra, pp.53-56

Chapter 16: Concept of Positive and Negative

1. The Book of Mormon, supra, 2 Nephi 5:21-24
2. The Book of Mormon, supra, 2 Nephi 13:9
3. The Book of Mormon, supra, Alma 3:6-8
4. Signs and Symbols of Primordial Man, supra, p.409

Chapter 17: Illuminati: The Resistance Movement Against Anunnaki/Elohim/Nephilim Control

1. Plomer, William, Cecil Rhodes (1933), pp.25-26
2. Rule by Secrecy, supra, p.250, quoting Manly P. Hall, What the Ancient Wisdom Expects of its Disciples (1982), p.27
3. Genesis of the Grail Kings, supra, p.118 citing Journal of the American Medical Association, Vol. 270, No.18 (November 10, 1993)
4. Gardiner, Philip, and Osborn, Gary, The Serpent Grail: The Truth Behind The Holy Grail, The Philosopher's Stone and The Elixir of Life (2005), p.79
5. Ibid. pp.78-80 citing The Caduceus vs. the Staff of Asclepius, by Dr. Keith R. Blayney, MBChB
6. Ibid. p.85
7. Ibid. p.141
8. Atrahasis (Clay), supra, p.36
9. Flavius Josephus, Antiquities of the Jews, bk. 1, chap.4, sec.2

10. Rule by Secrecy, supra, p.407; Sutton, William, The Illuminati 666 (2008), p.102
11. The Illuminati 666, supra, p.6
12. Epperson, Ralph, The New World Order (1990)
13. Occult Theocrasy, supra, pp.220-221
14. Encyclopedia Britanica, Vol. 6, p.373 (1915)
15. Pike, Albert, Morals and Dogma, p.321
16. The Illuminati 666, supra, p.120 citing Aleister Crowley, Magick in Theory and Pratice
17. The Biggest Secret, supra, pp.47, 208
18. Morals and Dogma, supra, p.741
19. Occult Theocrasy, supra, pp.363-367
20. Ibid. p.221
21. Morals and Dogma, supra, p.11; The Illuminati 666, supra, p.134
22. Morals and Dogma, supra, pp.15-16; The Illuminati 666, supra, p.111
23. Morals and Dogma, supra, p.375; The Illuminati 666, supra, p.138
24. Still, William T., New World Order: The Ancient Plan of Secret Societies (1990)
25. The Illuminati 666, supra, pp.233-234 citing The Daughters of the American Revolution Magazine, Hall, July 1982, p.485
26. The Biggest Secret, supra, pp.358, 208

Chapter 18: The Garden of Eden, The Tree of Knowledge, and The Good and Evil Knowledge that Man Learned

1. The 12th Planet, supra, p.366
2. Ibid. p.98
3. Ibid. p.106
4. The Epic of Gilgamesh
5. Adapa Tablet

Chapter 19: The Fountain of Youth

1. The Stairway to Heaven, supra, p.27, quoting Herodotus, Histories, Book III
2. Ibid. p.25
3. Ibid. p.11
4. Ibid. p.13
5. Ibid. pp.2-3
6. Ibid. pp.3-5
7. Ibid. p.3
8. The Book of Enoch, VII:4-5
9. Atrahasis (Clay), supra, pp.62,64
10. Flying Serpents and Dragons, supra, p.161
11. Ibid.
12. Caveman Cold Case, Secrets of the Dead, airing on PBS

13. Paraphrasing Matthew 26:27-28, Mark 14:23-24, Luke 22:17&20
14. The Gods of Eden, supra, pp.130-132
15. Bloodline of the Holy Grail, supra, p.35, citing A.N. Wilson, Jesus, ch 4, p.83; Genesis of the Grail Kings, supra, p.171
16. Merriam-Webster's Collegiate Dictionary, 11th Ed.
17. The Serpent Grail, supra, p.288
18. Realm of the Ring Lords, supra, p.123
19. The Serpent Grail, supra, p.288
20. Slave Species of the Gods, supra, p.18
21. Sinha M, et al "Restoring systemic GDF11 levels reverses age-related dysfunction in mouse skeletal muscle" Science 2014; DOI: 10.1126/science.1251152; and Katsimpardi L, et al "Vascular and neurogenic rejuvenation of the aging mouse brain by young systemic factors" Science 2014; DOI: 10.1126/science.1251141
22. Villeda S, et al "Young blood reverses age-related impairments in cognitive function and synaptic plasticity in mice" Nature Med 2014; DOI: 10.1038/nm.3569
23. theguardian, "Young blood can reverse some effects of ageing, study finds", by Alok Jha (October 17, 2012)
24. theguardian, "Infusions of young blood may reverse effects of ageing, studies suggest", by Ian Sample (May 4, 2014)
25. Genesis of the Grail Kings, supra, p.171, citing Grant, Kenneth, The Magical Revival (1991), p.133;
26. The Serpent Grail, supra, p.248
27. Genesis of the Grail Kings, supra, pp.186, 184
28. Ibid. p.131
29. The Serpent Grail, supra, p.53, citing The Magical Arts, by Richard Cavendish (1984), p.157
30. Genesis of the Grail Kings, supra, p.163, citing the Magical Revival, p.123
31. Ibid. p.186
32. Baigent, Michael, and Leigh, Richard, The Temple and the Lodge (1989), pp.128-129
33. Genesis of the Grail Kings, supra, p.162
34. Ibid.; Plate 19
35. Ibid. pp.163-164
36. Ibid. p.160 citing The Magical Revival, p.123
37. The Serpent Grail, supra, p.153
38. Ibid. p.149
39. Ibid. p.150 quoting W.J. Wilkins, Hindu Mythology: Vedic and Puranic (reprinted D.K. Printworld, New Delhi, 2003)
40. Ibid. p.152 quoting Rig Veda
41. Ibid. p.143; De Vere, Nicholas, The Dragon Legacy: The Secret History of an Ancient Bloodline (2004), p.65
42. Realm of the Ring Lords, supra, p.118
43. Ibid. pp.119-120 citing The Magical Revival, ch. 2, p.44 and ch. 7, pp.121-124
44. Ibid. p.121 citing The Magical Revival, ch. 8, p.148
45. The Serpent Grail, supra, pp.173-176

46. The Stairway to Heaven, supra, p.6
47. Ibid.
48. The Dragon Legacy, supra, p.130
49. Ibid. pp.191-192
50. Realm of the Ring Lords, supra, p.12
51. Genesis of the Grail Kings, supra, p.127 citing Graves, R., and Patai, R., Hebrew Myths - Genesis, p.53
52. Suares, Carlo, The Cipher of Genesis, Using the Qabalistic Code to Interpret the First Book of the Bible and the Teachings of Jesus (1970), p.21
53. Ibid.
54. Signs and Symbols of Primodial Man, supra, p.324
55. The Dragon Legacy, supra, p.136
56. The Serpent Grail, supra, p.222
57. The Dragon Legacy, supra, p.136
58. The Serpent Grail, supra, pp.143-144
59. Ibid. pp.188-189
60. The Lost Realms, supra, p.37
61. Heindel, Max, The Rosicrucian Cosmo-Conception (6th Ed. 1998) pp.518-520
62. Realm of the Ring Lords, supra, p.238 citing Miller, Elizabeth, Dracula: Sense and Nonsense (2000), ch.2, p.72
63. Ibid. p.238 citing Miller, Elizabeth, Dracula: Sense and Nonsense (2000), ch.5, pp.187-188
64. Ibid. pp.239-241
65. Ibid. p.242
66. Ibid. p.244
67. Ibid. p.243
68. The Dragon Legacy, supra
69. Realm of the Ring Lords, supra, pp.239, 241-242 citing Melton, J. Gordon, The Vampire Book, pp.758-759
70. Ibid. pp.241, 246
71. Ibid. p.240 citing Florescu, Radu, and McNally, Raymond, Dracula (1973), pp.9-10
72. Ibid. p.241 citing Dracula (1973), ch.7, p.151
73. Ibid. pp.240, 245, 248
74. Ibid. p.247
75. Ibid. p.237
76. The Dragon Legacy, supra, pp.80-81
77. Ibid. p.72
78. Realm of the Ring Lords, supra, p.131
79. Ibid. p.132 citing Graves, Robert, The White Goddess, ch.10, p.166, note 1
80. The Serpent Grail, supra, p.101
81. The Dragon Legacy, supra, p.221
82. The Serpent Grail, supra, p.104
83. Ibid. p.102
84. Signs and Symbols of Primordial Man, supra, p.234
85. Ibid. p.78
86. The Dragon Legacy, supra, p.222

87. Signs and Symbols of Primordial Man, supra, pp.68, 314
88. The Serpent Grail, supra, pp.78-79 citing Walter J. Friedlander, The Golden Wand of Medicine: A History of the Caduceus Symbol in Medicine (1992)
89. Fortune, Dion, The Mystical Qabalah (1935), p.34
90. Ibid. p.49
91. Ibid. p.51

INDEX

A

Aaron, 104, 107, 145, 228, 229
Abaddon, 169
Abigail, 115
Abimelech, 114
Abishag, 236, 237, 248
Abraham, 3, 90, 91-93, 95-101, 103, 104, 111, 113, 117, 122, 123, 137, 144, 145, 148-150, 238
Abram, 93, 94, 95
Absalom, 116
Abydenus, 76
Abyss, 169
Abyssinia, 185
Abzu (Apsu), 23, 26, 35, 37, 39
Achan, 110
Adad, 5
Adah, 99
Adam, 3, 37, 38, 42, 55, 58, 65, 137, 145, 170, 201- 205, 208, 212, 226, 244
    Generic Term, 37
    Physical Features, 37
    Worked, Not Worshipped, 32
Adam and Eve, 202, 203, 205
Adamah, 37
Adapa, 82, 203
Adonai, 194, 195, 201, 206
Adoni-Bezek, 114
Adonijah, 116, 237
Aegyptiaca, 20
Aesculapius, 190
Africa/African, 7, 15, 23, 26, 33, 39, 43, 44, 54, 58, 60, 62, 135, 153, 185
Africanus, Julius, 20
Afterlife, 139, 140
Ahinoam, 115
Ahura Mazda, 77
Ai, 114
Ainu, 43
Akhnaton, 102
Akkad/Akkadian, 1, 13, 14, 25, 35, 68, 82, 172
AL.A.NI, 39
Alchemical, 226, 228, 230, 241, 246, 247, 248, 250

Alchemical Medallion, 227, 230
Alchemist, 216, 227
Alchemy, 227, 230, 250, 251, 252
Alexander The Great, 209
Al-Khidr, 161, 162
Allah, 92, 144-146, 148-150, 152, 153, 155-163, 165, 166, 188, 192
All Seeing Eye, 197, 198
Al Qaeda, 153
Ambrosia, 232, 233
Amelu, 31
Amen (Amon, Amun, Ammon, Amon-Re, Amen-Ra), 167, 168
Amenta, 239
Ammonites, 114, 116
Amnon, 116, 167
Amorites, 96, 113, 114
Amram, 102, 111
Amrita, 233
Amsu, 133
An, 1, 9, 25, 100
Anak, 9
Anakim, 9
Anakites, 9
Ancient Astronaut Theory, 11
Ancient Mysteries, 175, 189
Andes, 8, 243
Ankh, 1, 41
Antioch, 136
Antu, 2
Anu, 1-5, 9, 13, 21, 23, 25, 28, 31, 70, 71, 82, 96, 100, 102, 128, 142, 189, 203, 248
Anunna, 4, 25
Anunnaki, 3-16, 19, 20, 23-40, 42, 43, 44, 48-53, 58, 59, 60, 65-70, 73-76, 79-84, 90-93, 96, 100, 102-104, 110, 112, 116, 122-126, 128, 129, 130, 131, 139, 140, 142, 150, 164-166, 172, 182, 186, 188-196, 199, 201-208, 211-216, 233, 237, 238, 244-246, 248, 251, 254, 255, 257, 258
    Pantheon, 5, 7
    Physical Features, 4
    Described as Annedoti, 38
    Prohibited Humans Access To Knowledge, Ch.19

275

N

T

Yima, 77
Yin-Yang Symbol, 253
Ymir, 77
Yucatan, 8

Z

Zadok, 116, 125
Zaphenath-Paneah, 100; see Joseph
Zapotecs, 135, 185, 251
Zephaniah, 137, 171
Zeus, 76
Zilpha, 99
Zipporah, 102
Ziusudra, 71; see Noah
Zodiac, 5
Zoroastrian, 77, 233

34729033R00162

Printed in Great Britain
by Amazon

GOOD and EVIL

Why
Judaism, Christianity, and Islam
Have Nothing To Do With God
and
Why These Religions Demonize the Illuminati

Good and Evil
Why Judaism, Christianity, and Islam Have Nothing To Do With God and
Why These Religions Demonize the Illuminati

Copyright Notice
© 2016

(ISBN-10 153-9593592)
(ISBN-13 978-1539533591)